SHOP!

OR CLOGS TO CLOGS IN THREE GENERATIONS – WELL, ALMOST

SHOP!

OR CLOGS TO CLOGS IN THREE GENERATIONS – WELL, ALMOST

by

BRIAN GREENWOOD

The Memoir Club

First published in 2009 by
The Memoir Club
Arya House
Langley Park
Durham
DH7 9XE
Tel: 0191 373 5660

British Library Cataloguing in
Publication Data.
A catalogue record for this book
is available from the
British Library

ISBN: 978-1-84104-214-5

Typeset by TW Typesetting, Plymouth, Devon
Printed by Cromwell Press Group, Trowbridge, Wiltshire BA14 0XB

*For Enid, my family and friends
who have made a long life very happy.*

The unhappy parts are other people's fault!

Contents

List of Illustrations

Acknowledgements

Grateful thanks to Nigel Watson for helpful advice. David Greenwood, James Lister and Dr David Fieldhouse for skilful proof correction and Nicky Martin for cheerful and patient secretarial help.

The Memoir Club for their professionalism and particularly to the Rt Hon. Lord Norman Tebbit CH for his admirable Foreword.

Preface

My family, particularly my grandchildren have always been interested in the stories and anecdotes which I have told them. A year or two ago they began suggesting that I should write down some of the tales of the widely varied events and activities which I have been fortunate – and in some cases unfortunate – enough to enjoy. This book is an attempt to answer that suggestion.

It is not a detailed autobiography but rather, simply a compilation of memories. Many of which, I hope will be amusing, some will be informative, others saddening but all, I hope, interesting.

Brian Greenwod
Bishop Thornton
Harrogate
Autumn 2009

Foreword

The rise of the Greenwood family fortunes began in Bradford in the 1850s when Brian Greenwood's great-great-grandfather took up the trade of hatter, which was carried on by his son and then grandson, who expanded the business into a gentlemen's outfitters.

Shop! traces the fortunes and misfortunes of his descendants -most notablyBrian Greenwood himself- through a hundred and fifty tumultuous years including two terrible wars, the devastating slump and depression of the inter-war period, the height and the fall of the British Empire and that of the Greenwood empire too.

The story has in it the stuff of a TV saga It is perhaps a bit short of real villains and sexual misdemeanours, though they are both there, and there is a touch of hubris and nemesis too, but its strength is the strength of character of a hard working Yorkshire family through good years and bad alike.

At its height when I had the good fortune to meet Brian and his wife, Enid, the Greenwood business was an outstanding medium-sized enterprise which allowed the family both to live in some style and put a great deal into the local community.

Sadly the division of the business into separate parts owned by Brian and his brother proved to be a costly mistake which left it vulnerable to the chill winds of the 1990s. Even worse an unwise diversion into a high tech medical project and an internal fraud compounded its difficulties.

The hard times seemed to have no end but even in his eighties Brian Greenwood finds it difficult not to think about business and not to be running a substantial mini conglomerate. Despite having seen a small fortune ebb away the message of his memoirs seems to me that just as to have loved and lost is better than never to have loved at all, so in Kipling's words to have known both success and failure and treated those impostors just the same, is better by far than to have never encountered them at all.

Anyway, the Greenwood family tree is not dead and another Greenwood may yet write another chapter of the family saga in another century or so. Yorkshire folk do not give up that easily.

Rt. Hon. Lord Tebbit CH

CHAPTER 1

Early Days

LET'S START BY BRINGING OUT the skeleton from the family cupboard. A herbalist, by name Titus Hirst, born towards the end of the eighteenth century, produced via one Sarah Greenwood, a son, James Greenwood, in 1823. I have no idea why my great-great-grandfather, James, took his mother's name rather than his father's. All I do know is that despite his rather inauspicious start he made a success of his life.

In the late 1850s James Greenwood – previously a woolcomber – worked as an assistant and general handyman in a small hatter's shop at 29 Westgate, Bradford. The owner of this modest business was Mr Stringer Lake and his trade was the sale and renovation of silk hats. In those days top hats were the normal headgear for Bradford's successful gentlemen.

Family lore has it that great-great-grandfather James got surprisingly lucky since, one day, Mr Lake simply disappeared. What prompted his departure was, and remains, a mystery. It has always been a mild anxiety for me that perhaps my ancestor murdered him in order to take over his business!

I think that unlikely since James Greenwood was a God-fearing man with family responsibilities. More likely, I think, Lake had simply moved on to trade elsewhere, possibly in nearby Shipley. Whatever the reasons for Lake's disappearance the fact was that James found himself with the business and premises and had learned enough as a hatter's assistant to be able to keep the business going. He was fortunate in having a bright twelve-year-old son, Moses, whom he soon set to work making hat frames in the Westgate shop. The Greenwood business began in this peculiar way in, we think, 1860 but not until 1863 did the name 'Greenwood' appear on the shop front; probably James was happy to trade on Stringer Lake's goodwill or perhaps he simply could not afford a new sign.

James must have done pretty well out of Lake's business since he acquired a few domestic properties around Bradford and was apparently able to live on the rents from them. Indeed, a directory of the period went so far as to describe him as a 'gentleman'. In any event, he took no further interest in the hatter's business and it was left to young Moses to find new

1

premises at 148 Westgate, Bradford which he opened for business in October 1865. At the end of his first week's trading his takings were £2 9s 2d, i.e. £2.49.

By 1868 business was booming and sales had leapt to an average of £10 per week! Hats and caps were then being sold in addition to the repair and very occasional sale of silk hats. The business progressed, albeit slowly and by 1875, the year's takings had almost reached that goal of small shopkeepers in those days – £1,000 per annum. The precise figure was, in fact, £981.

In 1889 my great-grandfather moved three doors to new premises at 142 Westgate, formerly a hairdresser's. The move proved a success and the shop's figures steadily improved. However, it was in 1896 that an odd incident produced the base from which, ultimately, Britain's largest privately owned chain of men's outfitters was to grow.

Moses' son Willie Greenwood worked at first for the Post Office delivering telegrams but by the time he was sixteen the business needed an extra pair of hands and he was able to join his father. Two years of selling nothing other than headwear, albeit now of all kinds, was clearly too much for young Willie. The eighteen-year-old got on his bike, pedalled through the city centre of Bradford, up the long pull of Leeds Road, out past Pudsey and into the middle of Leeds where he parked his bike outside the impressive premises of Holts – wholesale warehouse men. From there he bought a few boxes of ties and a few of braces, strapped them on to the carrier at the back of his bike and pedalled off back to Bradford. That was the start of the outfitting business.

It succeeded and Grandfather Willie enjoyed it. His father, a life-long hatter, was less enthusiastic and was happy to enjoy first semi-retirement and then full retirement during which he followed a variety of interests. He became a skilled photographer. He took an interest in astrology and cast horoscopes for all around him – I am told they were suprisingly accurate. He was a skilful joiner – I still have the mahogany cabinet which he designed and built so as to show pairs of photographs in a three-dimensional view.

Moses was a staunch Methodist throughout a long life and he and his family were regular attenders at the chapel in Daisy Hill, Bradford, which he had helped to finance.

Back at the shop, things were progressing for Grandfather Willie. He had married at the turn of the century, he had acquired the premises next door to expand his business and the first of his three sons – my father, was born in what was then the family home – over the shop. Up to the outbreak of the First World War the business marked time but Willie remained optimistic for the future and was able to afford a house rather than living over the shop.

Willie's cash book for August 1914 raises a sad smile. In the first week, opposite the takings and in the column for remarks Willie wrote, 'War declared on Germany'. The following week has the note, 'War still on'. Presumably Grandfather thought it would be all over in a matter of days.

Although the family business was reasonably successful, my father certainly was not born with a silver spoon in his mouth. He and his two brothers shared the same bedroom and shared the same clothes. My father, Walter's clothes were passed down first to brother Arthur and then to brother Harold, the youngest of the three.

Father was never very close to his father for Willie was a stern man, utterly opposed to smoking and drinking and careful – very – in spending money. Young Walter had to walk two miles to school and back to save the bus fares. He was never happy as a schoolboy at Carlton Street and later Belle Vue and his school reports were poor. He was never at the bottom of the class but certainly never near the top.

In 1917, at the age of sixteen, he saw an advertisement in the local paper – 'Smart boy required. Wages 12/6d (that is 62½p today) and commission'. It was the magic word 'commission' that attracted him so he took a morning off school and applied for the job at Hepworth's the clothiers at their Kirkgate, Bradford branch. The manager, Mr Carruthers, asked him a few questions, clearly decided the boy had potential and engaged him. Father was delighted to be able to leave school and start in a job which he had found himself. However, he soon learned that the job was not all he had hoped for. In the dark days of the First World War, male staff for the menswear trade were obviously in short supply and the staff at Hepworth's consisted only of the hard-bitten manager, Carruthers, and another youngster – Arthur Hargreaves – who was not much older than Walter himself who, of course, was number three on the team.

His hopes of doing well from the magic word 'commission' were soon dashed. He would only get commission on any sales which he himself made. Carruthers served every customer he could, Hargreaves was next in line and only rarely did Walter have the chance to develop a salesman's skills.

Nevertheless, young Walter was still very keen as evidenced by the occasion when he stepped briskly out from the rear stockroom with a welcoming smile and a cheerful 'Good Morning Sir!' only to disappear from the astonished customer's sight through the trap door behind the counter which led to the basement stockroom. Although both shaken and stirred Walter was not seriously injured and escaped with nothing worse than a telling off from Carruthers for alarming the customer.

Apart from the basement the shop was on two floors which meant that even the ubiquitous Carruthers could not always be watching over his two assistants who, therefore, had the chance occasionally to enliven otherwise dull days. The two youths would catch mice – there were always plenty in the basement – and then put the dead mice into neatly wrapped parcels.

The next step was to dangle the parcels on a string from the windows of the first floor clothing department. An ingenious improvised hook which could be shaken loose and then reeled back with the string, meant that the parcel could be lowered onto the pavement, the hook and string withdrawn, leaving it sitting there, just as if some passer-by had inadvertently dropped a purchase. Watching the reactions of people noticing the package afforded the two youths much innocent amusement. The majority of people either did not notice it or looked at it but still walked by. However, every so often a passer-by would stop, look around furtively and then pick up the package and put it quickly into bag or pocket. The thought of their reactions when they opened their find kept Walter and young Hargreaves happy on many a dull day.

Shop work was never easy in days long past. The hours were long and the work was often tedious and boring. Constantly brushing the hanging garments, re-stacking merchandise in geometrically perfect piles and the constant polishing of the windows, the floor, the fixtures and the counters took most of the time. On the occasions when the assistants were allowed to serve a customer they had to try their hardest to make a sale. Failing to make a sale was known as 'taking a swap' and in Mr Carruther's branch of the Hepworth's chain, taking a swap without having tried every trick in the book was an unforgivable sin. Young Walter and Hargreaves knew that if the potential customer seemed to be wavering and about to walk out, they were duty bound to call for Carruthers with such a phrase as – 'Excuse me Sir, I'll just see if the Manager can find what you are looking for'. Carruthers would step forward, usually kick the leg of the youth who had called him as a clear indication to get out of the way and leave him to handle the customer one on one. It was a fact then, it is a fact now and I should think always will be, that any customer prefers to be dealing with one person at a time, ideally a senior figure, the manager or manageress, as opposed to a mere assistant.

Carruthers was a remarkably skilled salesman in those days when salesmanship was a real and regularly practised skill. All too often the customer would leave Hepworth's having bought something that he had rejected when either Hargreaves or Walter was trying to sell it to him but after a short session with Carruthers he was convinced that the item now represented an excellent purchase.

Carruthers was not the only expert salesman who influenced young Walter. There was a trader on the other side of the street who had a novel and surprisingly effective technique. His was a jeweller's shop with a large single window and the door at the right-hand side thereof. There were no solid backs to his window displays but rather simply curtains. The jeweller spent much of his day looking out through a gap in the curtains. If he saw a prosperous looking window shopper pausing to look into his window, he would be out of the shop quickly and quietly, pass behind the customer so as to block the escape route and then with one hand he would tap the customer on his shoulder and with the other produce and flip open a handsome gold watch from his waistcoat pocket. He would glance at the watch and then ask the rather surprised window shopper, 'Sir, have you five minutes?' Anything other than a flat 'No' meant that within seconds the window shopper was ushered into the shop and usually would emerge a little later carrying a small package.

Shortly before the end of the First World War when Walter was still seventeen, he made a move which oddly enough was mirrored precisely by my experience some twenty-seven years later. He went to the recruiting office and volunteered to join the Royal Flying Corps. Luckily for him, the war ended before his eighteenth birthday and he was too young to serve.

In 1919 Walter left Hepworth's where, by then, he was regarded as a senior and valuable assistant and joined his father in the Westgate shop. The family had moved from the rooms over the shop to 50 Toller Lane, Bradford. The business did well in the post-war boom. Walter worked long and hard, often until 9.00 and 10.00 at night and, in 1921, the premises were extended and rebuilt.

Walter persuaded his father to attempt the wholesale trade and they began a wholesale cap business with some success until the slump came a year or two later. Walter had his share of carrying a case of samples around the north, particularly the north-east, for which area he always had great affection.

He constantly pressed his father to open more shops but the response was not very enthusiastic.

Walter met his wife on the top of a tram. Hannah Ivy Nellist (later always known as Anne Greenwood) worked as a model and assistant at Novello's gown shop in Kirkgate, Bradford (a business purchased by Walter as a property investment forty years later). The lights in the tram they were both using that evening failed and the confusion that followed gave him an opportunity to start a conversation which led to a marriage that spanned forty-seven years. They were married on Boxing Day, 1923, at St Barnabas Church, Heaton, and went to live at 44 Springcliffe Street, a house owned by Walter's grandfather and for which he charged a rent of 5/- a week. Their first home was nothing if not modest. It was one of a terrace of 'back-to-back' houses of which there were street after street in the Manningham Lane/Westgate parts of Bradford, which areas are today almost wholly Pakistani. They were very happy in their home and it was here that their eldest son, Denis Greenwood, was born in 1925.

Anne Greenwood was a very attractive woman as the nature of her work at Novello's suggests and remained so throughout her long and busy life. She was as ambitious and determined as Walter. She was uncomplaining about the long hours he worked and she shared his excitement as the business grew and prospered. Although never involved on a day-to-day basis she was very much involved behind the scenes. Coming from a large family (she was one of the elder children in a family of eight), she was accustomed to helping other people and taking responsibility and she was not afraid of hard work herself.

Turning back to the business story. In 1922, Walter was in partnership with his father and younger brothers and had persuaded them to open a branch shop at 53 Manchester Road, Bradford. Walter, as the oldest brother, received a yearly salary of £184, the younger brothers even less. The following year another branch was opened in Sunderland and in 1924 there was another branch in Manchester Road, Bradford at Number 162 and premises at 7 Otley Road, Bradford.

In 1925 Walter, who was nothing if not enterprising, opened a branch in London! In Shoreditch to be precise. We believe this shop was taken because the previous proprietor owed the partnership money for caps supplied through the wholesale business. It very soon proved to be uneconomic to have a branch so far from the centre of activities and it was closed the following year and replaced by a branch in Brighouse.

In 1927 Walter decided to go it alone. He had different views from his father and brothers as to how the business should be expanded and, therefore, the family enterprise split up and it was agreed that Walter would take the branch shops which had been opened largely by his own efforts and the main business would remain in the hands of his father and brothers, Arthur and Harold. Of the branches Walter took as his share of the family business only one was a freehold – 162 Manchester Road – and the stock in all of them was very much less than at the parent premises in Westgate, which remained a more profitable unit than all the others put together.

Walter was certainly prepared to take a chance. He had just moved into a new semi-detached house at Lynton Avenue, Bradford where his second son, Brian Greenwood, was born in 1927 and now, finding himself in sole charge of his ramshackle little group of businesses, he began to expand at a phenomenal rate. By the end of 1928 he had opened a second branch in Sunderland, two in Middlesborough, one in Darlington, one in Shipley and one in Heckmondwike. His personal bank book for that year shows that he had £29 outside the business at the start of the year and was obliged to withdraw £20 in the course of the year. Every penny that the business earned was ploughed straight back. Walter allowed himself a salary of £6 a week as he struggled to hold his business together and to expand it. His head office was one room above 162 Manchester Road shop, his warehouse was the same room, his transport was a Morris Oxford car and his executive staff, his window dressers, his stocktakers, his buyers, were – himself!

These were the days when he dare not meet his bank manager and if he saw him in town he would run up the nearest side street to avoid him. At the beginning of every week he would add up the sales for the previous week and then decide which of his suppliers' accounts he could afford to pay. The branches were ill-equipped, window fittings were mostly home-made, interior fittings were either second-hand or simply open shelving.

His hours were long. Normal procedure on Wednesday (early closing day in Bradford) was for him to leave Bradford with a car full of stock for

Sunderland or Darlington and to dress windows there throughout the night before driving back to open up in Manchester Road the following morning.

His risks and gambles paid off and with each year that passed the branch list grew longer so that by 1932 he had no less than twenty-six shops and the time had come for two more very important steps. First, his father retired and the original family business in Westgate, Bradford, became again part of Walter's firm and, indeed, his headquarters. His brother Arthur, had left the retail trade and was established as a hat maker in Preston, and younger brother Harold rejoined Walter.

For years the family legend was that Grandfather's retirement followed a heart attack caused by the excitement of rescuing my brother, Denis, from the path of an on-coming car whilst we were picnicking at the side of Harewood Avenue. I must have been in my fifties when my last surviving aunt told me the truth. Whilst the car rescue had, in fact, happened it was not that which caused Grandfather's heart attack. It was the fact that Grandmother returned home one afternoon to find her husband in what is, I believe, delicately known as *in flagrante delicto* with the parlour maid! I am not surprised he had a heart attack! In any event, he retired at that time and lived for forty odd more years into his nineties.

For most of his life he had a billiard room at every house into which he moved including the small retirement bungalow where he spent the latter part of his long life. He taught me to play the game as a boy, reminding me constantly that billiards was a game for gentlemen whereas snooker was a rough sport played by nasty people in the rooms over Burtons. Unfortunately I have found very few billiards players among my friends and therefore the billiard tables which I have owned – and still own – have been used mainly for snooker, though I still enjoy playing the very skilful and much underrated game of billiards.

The second big change was to form his business into a limited liability company known as Greenwoods (Hosiers & Outfitters) Limited with an Issued Capital of 1700 Preference Shares of £1 each and 4,200 £1 Ordinary Shares of which Walter held all save 200. Shortly before establishing his business as a limited company, in 1931 Walter again moved house, this time to Briaden, Shipley Glen, where we lived until 1934. This was a very pleasant stone-built bungalow but with dormer windows providing first-floor space and a large garden behind. The location was and still is a sought-after Bradford suburb. Its name, used also for the family's next home, comes, of course, from the names Brian and Denis.

In 1933, for the first time, the business was operated from central headquarters as opposed to a room above a shop. In that year Walter bought premises at 17 Drewton Street, Bradford, which were formerly a dance hall. They were ideally suited for his purpose since the ballroom area provided ample space for warehouse stocks, branch fixtures etc. and the other rooms provided office space for the handful of staff who were now essential to deal with the administration of the steadily expanding chain.

It must be remembered that this growth in the business from a handful of ill-equipped half-stocked branches up to a group of more than thirty shops operated from a central headquarters, took place in the middle of the worst trading period that the century saw – 1927 to 1933 – and perhaps his efforts in this period were his finest business achievement. All around him businesses were failing, the unemployed were counted in millions and yet, from nothing, he had built the foundations of a major business.

In the twenties and early thirties as well as his ever-increasing chain of menswear shops Father had a modest wholesale trade in men's caps. He invented an unusual form of tweed cap which he christened the 'Fitzall'. These caps simply had an elastic section at the rear. The design was very much like that often seen nowadays on baseball caps – what a pity he didn't patent it!

As well as being hard-working and enthusiastic, Father must in those days have been quite a hard case. For example, the tenant of the chemist's shop which he owned next door to one of his northern branches – Middlesborough, I believe – didn't pay his rent. Father's solution was simple and effective – he had a key to the premises so he went there one night and helped himself to what he judged to be the amount owing, from the chemist's stock. Thereafter any commercial traveller calling at his office and warehouse in Bradford found himself obliged to purchase a few packets of Beechams or bottles of Aspirin, or whatever chemist's item Father could wish on him.

Adjoining Drewton Street headquarters was Hemingway's shirt factory. It was in the thirties that Hemingway's produced that remarkable item, a shirt with the collar attached! Not only that, but it was a shirt that you could put on like a coat. A coat shirt, in fact. Since the style had, of course, originated in the USA, Father and Jimmy Hemingway christened this new product the 'Yankee' and it sold very freely at all the Greenwoods shops. Normal shirts at that time were pulled on over your head like a tunic, hence the trade term, tunic shirts. They had separate collars secured with two studs.

Apart from introducing the 'Yankee', Father came up with another shirt design known as the 'Reversit'. This was a shirt that could be turned inside out since the buttons were on a separate strip of cloth. It came with the usual two separate collars. The theory was that when one side of the shirt showed signs of wear, you simply reversed it. In fact, 'Reversit' shirts were often known as 'mucky men's' shirts since reversing a garment meant the same shirt could be worn for days.

In 1934, as the trading depression began to lift, business improved. Thirty-six branches were open, operated from Drewton Street, and the familiar green and black shop fronts had been introduced at a handful of branches. Of the thirty-six shops no less than sixteen were in Bradford itself but the others were now spread to such towns as Blackpool, Morecambe, Lancaster, Glossop, Keighley, Skipton, Barnoldswick etc.

CHAPTER 2

Young Days

I ONLY HAVE A FEW MEMORIES of life at Shipley Glen where we lived for three years of my young days. I suppose I would be about three when we moved there and six when the family moved on and, perhaps one could say, upwards.

I made my first public appearance whilst we lived at Shipley Glen. The local amateur dramatic society put on a performance of *The Desert Song*. As a four-year-old I was taken to see the show and apparently I enjoyed it so much that I insisted on taking part. The only way my parents could quieten me was to promise that I could go on the stage during the interval. Since the producer of the show was in fact my father's general manager, one Walter Woods, I suppose influence gave me preferential treatment. Anyhow, one way or another I was allowed up on the stage and I gave the audience what I am sure was a spirited rendering of the song – popular at the time, I believe – called 'Riding on a Camel in the Desert'. I must have got thespian urges out of my system at that early stage as I have never again wanted to be involved in any kind of theatricals.

I was too young to go to school but my brother, Denis, was not. He was sent off to the school in Baildon Village but, shortly after, he departed the school in some disgrace having tried to fight his teacher. He would only be about six but he was a tough little boy and I can well understand his lady teacher being alarmed.

Shortly after that incident – possibly because of it – we removed to Cragg Woods, Rawdon, near Leeds, to a house which my parents promptly renamed, Briaden. This Briaden must have been one of the biggest semis in Yorkshire. It was a large stone-built Victorian house, built in the middle of the nineteenth century for, I believe, two brothers, one of whom had lived in the slightly larger eastern side and the other had occupied the rather smaller western part. Both parts had large gardens and I suppose my childhood there was idyllic. Father was only in his early thirties but the standard of living which we then enjoyed was very high. There were two maids living in the attic, a gardener in the lodge at the bottom of the drive and a chauffeur who came to work daily.

11

For a few months when we first lived there, the domestic staff were supplemented by a governess for Denis and me. Looking back, it was an odd experience to begin one's education at home with just one teacher and only my elder brother as a school-mate.

The joy of my early days at Briaden was the large garden of two or three acres in which to play. Sometimes our play brought us into direct contact with the neighbours – that is to say the old man, Mr Jessop, who lived very quietly in the smaller part of the building cared for by a very fierce housekeeper who most certainly was not having the two small boys from next door climbing over the garden fence to retrieve lost balls – or for any other reason. Incidentally, shortly before the war, Mr Jessop died and, of course, Father was the obvious purchaser for his property. Briaden then became a very substantial house in a very large garden in a quiet and peaceful location.

May 1934 saw my schooling begin. In the months that we were in her care our governess had given both Denis and me a fair grounding. At eight years of age it was obvious that Denis was overdue for school, and it would not have been too soon for me, two years his junior.

In May 1934, Woodhouse Grove School, Apperley Bridge, only one mile away from Briaden – in those days primarily a boarding school supported mainly by Methodist parents – opened a junior school. In 1933 its governors had purchased a fine Victorian mansion known as Ashdown House built in 1878 on the site of an earlier mansion – Upperwood House – where Charlotte Brontë once worked as a governess. That fact, and other Brontë connections with Woodhouse Grove School prompted the governors to name their new preparatory department, Brontë House. It was there on 5 May 1934 that Denis and I were part of the small group of boys on show at the official opening.

Unfortunately, we were rather a prominent part since Mother had made a mistake. The advice to parents of new boys had been that they should attend the opening ceremony in black or grey suits. Mother had assumed that since it was May-time, light grey suits would be appropriate for her sons. The result was that in all the photographs of the opening ceremonies two boys stand out brightly in silver grey suits which photographed as almost white.

I was the youngest and smallest boy in the school and was there for two reasons. First, the school was desperate for pupils – so much so that only a handful of genuinely new pupils enrolled at the new preparatory school.

The bulk of the boys there had been pushed back from the lowest form of the senior school half a mile down the hill of Apperley Lane. The other reason I was sent to a school where the official entry age was eight, was that it was obviously very convenient for my parents to have us both going to the same place.

It is interesting to look at some figures as regards Brontë House in the dark days of the 1930s. First it should be noticed that when the house was built in 1878 it had cost £30,000 – a very large sum indeed at that time. When the Woodhouse Grove governors completed the purchase of Ashdown on 1 October 1933 the price was only £3,000. Today, Brontë House, even without the various additions made since the war, would be worth well into seven figures.

It is perhaps as well that Brontë House cost very little, since, in its early days the school certainly struggled for pupils. In my first term there were only eleven boys in my form but for the following autumn term we were down to seven. The headmaster of the senior school, Clifford Towlson, gave his opinion on each pupil's progress at the foot of the termly reports. It is gratifying to see that, as a six-year-old, he thought me, 'Keen and intelligent – shows much promise.' Two terms later I was still described as 'intelligent' but Dr Towlson added the comment, 'Sometimes untidy'.

We were measured and weighed at the end of each term and I see that at the end of 1934 I was still only 3ft 10½ inches (1.18 metres) tall and weighed in at only 3 stones 4½ lbs (19.3 kilos). It was then – and for several years after – that I was known to all my schoolmates as 'Titch' Greenwood. Although I was small and light, I was certainly fleet of foot and could outrun significantly bigger boys. I must have had some sort of a reputation – like my older brother – of being a fairly tough little boy since on one occasion I found myself fighting for the school.

A new boy – his name was Craddock – was thought by his contemporaries to be too cocky and not sufficiently respectful of them or, indeed, of the school. Somebody had the bright idea that it would be a fair humiliation for Craddock if he were thumped by somebody significantly smaller and, of course, 'Titch' Greenwood was the chosen one.

I had hardly met the boy but I found myself inside a ring of cheering schoolboys squaring up to someone quite a bit bigger than me. Neither of us really wanted to fight the other but we had no choice, so went at it hammer and tongs until the voice of authority broke up the fight. Both of us appeared first before Matron who tended our sundry wounds with iodine and sticking plasters and later before the Head who gave us the hard word but spared us the cane.

Corporal punishment was, of course, standard practice in schools at that time and in the senior school older boys, in the capacity of prefects, were allowed to beat others – not a good idea. Happily, throughout a wide variety of misdemeanours during my school life, I managed to avoid being caned.

The 1930s were a hard time. I was leading a spoiled and very fortunate existence during what were bleak years when the country was deep in depression. I can clearly remember seeing children playing in the Bradford streets without shoes – just as I remember seeing, when Father took me on business trips, Lancashire children, some in clogs and some with nothing on their feet in winter weather. Looking back I find it remarkable that Father managed to build his chain from a handful of shops to a significant size during that very difficult period.

In 1938 two things happened which certainly affected me for the rest of my life. The first was that my mother was increasingly concerned at my small stature and apparently frail physique. The family doctor examined me as thoroughly as the primitive medical equipment and techniques of those days permitted and he pronounced that I had 'strained my heart' – whatever that might mean, and it would be a good thing if I were taken off games for a lengthy period. That decision, based on I know not what real evidence, meant that I played no sports until I was fifteen – except for teaching myself to play tennis banging a ball up and down against the wall at the back of the Briaden tennis court. When – some seven years later – I was allowed to play games my speed, coupled with some fairly grim determination, enabled me to progress well as a player at some sports.

My self-taught tennis stood me in very good stead but I was inevitably useless at cricket, not even having held a bat or bowled a ball since I was seven. The senior school had no facilities during the war for teaching fifteen-year-olds the very basic elements of cricket which all my contemporaries had acquired over the years. It has been a source of real disappointment to me all my life that I never had the opportunity to play cricket seriously since I think it is probably the finest team game ever invented and it gives me great satisfaction as a spectator, be it in a test match crowd or, more usually, watching TV coverage or listening to that splendid part of the BBC's otherwise often so dreary output – 'Test Match Special', on the radio.

I have one or two interesting memories of pre-war life in the happy surroundings of Briaden, Underwood Drive, Rawdon. Not all of them were happy. I remember playing on the front lawn underneath the magnificent oak tree, which no doubt still stands, when a dog from the farm down the road came up the drive, across the lawn, and for no good reason at all attacked me. I would be about seven or eight at the time. The dog, which was of a fair size, a crossbred sheepdog, I suppose, bit me viciously around the left knee and literally tore a piece of flesh from me. To this day my passport contains the remark, 'Identifying feature: scar above left knee'. My parents rushed me to Bradford Infirmary, which would be a half-hour drive, and I remember that the doctor there poured something into the open wound which seemed to produce smoke. I was told afterwards that this was silver nitrate to cauterise the wound. My parents and the medical staff were surprised that throughout the whole painful business I neither screamed nor cried having decided to myself that I would not do so, however much it hurt.

Another example of the grim determination which, for some reason, seemed to be bred into both my brother and me, came when I nearly killed him. To add to the pleasures of the Briaden garden, Father had taken what was originally a 'sunken garden' and turned it instead into a concrete pool of some 50 or 60ft diameter and with a water depth of about four feet. Around the pond was a tarmac path and we would frequently ride our bikes round the edge of the pool. Brother Denis was doing just that when I decided to get my own back at him for some recent slight. I therefore took a stick and shoved it firmly into the front wheel of his bike as he cycled round the water's edge. The effect was spectacular. Naturally the bike came to a sudden halt. My brother continued but by this time he was airborne. He went straight into the water and the bike fell on top of him. Only then did I realise that what I had done was both pretty stupid and highly dangerous. Happily he soon surfaced and clambered out of the pond with one clear objective in the forefront of his mind – he was going to beat me to a pulp! My speed of foot served me well and I was up the path onto the drive and into the house in a flash.

On the right-hand side of the porch at the eastern entrance to Briaden was a door which led into the conservatory. I was through the door in a flash and locked it behind me. The upper part of the door was leaded light glazing which, of course, enabled me to grimace at Denis who, seething with rage, was locked on the other side. A lesser boy than my brother would have accepted temporary defeat and awaited another opportunity to have his revenge for my dumping him in the pond. Not so Denis. Without hesitation he drove his fist straight through the leaded light window and I found myself – deservedly, I suppose – on the receiving end of a shower of glass and a hard fist.

I did something good whilst a small boy and looking back on it gives me as much satisfaction as many much larger and more important events. I was in the house alone – not unusual in those days when houses were frequently unlocked and there was no fear of casual burglary etc. The front door bell rang and standing on the step was a shabby little man with a tray of boot laces and other 'sundries' around his neck. In his lapel he wore the round silver badge that indicated he was an ex-serviceman and a row of medal ribbons from the First World War was fixed to his tattered jacket. Those were hard times and this man had obviously been reduced to little more than a beggar. I told him, 'I don't want anything, and my mother is out.' He turned on his heel, trudged down the drive and began the long walk back to other houses and Apperley Lane.

I suddenly felt desperately sorry for him. I ran upstairs, found my money box, broke it open and took everything I had in it in both hands and ran after him. I didn't speak, I just caught him up and gave him all my savings and then ran away. Seventy-odd years later I think it was probably one of the most generous things I've done.

In front of Briaden, across the quiet road, Underwood Drive, was a field of some five or six acres. This sloped downhill, in parts quite steeply, to a footpath along the northern bank of the River Aire. In those days the Aire was a filthy, polluted stream, thanks to the mills at Shipley and Keighley and other businesses which used it to carry away all kinds of noxious waste. The river, therefore, was not somewhere small boys could play but the field sloping down to it most certainly was. Each winter we made various sledging tracks down that field, making them even more exciting than the good downhill velocity provided, by creating jumps. Old doors racked up on piles of stones or bricks and then given a covering of snow could, when strategically situated, get your sledge airborne for quite a distance.

I particularly remember the idea we had one winter to continue sledging by night and I commend this to any youngsters – or their parents – reading these words. We collected a large number of jam jars and put half a candle inside each. Then, when the candles were lit, we set them out to provide a kind of miniature runway lights.

Even as small boys my brother, my friends and I knew in 1938 that all was not well in the world. We heard anxious discussions between our parents and their friends and, of course, a lot of schoolboy literature involved exploits from the Great War which less than twenty years previously had been very much in progress. The possibility that there might be another war with Germany was ever present, even in our young minds.

I remember clearly seeing a German airship fly slowly up the valley of the River Aire and I can still see the enormous black swastika on its tail. I suppose 99% of the world's population has never seen a full-scale airship. The advertising blimps which are today described as airships are a fraction of the size of the 'Graf Zeppelin' which, with a capacity of 3.7 million cubic feet, was half as big again as the zeppelins of the First World War. The last of the airships, the 'Hindenberg', was almost double the size of the 'Graf Zeppelin'. I do not know which of these monsters it was that in about 1936 I saw flying almost overhead. Both those airships made transatlantic voyages and their route took them across northern England. In fact, the view was that part of the purpose of their voyages was aerial reconnaissance for use by the Luftwaffe in the war that was to come.

At the end of the summer term in July 1938, I was still significantly undersized. I weighed 64 lbs, that is 29 kilos. I was 4ft 5½ inches tall (just under 1.36 metres) and continued to be the smallest of all my contemporaries. I ended that school year seventh in a form of twenty-seven and with good grades – although I was slightly under the average age. Unfortunately, my mother decided that I must remain for a further year at Brontë House rather than transferring to the senior school. The headmaster also wanted to keep several boys back for a further year in Brontë House otherwise the numbers there would have been too thin.

This was the second of my 1938 misfortunes. The other, of course, being the 'off games' decision.

The result of this one was that I repeated a whole year's work which was a complete waste of time since obviously the second time round the work was easy.

The following September, in what was presumably an attempt to correct a serious mistake with the education of those boys who had unnecessarily been obliged to repeat a year's work, the school authorities placed the small group of us who had been so affected not in the bottom form of the senior school but in the second form. This was, of course, an educational nonsense since we found ourselves in a class where the other members had had a year of such subjects as French, algebra and geometry, as well as other subjects, about which we had been taught absolutely nothing. To this day, I am angry that this mistake meant that all my middle years at school were spent in the Lower Fourth, Transition B, and the Lower Fifth. It was not until I passed School Certificate reasonably well that I was able to join the Sixth Form on equal terms with my friends who had gone through the upper of the two streams which then constituted Woodhouse Grove School.

The only good thing that happened to me before I moved into the Sixth Form was that, shortly after I had turned fifteen, I was at last allowed to play games and enjoyed a season as full back for the second XV. Not having played the game previously, my technical rugby skills were sparse but the 'grim determination' attitude cannot have gone unnoticed since I see at the foot of my old school report for December 1942 that the headmaster has added the words, 'a plucky full back'.

The war that was then raging had only marginally impacted on my family and on my school life. I remember that on 3 September 1939, the day Britain went to war, we had left St Barnabas Church, Heaton, Bradford – my mother's family church, where my brother and I had been christened – and had called on our maternal grandparents, Grand-father and Grandma Nellist. They lived in a small cottage at Highgate, Heaton. This grandfather's working life had been spent as a gardener and it had been a struggle for him to bring up eight children. He was a dignified and upright – in both senses of the word – man. But on that Sunday morning, when we listened to Prime Minister Neville Chamber-lain's broadcast, there were tears in his eyes. His wife, and one or two of their daughters who were there that morning, were all weeping – not least because one of Grandfather Nellist's two sons was already a regular soldier in the Coldstream Guards. It was obvious that he would be off to war immediately and would almost certainly be followed shortly there-after by the other son, and probably the husbands of one or two of the daughters.

The outbreak of war stopped the expansion of Father's business in its tracks. There was no time for expansion or improvement of the business. It was a matter of survival which depended mainly on finding enough merchandise to sell and also finding people, elderly men, youths and – for the first time – female assistants and manageresses to replace the men who had gone into the services. This expansion in the years immediately before the war had been dramatic. By 1935 there were fifty Greenwood's shops.

Up to the outbreak of the war rapid growth was the order of the day. At one period a new Greenwood's branch was being opened somewhere every month. All the branches were within a 100-mile radius of Bradford with the exception of an ill-fated attempt in 1936 to open a flagship branch in Oxford Street, London on the corner of Dean Street. The rent of that shop was as much as any ten of the northern branches and unfortunately, Father found that north country policies aimed primarily at producing merchandise of the keenest possible value did not seem to work in London. For example, on one occasion he found that a standard line of ties priced at 1/6d – the equivalent of 7.5p today – simply did not sell in Oxford Street at all. As an experiment he marked them all up to 2/6d. – or 12.5p – whereupon they began to sell freely.

The London experiment did not survive the start of the war, neither did some of Father's favourite branches in Sunderland and elsewhere in the north-east. Some shops had to be closed due to shortages of supplies and also problems with deliveries. One or two shops were damaged during air raids but only two – Chariot Street, Hull, and Grimsby branch – were blown out of existence.

I was a very patriotic boy during the war. In the dark days of 1940, when invasion seemed imminent, I persuaded an uncle to lend me a .22 rifle. It was a single shot, cheap weapon but I practised hard so as to ensure that I could kill at least one German with a clean head shot at up to fifty or sixty yards. My reasoning was that they would no doubt shoot me thereafter but there would have been one German officer less. (I did not intend to waste my single shot on anything less than officer material!)

It seemed to my mind likely that, if the invasion succeeded, our fairly large home would probably be requisitioned by the Germans and I therefore prepared an alternative method of killing one – or better still, several – of the enemy. I stole – I now admit it – poison from the school's chemistry laboratory and kept this hidden with a view to poisoning any Germans billeted on us. Thank heavens these desperate moves were never needed since clearly my life would have ended before my fourteenth birthday.

Father worked desperately hard during the war and managed some war work in addition to his business struggles. He spent numerous nights on duty as a Special Constable at the Arrow aircraft factory a few miles from our home.

He was also able to put one of his hobbies to useful war service. He had long enjoyed making what we now call 'home movies' and he had more than one cine projector. During the darkest days of the war military camps and units such as anti-aircraft gun sites were places which the occupants left only very rarely. Consequently any kind of entertainment was very much welcomed. Father obtained films from the Army Kinema Corps and visited numerous camp sites in the West Riding of Yorkshire giving evening film shows to those for whom the only other entertainment was the NAAFI. I was his assistant projectionist on several of those trips.

An additional burden for retailers during the war was, of course, rationing. Food rationing began in 1940 and in 1941 clothing and footwear also went 'on the ration'. Taking the right number of coupons for every item sold was almost as important as taking the cash for the sale. When new supplies were obtained from a wholesaler or manufacturer, the appropriate number of coupons had to be transferred together with the cheque in payment.

Whilst Father was struggling with his wartime problems and whilst – much more importantly – Britain was suffering defeat after defeat in 1940 and 1941, life at Woodhouse Grove School continued on broadly similar lines to that before the war but with a steady and progressive deterioration in a variety of areas.

First, and probably most important was the inevitable deterioration in the quality of the teaching staff. The young, able teachers were away to the war and their replacements were increasingly unfit men or older men. The school maintenance staff, cooks, cleaners etc. became fewer and fewer. Food rationing meant that school meals were of an even lower quality than the levels which harsh economic factors had necessitated before the war. The school became shabbier. Tired old equipment could not be replaced but, nevertheless, the school numbers actually increased from a total of 255, split almost equally between boarders and day boys in 1940, to a figure in 1945 of 325 in total of whom two-thirds (212 to be precise) were boarders. By that time I was one of them.

In summer 1943 my brother left the school and my parents agreed that I should return after the summer holiday as a boarder and thus spend my final two sixth-form years in that capacity. This was a wise decision and the fees (£100!) was money well spent.

CHAPTER 3

Youth – Wasted on Young People

I AM NOT SURE FROM WHOM the above is a quotation, perhaps I dreamt it up myself, but without doubt the five years or so of my life between entering the sixth form at WGS and becoming a young married man were in the main highly enjoyable, sometimes quite exciting and I certainly wish I could have them over again – as do we all.

I had grown five inches in a year and put on a stone and a half in weight which I badly needed. I should have mentioned that, when the headmaster thought me 'a plucky full back', and I was tackling hefty boys weighing as much as twelve or thirteen stones, I was just over five feet tall and weighed in at about six and a half stones, i.e. about ninety pounds – about forty kilos. Now in the autumn of 1943 with my height moving towards 5ft 7ins and my weight around eight stones I had a reasonable chance of surviving the role of a boarder at WGS in the middle of the war.

As a new boarder I was lucky in that I was already a senior boy in the sixth form, in the first XV, and had been around the school for a long time. Nevertheless, the initiation ceremony had to be performed and therefore, just like the already-homesick eleven-year-olds who had arrived at the bottom end of our dormitory, I was obliged to entertain the company standing on the lockers with a chamber pot – on my head, – and singing an appropriate song. I was spared the fate which befell some of the genuinely new boys whose singing was not appreciated.

They were kindly invited by the prefect in charge of the dormitory to bang their head against the lockers until he told them to stop! You will gather from this that bullying and intimidation of small boys was rife – partially, I think, as a consequence of the low calibre of the wartime teaching staff, some of whom simply could not impose reasonable standards of discipline.

On this unhappy topic of indiscipline and bullying, I must mention three examples. In most of the classrooms in front of the long blackboard on the wall, there stood a wooden dais about eighteen inches high. On several occasions boys who earned the disapproval of their fellows were pushed underneath the dais and left there sometimes throughout an entire lesson – not very nice.

More amusing and less objectionable were the scenes that frequently took place during the boarders' supper. The last duty of the master in charge for the day was to supervise that evening meal which comprised very little in the way of good food but always a small bottle of milk. Depending upon who was the master in charge, supper could be taken in almost complete calm and silence or, alternatively, in organised chaos. One master who, although by far the best-qualified teacher in the school, was very weak on discipline, was Herr Doctor Mendel, a German Jew who had been able to escape from Nazi tyranny shortly before the war began. 'Doc Mendel', as we called him, taught German but by 1943 his subject was fairly unpopular and he was down to only one pupil – me. He also taught other subjects and in every respect save his inability to keep order, he was a good teacher and a kind and friendly man. Thus it was with fairly typical schoolboy cruelty that we came to regard supper with Doc Mendel in charge as the time for all kinds of bad behaviour. On occasions the dining-room air was thick with flying milk bottle tops. The circular cardboard bottle tops could, if you knew how, be thrown quite a distance, pretty well the length of the dining hall. There was much shouting and laughter, particularly if someone had managed a successful table bump.

The dining-room held a number of long tables with ten boys seated on benches down each side and a senior boy, a prefect or sub-prefect, sitting on a chair at each end. Other sub-prefects and I had – over time – trained the boys on our end to lift our end of the table just a fraction of an inch clear of the floor. On the word of command they would swing the whole table towards me – I had previously edged my chair back a foot or so – and then let the whole table swing through so as to thump the boy in the chair at the other end firmly in the midriff. Properly executed, this manoeuvre could be guaranteed to knock boy and chair over and yet, from the master's viewpoint, nothing had happened except that, for some reason, one of the prefects had fallen over the back of his chair.

Dining-room disorders included such pleasant customs as taking the large metal teapot and gently inserting the spout into the jacket pocket of one of the boys on the adjoining table sitting with his back towards you. It is quite amazing how much tea a jacket pocket will hold before the wearer feels the heat and the damp and reacts appropriately.

One final example of the appalling disciplinary standards which enlivened my boarding years in the dining-room would be the fate of the school maids. By 1943/44 the school was down to only two maids, part of whose duties were to assist with the serving of food and clearing of dishes. By that time most of such tasks were met with boy-power.

A wartime boys' boarding school with strict bounds inevitably produced a monastic feeling but celibacy was not in the minds of sixteen and seventeen-year-olds for whom sex had begun – as they say – to rear its ugly head. The upshot of all this was that when the two maids ventured to the far end of the dining-hall, albeit to deliver food or retrieve some crockery – they were in constant danger of having their bottoms pinched or hands up their skirts.

I greatly admired the way in which the two girls coped with this situation. They armed themselves with the long and large soup ladles from the kitchen and gave offending boys a hearty thwack and comments such as, 'Keep your hands to yourself, you nasty little b . . . . .!' All of which goes to show that there were times when WGS was anything but a breeding ground of refinement and good manners!

Bullying was and always will be a nasty business and sometimes it went too far with spectacular results. We tended to think of the school as being something like a prisoner of war camp. Indeed, I frequently headed my compulsory weekly letter home with the address, 'Stalag Luft III'. One boy who had been on the receiving end of far too much bullying decided to attempt what wartime POWs called a 'home-run'. He left his dormitory in the middle of the night and – so the story went around – went up to the railway bridge, waited until a goods train was passing underneath and dropped down into a tarpaulin-covered railway wagon. He left the train in – I seem to remember – Sheffield, found somewhere to stay and then made contact with his parents – telling them that only if they swore not to send him back to school would he return home. His parents were to put an advertisement in the personal ads. column of the local evening paper if and when they agreed to his terms.

That was the story that went round the school and I believe it to be fairly accurate. One thing is certain, we never saw the boy again and thus he had indeed achieved a successful home-run.

It was not all bad behaviour and ill-discipline. There were some masters with whom you definitely did not tangle. I remember one, a science master by the name of Roberts, who the boys christened 'Sissy' Roberts for the very good reason that that was exactly what he was not. On my first day, in one of his algebra classes, I was doodling on the cover of my algebra exercise book, little knowing that 'Sissy' Roberts, who made a habit of patrolling up and down the classroom while he spoke, was approaching me from the rear. My first intimation of his proximity was a heavy blow which knocked me clean from my desk chair and left me sitting on the floor, somewhat shaken. Such treatment would probably put the master behind bars today but it was not unusual in my schooldays and in that particular case it had the desired effect since, thereafter, I behaved myself impeccably in that man's classes.

School discipline, or the sometimes the lack of it, did not always involve violence. I remember with a smile the occasion in a physics lesson when I was speaking to the boy next to me, who was named Beevers. The master saw Beevers' head turned towards me and immediately said, 'Beevers, stop talking! Take a page.'

A 'page' was the standard WGS imposition. All boys had a page book consisting of landscape-shaped pages ruled with about fifty lines per page. When given lines as a punishment, unless the master decided otherwise and requested, say, a carefully written page of history or Shakespeare, or whatever, one had to fill the page with the same old Latin tag repeated time after time. If nothing else, this ensured that every Grove boy had at least six words of Latin – although they would have been of little use in general conversation. The phrase we had to write was, *Ante adventum magistri nobis tacendum est*, meaning 'Before the arrival of the master it is imperative to be silent'.

Back to Beevers and his unjustified imposition of a page. He replied at once to the master, 'But, sir, it wasn't me!'

'Don't answer me back, boy,' came the reply. 'Make that two pages.'

'But, sir, it wasn't!'

'Make that four pages, Beevers.'

'But, sir –'

'Eight pages, Beevers.'

Even then Beevers had not accepted that he was on a definite loser. He managed one more strangulated, 'But . . .' which resulted in sixteen pages which fully occupied much of his spare time for a couple of days.

We had one master who made himself thoroughly unpopular. He used to drive a little Austin Seven car and it was decided that this provided an opportunity for revenge. At the end of the school day he went to the staff car park and found his car was missing. He discovered it a little later, parked in the middle of a tennis court, which was down a flight of steps, to which site it had been carried bodily by a dozen of his pupils. Another example of the indiscipline of wartime schooldays.

In 1941 a unit of the Air Training Corps had been formed at the school and I was very happy to join it since, by the time I was sixteen, I was quite determined to get into the RAF and, like very many British boys, I dreamt of flying a fighter – ideally, a Spitfire. I did rather well in the ATC, quickly being promoted to corporal and then becoming something of an expert at aircraft recognition. My good friend, Dick Atkinson, and I were selected on two occasions to represent our unit at the Command Aircraft Recognition Championships held at Leeds University. Dozens of eager young ATC cadets sat in a semi-darkened lecture theatre while a succession of aircraft pictures from every conceivable angle was flashed on to a large screen for a few seconds. I see that in the last such championship my answer sheet, although written in a very untidy hand, nevertheless showed that I had correctly identified 72 out of the 80 images flashed at us. Some of those planes had names which have almost passed into the language – Spitfire, Lancaster, Dakota, Mustang, Hurricane, etc. Some others, more than sixty years later, have certainly passed into history – Firefly, Invader, Stormovik, Oscar, Black Widow, Betty, etc. Of all the planes we had to identify from all the fighting nations, those from Russia and Japan were harder for us to identify than those from Britain, America and Germany.

I was very serious indeed about my intention to get into the Air Force. In 1944 you had to be seventeen and a quarter to volunteer for the Forces. In December of that year when I reached that age I caught a bus to Bradford, made my way to the Mechanics' Institute in the centre of the city which was then the main recruiting office. I formally offered my services to King and country, was formally accepted and told to go back to school and await further developments.

I was not popular either at home or with the headmaster for committing myself to the Forces so hastily. However, a few weeks later – in January 1945 – I received an official communication inviting me to attend an aircrew selection board in Doncaster, return railway warrant enclosed. The letter advised that I might be away for as long as three days.

Of all places, the aircrew selection board was established on the upper floors of the main store of the Doncaster Co-operative Society.

Somewhere around two or three hundred anxious youths, or perhaps we can now say young men, were billeted in large dormitories and the following day the selection process began. Those of us who were in the ATC were in uniform and looking as smart as we could and we felt – rightly as it turned out – that our time in the ATC would give us precedence over those would-be fliers who had not had that experience.

A series of medical examinations came first. Those rooms above the Co-op had been sub-divided into numerous cubicles. You went into one and your eyes were tested. In the next one you were tested for night vision. In another room it was heart and lungs. And there was a particularly difficult test – blowing a column of mercury up a u-shaped tube and holding it for – I can't remember, was it one minute, or two? Or even three? One thing is certain, it was hard to do and many failed that test.

The system was very simple. If you failed any test, that was it. You were immediately – and I mean immediately – on your way home. It was thus that, within an hour or two, two or three hundred candidates had been whittled down by half. As the tests continued, they included intelligence tests, and such things as a Morse Aptitude Test, where you had to identify some Morse dots and dashes against a recorded background noise of engines roaring, anti-aircraft shells bursting and machine guns firing.

After two days, there were only three of us left. All three of us were NCOs in the Air Training Corps. We solemnly swore an oath of allegiance to King George VI, were issued with a pay book and given three days' pay for a rank of AC2 (Aircraftman Second Class) and – most important of all – we were told which way we had been graded. Those accepted for aircrew training were graded either PNB or WOP/AG. Those letters stood for pilot, navigator or bomb aimer in the first grading and wireless operator or air gunner in the second. I knew enough about casualty rates for air gunners and I also knew that commissioned WOP/AGs were rare birds. Consequently, I was absolutely thrilled to be told that I was graded PNB.

I was now officially a member of the Royal Airforce Volunteer Reserve, AC2 3044660 Greenwood G.B. I was able to wear an RAF VR badge with very considerable pride. I was sent back to the school with instructions to finish my education and told I would then be called for initial training and later aircrew training. They say little things please little minds and perhaps I was being small-minded when I took great pride in sporting in my ATC forage cap the white flash which indicated that I was potential aircrew.

However, AC2 Greenwood was still very much a schoolboy with several months to go before a successful Higher School Certificate exam would permit him to leave WGS. Naturally his hope was that he would go straight from school into the RAF.

Sport played a big part in the latter part of my schooldays. I had my first XV colours, I had run well in athletics and was looking forward to doing something outstanding in the forthcoming July 1945 school sports. It was a pity that tennis was not an inter-schools sport. We had only played inter-house matches but I was in the happy position that there was only one other tennis player who I could not confidently expect to beat. He and I were much of a muchness but since we were both in the same house there was no doubt where the inter-house tennis cup was going. Let's disregard chronology for the moment and get all these school sporting memories out of the way.

On the rugby field I had started as full back where I relied mostly on the 'grim determination' factor. During my second year in the school first team I played mostly on the wing where my speed came into its own.

In wartime, sporting fixtures with other schools had to be restricted to those which could be reached reasonably easily and, unlike today when WGS sends its rugby and other teams as far afield as New Zealand, Canada, Australia and South Africa, the furthest we got was a train ride up Airedale to play Giggleswick on a cold winter's day. So cold, in fact, that we were allowed to change in one of the boiler rooms at Giggleswick School and as we were getting into our kit, in came a very scruffy-looking individual in overalls to stoke the boiler. Our team wit, Chrimes by name, was short-sighted enough to think that a witticism might be in order. He politely enquired of the Giggleswick captain, 'Your headmaster, I presume?' The Giggleswickians were not amused and, having already been determined to beat us, they now were determined to thrash us – which they duly did.

Generally, however, we were in those distant days a reasonably good rugby-playing school. Nowadays, as I write these words, WGS is not a reasonably good rugby school. It is an excellent, sometimes superb, one.

I was enjoying my school rugby and was delighted to receive an invitation to play in Leeds on the old Headingley club's ground at Kirkstall in a Yorkshire Schoolboys' trial match. I was picked to play at full back and was having, I think, quite a reasonable game when, just after half time,

I tackled a particularly hefty opposing forward. When I picked myself up I knew I had sustained some damage since my left arm was hanging limp and I could hardly lift it. I had in fact broken my left collarbone. A wiser youth would have gone off the field and sought medical help. Grimly determined, Greenwood, thinking of the possibility of being selected for the Yorkshire Schoolboys' side, decided to play on. Rugby players reading this will appreciate that fielding high balls with only one hand, tackling with one arm, etc. are difficult things to do. Nevertheless, I saw the match out, managed to dress myself, went home (it was school holiday time) and played snooker that evening by lifting my left arm on to the table with my right and after each shot, letting it flop back and hang limply. Only the following morning, when I found I couldn't get out of bed with one arm completely useless, did I decide the game was up. The family doctor dealt with me with some help from a specialist and I returned to school with my left arm strapped across my chest. The break healed just in time for the close of the 1944/45 rugby season.

I received a kind letter from the then president of the Yorkshire Rugby Union, one 'Bob' Oakes, who for many years was a very significant figure in the rugby world. Oddly enough, Bob Oakes used the same adjective as my headmaster had used when I began playing rugby as a light-weight full back. He said, 'It was a very plucky thing to do, but you should have left the field.'

As previously mentioned, I simply hadn't a clue about cricket since no one had ever taught me anything about the game. Nevertheless, I had an eye for a ball and was therefore asked to play for my house team in the inter-house competition from which the real cricket players in the school XI were excluded. In one house match with the teens of runs required I was finally sent in to bat. I hit only four balls in quick succession – six, four, six, four – all of them agricultural-type shots to the mid-wicket boundary. On the strength of that very much one-off performance, the following Wednesday I was asked to play in what we called the First Club, namely the practice match for the first and second XIs. This was a splendid opportunity for all my pals who could play cricket to give me a hard time. I took a fair few body blows before Chrimes, who was a pretty good and hostile fast bowler, finally took pity and with little difficulty clean-bowled me.

On only one other occasion did I hold a cricket bat in my hands in a proper match and that was several years later when I was invited to play for the Greenwood Company Cricket XI in the Bradford Wednesday Afternoon (early closing day) League. I went in at number eleven with only two runs required for victory and with characteristic arrogance tried to get them with a boundary. My wild slog missed and I was clean-bowled with the first ball I had to face and – as they say – 'They never asked me again.'

Back to schooldays. Towards the end of the spring term in 1945 the school sports were held. Bubbles to false modesty, the bottom line is that I swept all before me. Boys were allowed to enter six events. I entered the 100 yards, the 220, 440, the half-mile, the mile and the 3¼ mile steeplechase. I won them all. I broke the half-mile record in the process and had actually broken the mile record in training but had no competition on the day to push me towards a record time when it counted.

The three-and-a-quarter-mile cross-country race was a different matter. In 1943 my brother, Denis, had won it and had established a record time of 20 minutes 54 seconds for the difficult course. In 1944 I had won that race but had not managed a particularly fast time. The year 1945 was my moment. I was fit, happy, full of confidence and, on the day, I finished the thick end of half a mile ahead of the next boy in a time of 19 minutes 51 seconds – a record which stood until, in later years, the race was abandoned following changes to the layout of the school campus. I did not realise it at the time, but my not-very-impressive physique was ideal for a long distance runner. Comparatively long strong legs were topped by a narrow-shouldered but deep-chested body which contained a good pair of lungs and, I think, a rather larger than normal heart.

Only one aspect of the school sports of 1945 caused me any pain. That was the year when the headmaster decided to abolish the long tradition involving the Victor Ludorum cup. For many years the boy who had done best on sports day had received this cup and then been chaired around the school. I was denied that honour since dear old Clifford or, as we called him 'Pop' Towlson, our headmaster, had finally decided that there should be less emphasis on individual sporting performances and more on team efforts. My mother, who took pride in her boys' achievements, shared my disappointment that I was not to hold the coveted cup. So she went out and bought a small silver cup, appropriately engraved with details of my triumph.

My father had never been a sportsman although he had quite good ball sense and, if time had permitted, I am sure he could have played a variety of games and sports. Time did not permit. He had been too busy first building up his business and then struggling to preserve it during the war years. Consequently, he was a very surprised man when, a few weeks after leaving school in the summer of 1945, I asked him to go with me to an athletics meeting in Huddersfield which I had seen advertised in the *Yorkshire Post* and, mainly out of curiosity, I had entered for the youths' half mile handicap race.

We are out of chronological order here but I'll get back to school and the closing days of the war – and their impact on my young life shortly.

Father took me to Huddersfield and was accompanied by one of his suppliers. I saw Father and his friend comfortably settled in the grandstand and then went to change. We went out on to the track which was, of course, a good quality cinder track and this would be the first time in my life that I had run on a decent surface. At school the running track was simply marked out around the rugby field.

Being a handicap race, the entrants were handicapped according to age and, since I was not far short of my eighteenth birthday, with two others I started just a yard or two in front of the normal starting point. The rest of the field – probably about a dozen runners – took their places at various distances in front of me. The gun went off and immediately my two fellow back markers surged away and began overtaking some of those who had been given a slightly shorter distance to run. A half-mile race is, of course, run over two laps. Nowadays we would think of an 800-metre event with two 400-metre laps. In those days it was half a mile with two 440-yard laps. At the end of the first lap on that memorable day at Huddersfield, as we ran past the grandstands, I suspect Father was greatly disappointed to see his younger son last in a comparatively large field.

I began overhauling those in front of me and on the back straight sailed past most of the field, thoroughly enjoying the feeling of running on a decent surface for the first time ever. We came round the top bend and I only had three or four in front of me. As we came off the bend and into the final straight only the local star – one Derek Ibbotson – was in front of me. I went past him like a train to – I think – his great surprise and to the amazement of the knowledgeable members of the crowd since, even as a youth, he was a rising star in British athletics.

In fact, Ibbotson went on later to become a world record holder for the mile and an Olympic athlete of international fame. I had to admit that for years afterwards I got a kick out of mentioning that in my youth I had done a bit of running and that on the one occasion when I came up against the world beater, Ibbotson, he came second.

Father was dumbfounded. For my part I was very proud to take home the prize which, of all things, was an extensive tea set which, of course, I presented to my mother. That day was a triumph but very foolishly I never followed it up. I realised years later that I obviously had very real potential as a middle or long distance runner — indeed the time I clocked that day would have won that year's British public schools' championship and this was without any proper training or coaching. I should have joined an athletics club and had some skilled help and advice and I do sincerely believe I could have got to, or at least very near, the peak of national and even international competition. In fact, the only running I did thereafter was in the Forces in cross-country events of which more will follow in due course.

CHAPTER 4

On Wheels and In Troubles

Now let's get back to my schooldays. In 1943 Father had bought brother Denis an MG PB two-seater sports car manufactured, I think, in about 1936.

Denis had remained a day boy at WGS and just as soon as he was old enough to have wheels he wanted them. He started out on two, in the form of a 150 cc elderly James motorbike on which he would chug up Apperley Lane to meet his girlfriend, Marjorie Bussey, with whom he celebrated sixty years of marriage in 2007. He took me on the pillion one day but the old machine didn't have the power to carry two of us up the hill and I had to run for much of the way.

Denis then moved from two wheels to three in the form of an old Morgan three-wheeler. A most impressive two-seater with the engine, a twin cylinder air-cooled job, open to the elements at the front end. The Morgan was pretty quick and I suspect that one of the reasons behind Father's generosity in buying Denis the MG was that it might be safer.

The good news for me was that since Father had bought Denis an MG two-seater when he was seventeen I could reasonably hope for the same. Father came through and shortly after my seventeenth birthday I was sufficiently spoiled as to become the very proud owner of a black MG Model TA. I realised I was very fortunate to be in that position since, unlike today when many sixth form schoolboys and girls arrive at school in their own cars, in those days it was a great rarity for a teenager to have his own vehicle. As I shall tell you in a moment I put the car to much good use whilst still at school.

My brother and I were both very interested in cars then and have been ever since. We probably inherited this from Father who, as soon as he could afford to do so, always kept several cars, some of them very interesting ones but none more so than the Rolls Royce Phantom III which he bought in the middle of the war. I was with him that day, returning from Preston where we had visited his younger brother's hat works which, of course, produced hats sold through Father's chain of shops as well as numerous other outlets. We stopped for petrol at a small garage a few miles outside Preston and as the garage man was filling Father's car (and taking petrol ration coupons as well as cash from him) we noticed that in the back of the garage there was some kind of large vehicle covered completely with a very large dust sheet. Father was curious. 'What have you got there?'

'That,' said the garage man, 'is a real car. Do you want to have a look at it?'

He pulled off the dust cover and underneath was the gleaming black body of a very large Rolls Royce. It was a car that had been made in 1938. In those days Rolls Royce owners bought the engine and chassis and then coachbuilders designed and added the style of body the car owner required. This car had a V12 engine of no less than 7,340 ccs. The body was by Gurney Nutting and its shape was nothing like the typical stately carriage appearance of most pre-war Rolls. The body was a four-door sports saloon with a beautifully swept rear end. The engine looked like an aero engine since there were two plugs to every cylinder and when one lifted the bonnet you looked at twenty-four plugs leads running from the immaculate engine housing. It was very fast. We later learned that despite its weight − approaching three and a half tons − the car was capable of 100 mph. The downside was that its petrol tank took thirty-two gallons and its petrol consumption was only around seven or eight miles to the gallon.

Father was bowled over by the car and he agreed to buy it on the spot. Because of its savage petrol consumption it spent the rest of the war on blocks in the garage but as soon as the war was over and obtaining petrol became a little easier it became an important part of our family affairs as you will read later.

My MG was a major asset during my final year as a boarder at WGS. As I have told you already, wartime discipline at Woodhouse Grove was pretty lax. We took advantage of this and for two or three terms there was an epidemic of competitive bounds-breaking in the school. The dormitories all had fire escapes. The fire escapes were, of course, locked but the key to those locks was in a small glass cabinet at the side with the usual instruction, 'In an emergency break the glass'. We all discovered that breaking the glass was quite unnecessary. Loosening or removing one or two screws meant that the glass could be lifted out and the key used whenever needed. The result of this situation was that almost every night, boys would be out of one dormitory or another, vying with each other to see who could do the most outrageous things. I was particularly fortunate in that my home, Briaden was only a one-mile walk from the school along the bank of the River Aire. Thus it was easy for me to go with two or three friends down the fire escape, to walk home and spend an hour or two in the middle of the night playing snooker on the three-quarter size table which Father had thoughtfully provided, mainly for the benefit of his sons and their friends.

Occasionally, I was able to bring my MG into play and shortly after lights out, when the school had settled down, it was down the fire escape, a walk to the spot between home and the school where I had earlier parked the car, and then away to a dance – usually in the Broadway Hall at Horsforth some five or six miles away.

Competition for the most interesting night out from school was intense. One boy got as far as Scarborough and back – some sixty miles each way – in the middle of the night. Another successfully organised a mass breakout. Every boy in one of the larger dormitories – about thirty in total – went out down the fire escape to walk some distance across the valley to Calverley Woods where ignoring black-out conditions, they had a camp fire and a nocturnal party.

Apart from getting out of school altogether there were other nocturnal events. Smoking was, of course, strictly banned and consequently everyone wanted to try it. A small group of us formed a smoking club whose prime objective was to meet in the headmaster's study in the middle of the night and puff away on the pipes, cigarettes and cigars that we kept hidden in Dr Towlson's room behind a row of his books.

In due time we came unstuck.

The nocturnal bounds-breaking was at its peak in the spring of 1945 when it was abundantly clear that the war in Europe would soon be over. A group of us began to prepare for the sixth form boarders' end-of-war party. We had various day boys bringing to the school, over a period of some weeks, a large quantity of bottled beer, bottles of cider, together with cigarettes and cigars. These were stashed away in some of the changing-room lockers as we listened to the news of the dying days of the Third Reich.

VE Day arrived and that night, from three different dormitories, small parties went down the fire escapes collecting the drinks and smokes and then headed across the playing fields to a small barn on the other side of the railway embankment. The embankment split the school's playing fields but through it there was access via the tunnel for the River Aire and the footpath along the river bank. Candles were lit, toasts were drunk, songs were sung, a haze of tobacco smoke drifted out of the barn door and inside it most of the teenage boys had drunk far more than they could handle.

Finally, bearing a large sack of empty bottles, the celebration party staggered back towards school. At the foot of the fire escape to my dormitory the question arose, who would take the sack of empty bottles which we should, of course, have dumped in the river on our way back. Foolishly – and I suppose drunkenly – I volunteered and as the others went their different ways I staggered up the fire escape singing happily (probably 'There'll Always Be an England' or some such patriotic song) and dragging my clinking sack behind me. I opened the fire escape door and fell into my dormitory, smashing most of the bottles and the dregs therefrom soon made the dorm. smell like a brewery. Fortunately, all the younger boys in the dormitory turned to and helped to mop up and tidy up the mess whilst I collapsed on my bed.

I had never previously drunk anything more than an odd glass and therefore it was no surprise that before victory night was over I had been very sick and the following morning, a Sunday, I felt ghastly. Somehow I managed to get dressed and we headed towards chapel. Two of my friends supported me as I staggered up to and into the chapel. Then during the service, whenever a hymn was to be sung, they lifted me up and at the end of the hymn dropped me like a sack of coal so that I could slump in the pew in a pretty well unconscious state. After chapel I was being helped back towards school when we ran into Matron who took one look at me and immediately instructed my pals to get me into the sanatorium.

I found myself in an upstairs room in the san. lying in bed feeling dreadful whilst Matron and her colleagues discussed what ghastly disease had suddenly afflicted Greenwood and might it be contagious. I believe my parents were advised that I was quite ill but did appear to be recovering, from some unidentified complaint. Some of those who had been with me the night before smuggled a note in to me imploring me to 'Say nothing at all about last night!' I needed no encouragement to keep my mouth tightly shut! A day's rest put me right. My fellow drinkers all had suffered heavy hangovers but none of them had been laid as low as I was. Although various members of staff had their suspicions as to how some of their pupils had celebrated VE Day there was never a serious enquiry which might, of course, have meant expulsion for some or all of us.

My luck finally ran out a few weeks from the end of my final term when – so I was told – 'Pop' Towlson came into my dormitory at about midnight, shone his flashlight on my empty bed – I think I was at a dance that night – and said out loud, 'Ah yes. As I thought Greenwood.'

Clearly the headmaster had finally been alerted to the fact of nocturnal bounds-breaking and he had concluded that I was a – perhaps the – ringleader. The upshot of it was that he spared me from expulsion but I was 'reduced to the ranks'. For my last few weeks at WGS I was no longer a sub-prefect (there used to be two full prefects and about eight or ten sub-prefects). I was instead devoid of any status or privileges and was confined to the large schoolroom which served as our morning assembly hall, at all times when I was not in a class, in the dining-hall or in the dormitory. I could not complain. All the nocturnal bounds-breaking had been great fun while it lasted and whilst I was certainly not going to leave the school in a blaze of glory at least I had not been expelled.

My last two or three terms at WGS had been enjoyable not least because, whilst still only sixteen, I had met a girl and come to regard her very much as my regular girlfriend. Her name was Renée Rhodes. She lived just half a mile from the school on Apperley Lane and although not yet fifteen was already working as a ladies' hairdresser in Bradford. During the school holidays we went to the cinema frequently, went dancing occasionally and walked hand in hand along the river bank and in Cragg Woods, the quiet wooded area beyond Briaden.

It's easy to mock youngsters who think they are in love at a very early age. Well, I don't knock young love. If a youth is fortunate enough to have a girlfriend who is not only attractive but sensible and, most important of all, kind, then he is very lucky. You'll hear more about Renée a little later but let us now conclude my schooldays with a few more memories that may give you a smile.

When I was confined to the schoolroom for the last few weeks of my school life there was very little to do by way of entertainment. However, there was a game popular at WGS at that time and by continuous practice – I had nothing better to do – I had become pretty good at it. We called it 'Shove Ha'penny' but it was not the normal form of 'Shove Ha'penny' played on a board marked with parallel lines. It was actually 'Shove Ha'penny football' and was played on the window sills of the schoolroom which were about five feet wide by two or three feet in depth – that is, about the size of a small table. The game consisted of two goals, each about six inches wide, marked at the end of each window sill, or table as the case may be, together with two old pennies and one old half-penny. With the aid of a comb or a six-inch ruler you used your penny to propel the half-penny towards and ultimately if possible through your opponent's goal. The players took alternate shots. There is a surprising amount of skill in the game and I would recommend young readers to give it a try on a table top (one where a few scratches don't matter). I'm not sure which of today's currency would be the most suitable coins. Perhaps a 10p piece propelled by two 50p coins would do the trick.

Another school pastime was knuckle fighting. This was not as bad as it sounds. For a knuckle fight the two combatants each clenched one fist – or you could use both. Having tossed up as to who would go first, the combatants put their clenched fists together. He who had won the toss would get the first blow. His object was to strike downwards on to the back of his opponent's hands. The opponent, of course, was moving his hands downwards, sideways, backwards as quickly as he could so that the attempted downward blow would miss. The striker went on striking until he missed.

I appeared to have been gifted with very quick reactions and once it was my turn to strike I could bang away at the back of my opponent's hand or hands usually until such time as he surrendered. If and when the positions were reversed and my opponent was trying to hit the back of my hands I seemed to be able to whip them away so quickly that he usually missed.

I enjoyed my success at this 'sport' until the day I was challenged by a hefty boy named, I think, Baxter. He had fists like hams attached to big strong arms. We began our contest before quite an audience and the situation developed that I was frequently hitting him ten or a dozen times to every once that he managed to catch me. The difficulty was that my blows were minor taps. His were hammer blows. We battled on until both of us had hands swollen to almost double the normal size and then by mutual consent agreed the contest was a draw and adjourned to spend hours soaking our battered hands in water.

A particular pleasure during the latter part of my schooldays was the chance to fly. Before I joined the ATC at Woodhouse Grove I had only once been in a plane, and that was when I was a little lad of about five or six for a quick joyride from the sands at Southport. I distinctly remember the first plane in which I ever flew. It was a de Havilland Fox Moth biplane. It had a tiny cabin which could seat four and the pilot sat in an outside cockpit at the rear of the plane, rather like the driver of a Victorian hansom cab. The pilot had the usual big goggles but rather than a leather flying helmet he simply had a flat cap which he turned round with the peak to the rear. Many years later when I flew fairly frequently on Concorde I used to recall that first flight and wonder at the progress that aeronautics has seen in one lifetime.

With the ATC we had opportunities to fly whenever we visited an RAF station. On two occasions we spent part of our summer holidays on RAF stations in East Yorkshire and flew in two or three types of aircraft. These were mostly old bombers such as Whitleys and Stirlings which were used to tow gliders into France on D-Day. However, on one occasion some of us got a ride in a much more user-friendly aircraft – an Airspeed Oxford, a small twin-engined plane and the pilot thereof was happy to let us have the controls for a while. That experience only strengthened my determination to get into the Air Force as soon as possible after leaving school and hopefully be successful with aircrew training.

One final school memory. As I have said, we were more than short of female company at WGS during the war. The only way we could meet girls of our own age was via Miss Dorothy Braybrook's dancing classes. To this day there are large numbers of elderly people in Yorkshire who are surprisingly good dancers and who owe that skill to Dorothy Braybrook's dancing classes which were a feature of Bradford life for many years. During the war Miss Braybrook brought a team of her more advanced students to the school for an evening dancing class which I can tell you was an extremely popular affair. It may seem hard to imagine beefy rugby players looking forward with eager anticipation to a dancing class, but we certainly did. The one-two-three, one-two-three of the waltz and the slow-slow-quick-quick-slow of the foxtrot became very familiar. It was a real pleasure to talk to these attractive young ladies and in fact several relationships were forged and continued after schooldays and into matrimony.

In the spring term of 1945, just before the war ended, our headmaster decided that the time had come to have a school ball which consisted mostly of the boys who were members of the dancing class, Miss Braybrook's troupe of young lovelies together with a few members of staff and possibly an odd parent or two. The function took place on a lovely evening and started with a swing, but after a little while it became noticeable that the ballroom – the school's Memorial Hall – was almost empty. Members of the dancing class and Miss Braybrook's lovelies were nowhere to be seen.

Dr Towlson rushed out of the hall and on to the school playground where he could look up towards the tree-covered mound which has always been a feature of the WGS campus. As befitted a fine Methodist preacher, and a man who enjoyed singing, 'Pop' Towlson had a splendid pair of lungs. At the top of his voice he shouted, 'Come back, you boys! I know where you are and I know what you're doing. Come back into the ballroom this instant!' He didn't get an immediate response, but, in small groups his sixth form and some of Bradford's most attractive young ladies emerged from the trees and bushes brushing leaves, blades of grass and twigs from their clothes and hair.

On reflection, let's have one more instance from those distant days.

In the ATC we were taught the Morse code and our unit had been supplied with Aldis signalling lamps. These were powerful hand-held spot lights, powered from a car battery and with an on/off lever which enabled you to signal the dots and dashes of the Morse code. One evening, two friends of mine, Atkinson and Ayers, and I decided to give our signalling techniques and the Aldis lamps themselves a thorough test. I carted one lamp and its heavy battery to the cricket pavilion which stood about a hundred and fifty yards away from the school. My two friends had the other lamp up in the east dormitory which looked out over the cricket field. They flung open the window and then, with an airy disregard for the black-out regulations, which were still in force although there had been no air raids for two or three years, we began some snappy Morse signalling.

Courteous messages in Morse of the 'How are you?' variety soon degenerated into vulgar abuse translated into dots and dashes. Similarly, rather than the two lamps being pointed directly one at another, the beams of light began to stray and messages were flashed in all directions.

It was a still, calm night and seated comfortably on the bench outside the cricket pavilion, flashing away happily, I clearly heard footsteps crunching into the gravel of the school front drive on the top side of the cricket field. The footsteps sounded at first a measured and steady tread and I immediately realised that they signified the return of our headmaster from some function or other. The steady and measured crunch-crunch of his footsteps was suddenly quickened into crunch-crunch, crunch-crunch, crunch . . . as 'Pop' Towlson broke into a gallop and raced into the school and up the stairs into east dormitory. He flung open the dormitory door and there at the other end, with the window wide open, were my two friends who had not heard his arrival, still flashing towards me, probably wondering why my signalling had abruptly ceased.

Dr Towlson charged down the dormitory shouting, 'Boy! Do you want to have me arrested? Give that thing to me.' My friend Atkinson duly obliged and the now somewhat winded headmaster almost collapsed beneath the weight of a 12-volt car battery.

We were in the headmaster's study the following morning and managed to persuade him that it was only our zeal and enthusiasm for the ATC training which had caused us to forget about black-out regulations and appropriate behaviour in dormitories after 'lights out'. We escaped with no significant punishment.

The term and my schooldays ended shortly thereafter.

After the summer holiday which saw VJ Day – the end of the war in the Far East – I was waiting impatiently to learn what was to happen to my hoped-for RAF career. I was going out with Renée Rhodes and was increasingly fond of her. Consequently, when I heard in September 1945 that a boy still at Woodhouse Grove was bragging around the school about his affair with her, I was not – as they say – best pleased. I resolved to teach the boy – Cooper by name – a lesson.

Quite improperly I returned to the school one evening without any authority so to do and I walked into the Memorial Hall where most of the boarders were usually congregated, pushing through the swing doors, rather like a gunfighter entering a saloon in a Western film. The babble of conversation amongst all the boys in the hall stopped at once. They immediately guessed what I was there for.

'Where's Cooper?'

'I think he's up in the dorm.' Some boy spoke up.

'Fetch him.'

I stood there with the room in complete silence. All the boys were wondering if they were going to see a vicious fight in a few minutes time. The swing doors swung open and Cooper appeared.

I simply said, 'Come with me,' and walked out into the school playground and headed towards the top of the school playing fields, a suitably dark and secluded area. As we walked I – rather ostentatiously – carefully removed my wristwatch and put it in a pocket. This piece of psychological warfare was not lost on Cooper who correctly assumed I was getting ready for a really serious fight. What he didn't know was that I was also loading the odds somewhat in my favour by filling my right fist with a handful of copper coins – the old style penny pieces weighed heavy and if you had to have a brawl a fistful would significantly improve the weight of your punch.

Where on earth did I learn all this!

'What do you want? What's the problem?' Cooper said.

I said nothing until we reached the top field and then I turned to face him, hands hanging free and ready to land the first punch and quite confident that it would be a good one. I put the case to him clearly, if not very courteously.

'I hear you've been bragging about Renée Rhodes. You've got a choice. You either promise me now you'll never speak to her again, or I'm going to beat you into a pulp.'

I should say that, although Cooper was a little younger than me he was certainly bigger. He was also wise. He only hesitated for a moment before giving me an appropriate promise and a few words of apology. I suppose it was all rather an anticlimax in the end but for a time it was all quite dramatic and, if nothing else, this story serves to confirm that I was quite aggressive as a youth. Aggression helped with all the sports I played then and later but, in fact, I have never had a meaningful bout of fisticuffs.

CHAPTER 5

The Post War Years

W HEN I LEFT SCHOOL the war in Europe was over and Europe was
beginning its slow recovery from nearly six years of horror.
However, in the Far East war was still raging although it was obvious that
Japan was on the road to defeat.

There was no such thing as a 'gap year' in those days. The expectation
was that you left school and either began some sort of working career or
found some part-time work until your entry into university or technical
college. For me, higher education was simply not an option. I was a
member of the RAF waiting to be called to begin my training. Father was
certainly not going to let me have a few weeks or perhaps months of
idleness. Quite the reverse. Within days of the end of term I was assigned
to Greenwood's Branch No. 1 in Westgate, Bradford, the original family
business.

By the time I began there in 1945, Branch No. 1 was physically the
largest shop in the chain which was now more than seventy branches
strong. Westgate branch on the corner of Drewton Street, only a few
hundred yards away from the company's head office lower down that
street, had a total frontage of about 70ft. The ground floor was devoted
to the sale of men's outfitting – shirts, ties, socks, underwear etc. – and
the first floor was stocked with clothing and also a range of boys' wear.
Boys' wear was never a major part of the business and by the post-war
years was stocked only at some of the larger and older branches. It was
completely phased out a few years later.

My father had given clear instructions to Mr Jones, the manager who
was one of his very first employees, that I was definitely to have no kind
of preferential treatment. This certainly proved to be the case. I worked
for two or three weeks before Mr Jones was prepared to let me attempt
to serve a customer. I washed the windows every day, mopped both
floors, cleaned the brasses of the counters and when my cleaning chores
were over, I spent the rest of my time brushing and tidying stock. At
appropriate intervals, Mr Jones would give me lengthy lectures on the
sizing of different garments, where items were kept in stock, some general

advice on window dressing and all the other skills which a men's outfitter then needed.

Came the great day when he told me, 'You can serve the next customer whilst I have a cup of tea.' I waited eagerly and in due course in came a lady. She wanted nothing more than a pair of socks for her husband which I duly supplied. I then tried to interest her in something else but without success so I took her money, handed her the socks and her change, thanked her warmly and remembered to open the shop door for her as she went out into the street.

I walked back to the till into which I had put her money and then the awful realisation dawned – I had given her change for one pound and she had only given me a ten shilling note. Ten shillings was a quarter of my weekly wage so I dashed out on to Westgate hoping to find her and correct my mistake. No such luck. She was well gone. No doubt congratulating herself on a successful bit of shopping. I, of course, had to make good the loss. At least that incident taught me one thing. Thereafter I always handled money with care but it was not an auspicious start to a career in retailing.

Within a month or two Mr Jones had taught me the basics of operating a Greenwood's branch and Father decided that my experience should be widened. Amongst the fourteen branches operating within the Bradford city limits at that time were two where we did not trade under the Greenwood's name. One was a business Father had acquired just before the war, a large shop on the corner of Westgate and Godwin Street, trading as Hey's Corner. This shop stocked rather more expensive merchandise than the rest of the Greenwood's branches. Halfway along Godwin Street at the entrance to what was then Kirkgate Market, a fine example of a municipal covered market hall, was the second differently named shop. This was Henderson's, the junk shop and clearing house for all the oddments, faded and damaged stock, which the rest of the chain inevitably accumulated. Not only did Henderson's sell all such items, it also was the place to which Father would send any unusual purchase which he had been able to secure at a very keen price. In 1945 this was beginning to include government-surplus items of clothing and footwear.

The manager of Henderson's before, during and for a number of years after the war, was a quite remarkable man – Mr Ronnie Buckley. Ronnie Buckley was without doubt the best salesman I have ever seen. If he had been lucky enough to have been born in better circumstances, to have had a better education than leaving school at fourteen, and a good opportunity, he might have used his instinctive psychological know-how to enormous effect. Much the same skills as he used for selling shirts and socks etc. could have been applied if he had been selling motor cars, insurance, shares, or even companies. He taught me a very great deal.

I went to work with him for a few months in the latter part of 1945 and soon saw what a good salesman can do. Henderson's was a very busy site. Godwin Street was in the heart of Bradford and the massive Kirkgate Market had one of its four main entrances immediately adjoining Henderson's. Customers poured down the steps into the vast market past the side window of Henderson's just as a steady pedestrian flow along Godwin Street walked past the front window. The shop had two doors, one on to Godwin Street – the main entrance – and a secondary entrance at the top of the market steps.

Buckley could weigh up a customer as soon as he or she entered the shop. It was taken as a 'given' that he would never take a swap. Of course he would sell the customer what he or she had asked for but usually if they had asked for one he would sell them two or even three. His skill lay in introducing other items which had never been in the customer's mind, but by the time they left the shop they had been so well 'sold' that they either went away thanking Buckley for his kind help in suggesting this, that or the other, or else they found themselves believing that they had been intending to buy those items all the time.

One of Buckley's favourite transactions was selling underwear. Half-sleeve vests and the pants that we now describe as 'long johns' were still in great demand. To Buckley, an enquiry for a vest or a pair of pants meant that he would expect to sell a minimum of two full sets before moving on to introduce some other – probably quite unrelated – item which he anticipated the customer could use. For example, a man who was obviously a working man would never leave Henderson's without the offer of some army-grey working socks regardless of what his original enquiry had been.

Buckley delighted in showing off his skills. He once invited me to pick any item I liked in the shop and guaranteed he would sell it before the day was out. I pointed to a slightly faded, ginger-coloured tweed overcoat that had been burnt by the sun in the window of some Greenwood's branch. He sold it to a very happy customer, who thanked him profusely, before the day was out. The customer had only wanted a cap.

I could fill a book explaining the techniques of introductory selling and how Buckley exploited them but let me settle instead for just three stories.

First, there was the customer who bought two left boots. On checking our stocks one day we found that we must by mistake have sold somebody two right boots since we had a 'pair' of left boots remaining. Either that or the original delivery of what must have been one of Father's cut-price orders had been incorrectly assembled. One way or another we had two left boots to shift.

Buckley, unlike any other Greenwood's manager, had the power to vary prices if he so wished. He took one of the boots and put it in the front of the window, marked down to a very low price – just a fraction of what one would expect to pay for a pair of boots in those days. Buckley was quite an artist and his hand-written tickets were always well done. That particular ticket included the phrase, 'Last remaining boots only . . .'.

In due course, a man put his head round the door and enquired, 'What size are your boots?' Buckley's reply was typical,

'What size do you take?'

'Size nine,' said the customer.

'Well, come in then, I think we can fit you.' Rule one. You cannot practice salesmanship until you've got the customer in the shop! In fact, the boots were either size nine, or maybe one size larger. They were on the counter and Buckley was beginning to parcel them up when the customer said, 'Hey, just a minute. They're both the same. They're two left boots.' To this Buckley's immediate answer was,

'Of course they are. You don't think there's anywhere you could get a pair of ordinary boots for a price like this?'

'Well, what would I do with them?' asked the customer doubtfully.

Buckley fixed him with an earnest look. 'Now, tell me, have you ever had a pair of shoes or boots where one's worn out quicker than the other? Have you ever lost a shoe or a boot? Have you ever damaged a shoe or a boot? Of course you have. Now, what you've got here are two spare boots. They're costing you next to nothing. It'll be well worth your while to put 'em on a back shelf and, sooner or later, you'll have such a problem and you'll have solved it very cheaply indeed. Now, that's got to be a good move, hasn't it?'

The customer was convinced and departed, smiling. As did so many.

Given his special freedom to set his own prices, Buckley was also free to put on a sale whenever he thought the state of trade needed it. We would strip the windows bare on the Saturday night and then, on the Monday morning, with the shop closed, begin filling them with the centre piece of each window a line, or lines, at an absolutely silly price. These he called his 'sprats to catch the mackerel'. We would, of course, have a few of those items in stock but almost always only in weird sizes. For example, men's shirts with a thirteen-and-a-half-inch collar size or trousers with an enormous waist size. If sooner or later a customer of the right size did appear then of course we would sell the garment and that customer had a wonderful bargain. But the last thing we wanted to do was to sell the 'sprats' because the longer they stayed in the windows the more 'mackerel' they might attract.

By the Monday night our window dressing would usually be complete. We would put up posters with the usual types of slogans but would also have added slip bills – SALE STARTS 10 a.m. THURSDAY. COME EARLY!

Buckley's ticket writing skills would have been exploited to the full. A typical example might be, say, a sports jacket on offer at perhaps half-a-crown (12½p) and the price ticket would include the words, 'NO WEEKLY PAYMENTS TAKEN!'

We would finish the windows on Tuesday and Wednesday morning and also complete arrangements inside the shop. Wednesday afternoon was early closing day then – six or seven day trading was years away. On the Thursday morning we would expect to find – and always did – a long queue of bargain hunters stretching for many yards along Godwin Street. The shop's doors would be firmly locked and Buckley would be enjoying a leisurely pot of tea. I used to bring him pint pots of tea from one of the cafes inside the market. At around 10 o'clock he would ask me to go out of the side door and see how long the queue was. I would come back and probably report, 'It's nearly to the end of the pub.' (There was a public house two or three doors to the right of Henderson's and a respectable queue would reach to the far side of it.)

Buckley would say, 'Well, I'll just go and stir them up a bit, and then we'll think about starting.' Off came his glasses, on went a trilby hat pulled well down and a raincoat with collar well up. Out through the side door went Buckley and in a moment he was mingling with the customers looking into the front window over the heads of, and through, the queue.

'Look at that!' I would hear him say. 'This stuff must have been stolen. I've never seen such prices. They're giving the stuff away!' Etc. etc. Having now got the front of the queue even more anxious to get in and

1. The first Greenwood shop in Westgate, Bradford in the 1860s

2. The family shop Westgate, Bradford.
W.H. Greenwood born over the shop 1901

3. 44 Springcliff Street, Bradford.
Denis Greenwood's birth place 1925

4. L to R Walter, Willie and Moses Greenwood with Denis and Brian

5. Denis, Anne and Brian c. 1930

7. Briaden, Shipley Glen near Bradford.
Home 1931 to 1934

6. Lynton Avenue, Heaton, Bradford.
Brian Greenwood's birthplace 1927

8. Briaden, Underwood Drive, Rawdon, Nr Leeds. The family home for 40 years

9. *The Opening of Brontë House 5 May 1934 by Edward Lamplough with Dr C.W. Towlson MA, DD Headmaster. D.W.G. and G.B.G in light grey suits*

10. Denis, Anne, Brian and Walter at Briaden 1943

11. Woodhouse Grove School 1st XV 1945. G.B.G. seated second from left

13. *Newark – a typical corner branch*

12. *Bridlington Branch. A typical example of the green and black shop front style*

14. *Accrington – an example of the shop front style used from the mid 1960s into the 1980s*

15. *Clitheroe, Lancashire with the timber style of shop front used a little later*

*16. Daisy Hill, Bradford Methodist Chapel. Originally part-funded by M. Greenwood.
Latterley owned by W.H. Greenwood as his* Songs of Praise *centre*

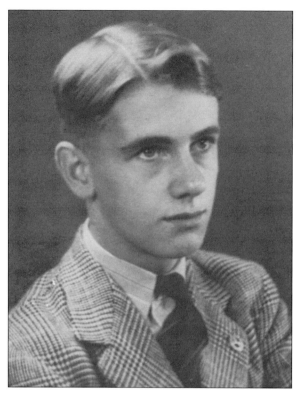

17. 17 year old G.B.G. complete with A.T.C. badge and school colours tie

18. G.B.G.'s 15 year old girlfriend Renée Rhodes

snap up bargains, and having added a goodly number to the back, Buckley would sidle back through the side door, take off his hat and raincoat, put on his glasses, smooth back his hair and then say to me, 'All right, Brian, let the first four in.'

Four customers were admitted, the door was locked once more and after the first four had had their wallets or purses fairly well emptied and been seen out through the side door, in would come another small group. And so on throughout most of the day.

We cheerfully closed for lunch, telling those still queuing that we needed a break in order to make further reductions and we would be re-opening at, say, 2 p.m. There was no way the queuing customers were going to go away and what usually happened was that the queue rebuilt itself and sometimes, if we still had a queue at closing time, we would nevertheless close the shop on time pointing out that we had lots of re-marking and stock re-arranging to do and that those still queuing must come back in the morning.

Henderson's sales were hard work but we took an awful lot of money, frequently exceeding the sales of the posh shop – Hey's Corner – further up the street.

One final word about Buckley which gives an insight into a real salesman's mind was an incident several years later. By that time I was Buckley's boss but I still very much enjoyed a chat with him. I was walking down Rawson Place in Bradford towards Henderson's and Godwin Street when I saw a goodly crowd looking into Henderson's window and then walking away smiling and laughing. What's he up to now, I asked myself. This was in fact the day after the Great Train Robbery when millions of pounds in cash were stolen from a mail train. Buckley had added to his window display with its usual cartoons and jokes, a very large hanging show card which bore the words, 'FIVE POUND NOTES TAKEN HERE. NO QUESTIONS ASKED'.

After my time with Ronnie Buckley, I had a short spell acting as a relief manager, that is, taking temporary charge of a shop whilst the regular manager was on holiday or off sick. I enjoyed the freedom and responsibility but at eighteen was probably not the most dependable of managers in the Greenwood chain. For example, when relieving at Queen's Arcade, Leeds, branch, I succumbed to the temptation to close the shop for a kiss and a cuddle with the very attractive young lady assistant.

Then there was the time when I was relieving at a suburban Bradford branch, Laisterdyke. At the end of the day's trading I went back home to Briaden and on that occasion both my parents were out when the telephone rang asking for Mr Greenwood, I promptly answered, 'Speaking.' The caller was Bradford City Police who felt they had trapped a burglar in one of our Bradford branches.

'Which shop?' I asked.

'Laisterdyke,' came the reply.

'I'll be there in fifteen minutes,' I said. 'I have the keys.' (I did not tell them why.)

I jumped into my little MG two-seater and was indeed there in a quarter of an hour. Two or three policemen led by a sergeant were covering the property from all angles. Also on the pavement was the female tenant of the flat over the shop. It was not easy to see into the darkened shop but there was a low light and some kind of movement visible towards the rear of the premises when you looked through the plate glass front door. I produced the keys, unlocked the front door and the police charged in. There was nobody there but a light had carelessly been left burning in the stock room and the door moving gently in a draught gave an impression that a person was moving about.

We reconvened on the pavement with the police not best pleased and my assuring them that the manager of the branch would be severely reprimanded for his carelessness which had resulted in a waste of police time.

The lady from the flat upstairs added her five cents' worth by commenting, 'It's only a daft young lad who's in charge here at the minute. I don't know what Walter Greenwood's doing letting somebody as gormless as that look after one of his shops.' Grateful for the semi-darkness which made my recognition impossible I heartily agreed with the lady.

Apart from working in the shops, I had a short stint at head office. The front portion of what had been a ballroom provided a modest amount of office space. The basement was where goods came in and the original ballroom area, with floor to ceiling wooden racks and long solid counters for making up deliveries, provided good warehouse space. Apart from the sections of racking which held reserve stock waiting for orders from the branches which came with their weekly 'Returns' envelope, each shop had its own numbered bin. Father was still doing nearly all the buying personally and with his intimate knowledge of every shop, he often bought lines specifically for one branch or a particular group of branches.

For example, the seaside branches, Blackpool, Morecambe and Scarborough, would obviously be favoured with summer and light-weight garments during the season. At Christmas time, when we had a massive sale of ties Father would have dozens of boxes of ties lying open on the warehouse counters and he would look at a particular pattern and say, 'That's just right for Branch 33. Give him five dozen.' Immediately five dozen boxes of that particular pattern would go into Bin 33 and be added to what the manager thereof had specifically ordered for his next delivery.

Whilst the firm was big enough to be regarded as a significant multiple retailer, nevertheless there was a lot of this internal sub-division as to the types of merchandise sold. To give one fairly obvious example, there were a number of branches in mining areas. There were three items which sold particularly well in mining towns. One was a white shirt – an obvious reaction to a dirty job. A second would be flat caps. The cap trade was always significantly better in, say, Barnsley than in a country town such as Skipton. A new cap for the weekend was a little luxury that miners often aimed for. Similarly, white artificial silk scarves, which were manufactured with the anticipation that they would end up being worn with evening dress – and indeed were very much a part of dressing for an important social function – these were hot sellers in the mining districts where miners would only occasionally wear collars during their leisure hours, preferring instead to have a white silk scarf knotted around the neck.

The Drewton Street premises were overfull with merchandise despite the continuing difficulty in obtaining new supplies. It was obvious in 1945 that if the business were to continue to expand, then a larger headquarters would soon be needed.

Apart from some time in the warehouse and also in the cramped department where price tickets and show cards were produced, part of my time at head office was spent on the boring task of counting clothing coupons.

Each week every branch posted its returns envelope to head office. This envelope contained the small envelopes each containing one hundred clothing coupons (or if less than that with the number clearly thereon) together with other important records. There was a simple cash account form which showed on the left hand side the daily receipts into the branch and such items as rentals collected from flats upstairs or staff contributions to the company's staff benefits society, known more popularly as the 'Sick

Fund'. On the right hand side of the cash account were detailed the wages paid, the commissions earned and any other outgoings. The balancing amount was the cash paid into the bank locally and had the corresponding bank slips attached.

The other major item was the simple, but nevertheless effective and efficient branch paperwork known as the 'Stock Summary'. This simple form was headed with a space for the commencing stock – that is, stock at the branch as at last Saturday night, with spaces below to add deliveries during the week and the numbers of the invoices thereof. Then a space for the deduction of that week's total sales. A sub-total followed after which the lower part of the form provided a space for any credits where goods might have been either reduced in price or transferred out of the shop. The bottom line of the week's Stock Summary was the total selling price value of all the stock in the branch at that time and it automatically became the commencing figure for the next week's Stock Summary.

From June 1941 until well after the war clothing, like food, was rationed. The ration was set originally at approximately two-thirds of pre-war consumption levels and this was later cut back to 48%. All of which was to say that the clothes ration ended up at around half of what people wanted to buy.

Clothing ration coupons were a damned nuisance. They were small fiddly bits of paper in more than one size and shape and they had to be accounted for. At head office every envelope from the branches had to be checked so that envelopes containing one hundred coupons could be passed on in bulk to the appropriate authority – an offshoot of the Board of Trade, I suppose.

Father learned that there was a 5% tolerance and that an envelope with only ninety-five coupons in it was perfectly acceptable. From then on there was no way we ever sent in an envelope with more than ninety-five coupons. With more than seventy branches taking coupons for every sale the total number that we were handling was enormous and even 5% thereof was a significant number. It was not long before Father thought we should experiment by not bothering to count the coupons accurately but just stuffing approximately ninety into each envelope. When he found that these were never queried he was in the happy position that one coupon in every ten taken by all his shops was available to him.

From the day clothes rationing began there had been an unofficial market in clothing coupons. People would sell their coupons to a neighbour. Drapers and outfitters would – like Father – find that they could get hold of surplus coupons as a consequence of, firstly, the 5% allowance and, secondly, the lax or non-existent supervision of the system. Coupons had a value of several pence each which value changed from time to time following the laws of supply and demand and also as regards the nature of the coupons. Some clothing coupons could be tendered loose. Others were supposed to be cut by the shop keeper from an actual ration book (a rule that was very frequently ignored).

After the war, with servicemen returning home, and the public having a little more to spend, there was an increasing demand for the still-modest amount of clothing that was being manufactured and supplied in the UK. Demand for clothing coupons became brisk. Now that more than sixty years has passed and Father is sadly long gone, I can tell you that he had a thriving business which he developed in the sale of clothing coupons for cash.

It must be remembered that, in the early post-war years, taxation was at a ludicrous level. Businesses suffered from EPT – Excess Profits Tax – which basically meant that every penny of profit above a standard based on pre-war levels would be taxed at a rate of 100%. Not many businessmen were happy about that! Similarly rates of personal taxation moved up to really excessive levels. The official top rate of tax on a substantial income was 98% but, as a matter of interest, even that level was exceeded in 1947/48 when the Labour government decided that there would be a special levy on high tax payers which produced an effective rate of . . . wait for it . . . 147.5%! I shall never forget my father's look of shock and horror when, in answer to his question to our accountant, Harry Clough, 'Does this really mean that whatever I earn I have to pay more than that in tax?' The reply was a flat, 'Yes'.

When taxation reaches intolerable levels, people inevitably move from legitimate schemes of tax avoidance into illegal procedures of tax evasion. An awful lot of British businessmen made that move.

Father generated cash through a contact who would call to see him every Saturday morning in his Drewton Street office. The first question was always, 'What price are they today?' The answer might be, say, 'Seven pence for ordinaries, nine pence for specials.' The specials were those that could be used anywhere. That was the 'wholesale' price of clothing coupons acquired in bulk by Father's rather shady visitor. I assume that man had distribution channels leading in some cases to individual shoppers, particularly ladies, and probably to other retailers who had the opportunity to increase their stock holding but lacked the coupons to go with the purchase.

When buying goods from a wholesaler or manufacturer, a shopkeeper had to pay against the invoice, but he had also to supply the coupons. Sometimes you had a situation where the manufacturer, over-burdened with excessive taxation, wanted cash rather than a documented with-coupons transaction. There were certainly circumstances where some supplies could only be purchased if you were able and willing to pay cash for goods that would be delivered without an official invoice.

Thus the cash from Father's coupons-for-cash transactions mostly found its way back into the system as he persuaded some manufacturer or other to let him have some scarce clothing – let's say a thousand pairs of flannel trousers – for a wad of used pound notes. Cities such as Leeds and Manchester which were centres for clothing manufacture and wholesaling were awash with cash in those days. Shopkeepers great and small struggled to extract cash from their businesses and then used the bulk of it to compete in this – I suppose you must call it – Black Market. All I know is that in early 1946 I made more than one trip to Leeds carrying a briefcase stuffed with pound notes whilst my father visited various clothing manufacturers. The briefcase was usually empty when I returned. I'm pretty sure that the majority of shopkeepers throughout the land found themselves involved in some kind of cash trading in those over-taxed post-war years.

The situation continued as regards coupons until clothes rationing was abolished in 1949. The sudden end of clothes rationing came as a considerable shock to Father's system. I was the first to tell him that it had just been announced that clothes rationing was to end. His pain was pitiful when he told me, 'I've got hundreds of thousands of coupons up my sleeve!' They would have been worth a lot of money – several hundred thousand pounds in today's currency – if they had been sold into the unofficial coupon Black Market.

Let's jump ahead in time a little and whilst we are about it cover all the main stories of the cash trading days. As a consequence of fiddling coupons, purchasing uninvoiced stock for cash and taking cash from their businesses without any records, the fact was that in the later 1940s and into the early 1950s, most menswear retailers had the stock in their shops very considerably undervalued. This had been all right for them as a matter of successful tax evasion, but what was the position if they wanted to sell their business?

Many Greenwood's branches were originally independent outfitting businesses and Father – and I can immodestly say that later myself – were experts in buying existing businesses. All too often we had no problem in agreeing the value for a retiring menswear retailer's shop property, or for his fixtures and fittings. But how could we deal with his stock when he assured us that the figure shown in his books was only half or two-thirds, or whatever the proportion might be, of its true value? There were all kinds of interesting ways of resolving that problem and none of them matters now, but it is interesting to remember – without any details – one such situation when the retiring retailer had several shops and the amounts involved in a possible purchase were very significant. Like some of the clothing manufacturers mentioned above, that particular retailer wanted to get his hands on a substantial sum of cash and would only sell his shops with their equipment and stock if his 'hidden' stock was at least partially paid for in pound notes.

We therefore found ourselves travelling north in the magnificent Rolls Royce which I described earlier, the company chauffeur at the wheel, my brother in the front seat, Father and I in the back and on my knee I had 'the parcel'. 'The parcel' was a brown paper-wrapped cube of significant size which contained solid money. In other words, stacks of one pound notes. I'm not sure how many, but it was certainly a lot. When we made a stop journeying north, my instructions were strict: 'Do not leave the car, and keep hold of "the parcel".' Similarly, when we reached the retailer's head office and negotiations began, I put 'the parcel' in the middle of the table where it sat throughout lengthy and complex negotiations between my father and the business owner. When the negotiations finally broke down – I gathered that 'the parcel' was not big enough – I had to nurse it all the way back home where its contents duly disappeared into the old safe which Father kept in the basement of Briaden.

It had been a severe shock to Father's system when he lost out on his several hundred thousand coupons, but he was at least as shocked once again when the time came that the government – by now fully aware of the fact that a major part of the nation's economy was 'off the books' – decided that from an early date blue pound notes would cease to be legal tender.

A few interesting weeks followed the shock of that announcement. I don't think my mother ever quite understood why she was to have a new mink coat, various pieces of jewellery and silver when it was not her birthday. These items were, of course, being bought by Father using his stash of blue pound notes, many of which had been in his safe in the damp Briaden cellars for so long that they were going mouldy.

Father had always been sensible about money. He knew well, from his early days, what it was like to be hard up and therefore, whilst he could be generous he was never silly or careless in his spending until . . .

He took the family – I was married by then as was my brother – a party of six, to the Park Lane Hotel in London. Soon after checking in we went out for dinner. Father took us to Manetta's restaurant and night club in a side street just off Piccadilly. I was amazed that, as we walked in, the doorman and the hat-check girl greeted Father warmly. Then the head waiter rushed forward to tell Father how delighted he was to see him again and, 'Please come this way. I have the best table for you, Mr Greenwood'.

As we walked across to the table, the leader of the dance band noticed Father, smiled warmly at him and immediately had his musicians change the tune they were playing into a jazzed up version of 'On Ilkley Moor bar t'at'.

What on earth had been going on, I asked myself. And then I noticed there was a faint smell of mouldy paper in the air. Father had been distributing mouldering blue pound notes in all directions, not only on this occasion but obviously on at least one previous visit and clearly all the staff at Manetta's regarded him as very much a big time spender.

CHAPTER 6

Shops and Styles

BEFORE GOING BACK to my personal activities immediately after the war I think it may interest you to be reminded of what the retail scene – particularly the menswear retail scene – was like in the late forties and early fifties.

Perhaps the first thing to point out is that, at that time, there was no such thing as a supermarket. There were no out-of-town shopping centres. There were no purpose-built town centre precincts, although a number of cities – Leeds being a very good example – had various covered arcades each containing a wide variety of different shops, and in principle, such arcades were not vastly different from a modern town centre shopping development.

There were far more independent traders in those days and many shops, including some in prime positions, were owned and operated by the man or woman who stepped forward to serve you when you entered as a customer. As a consequence of the very large number of independent retailers purchasing their goods in comparatively modest quantities there was a very significant wholesale trade with large wholesale warehouses near the city centres, not on out-of-town sites, in most of Britain's cities and major towns. The wholesale trade has now largely disappeared since the ever-increasing number of large-scale retailers buying directly from manufacturers and frequently at lower prices than the wholesalers might have to pay has driven much of the wholesale trade to the wall. However, that was not the case in the 1940s and 1950s.

Departmental stores were major elements in city centre shopping and they were to be found in the busiest streets of towns and cities. The complete absence of out-of-town shopping was a consequence of the fact that car ownership was pretty well limited to the better-off with most of Britain's shoppers going into town by bus, tram or train.

There were, of course, many multiple firms. The definition of a multiple retailer in those days, and probably still, is a retail business with at least five separate branches. Many of the multiple firms were already fifty or sixty years old by the time we are now considering. The first multiples had been in the shoe trade for the obvious reason that shoe boxes are all of similar size which made shop fitting very much simpler. However, there were multiples in almost all retail trades and in the menswear trade some of these went back a long way – as evidenced by the fact that Hepworths, where my father served his apprenticeship, was a major chain even before the First World War.

Multiple shoe shops included such names as Freeman Hardy & Willis, Stead & Simpson, Timpsons, Saxone, Barratts, Dolcis, Benefit, Stylo Shoes etc. In the menswear trade there was a division between multiple tailors with Montague Burton leading the field with their 600 or so branches. After them came the 500 shop Fifty Shilling Tailors, a name which obviously had to be changed at a later date to John Collier since the time had already passed when a suit to measure could be produced for as little as £2.50. Weaver to Wearer and Alexandre were well known as tailors and in the north-east Jackson the Tailor was a chain which led the way in changing window dressing styles.

As for the men's outfitters, some of them offered a bespoke tailoring service as a sideline, but their business was primarily the sale of ready-made clothes – usually with the greater emphasis on outer clothing as opposed to shirts, ties, socks etc. Hepworths, the ancestor of 'Next', was one such. Foster Brothers of Birmingham had some 150 branches, as did Bradleys of Chester. In the south, Rego Clothiers had around 150 shops in London and the Home Counties. There were dozens of smaller regional multiples and in that group, came Greenwood's which was approaching the 100-branch mark, a milestone finally reached with the opening of the 100th shop in Victoria Lane, Huddersfield in 1951.

I must also mention G.A. Dunn & Co., the hatters, who had built up a nationwide chain of around some 200 units as specialists in men's hats and caps. Only gradually in the post-war years did Dunn & Co. add ready-made clothes to their range of headwear.

Another specialist multiple in the menswear trade was Moss Bros. who then, as now, operated a business based primarily on the hire of formal wear for weddings etc.

In all these menswear retailers, and in all the independent menswear retailers – of which there were thousands – the emphasis was on personal service. Self-service or self-selection had hardly made an appearance. If a man entered one of the multiple tailors he would immediately be greeted by an experienced man, probably with a tape measure draped around his neck, who would soon be showing him pattern bunches and lengths of cloth before – if all had gone well – skilfully measuring him and entering the measurements on a carefully standardised order form and then sending the top copies thereof to the company's factory.

Leeds was very much the centre of the multiple tailoring industry with many thousands of cutters and machinists translating the order forms from their companies' branches into suits, jackets, trousers, overcoats etc., the overwhelming majority of which would prove to be an excellent fit when the customer called a few weeks later at the branch where he had placed his order.

Display techniques in the multiple tailoring trade had hardly changed from pre-war days. The expression, 'like a dummy in Burton's window' rightly remained in use since they and most of the multiple tailors used life-sized dummies on which to display the sort of garments they would be happy to make for you. The rest of their display would be mostly lengths of cloth.

It fell to Jackson the Tailor to be the first to realise that lofty plate glass windows and life-sized dummies were not as effective as plastic jacket shapes, known in the trade as 'jacket busts'. A full-sized dummy, standing on a window bed eighteen inches or two feet above pavement level had the customer looking up to the dummy's head some eight feet above pavement level – higher if the dummy had been mounted on a plinth as was often the case. A jacket bust with perhaps a pair of trousers laid beside it was right in front of you at eye level. It was not long before full length dummies largely disappeared from the multiples' windows and their shops fronts and the height of their facia signs became lower. Amongst the men's outfitters, both multiple and independent, it was a fairly sound generalisation to say that the higher the class of trade, the less you put in the window. Indeed that generalisation broadly speaking still applies.

In the late forties and early fifties the better end of the multiple trade, such as Austin Reed, Hope Bros. and Horne Bros. would have fairly lightly dressed windows. Fosters, Bradleys, Rego and Greenwood's were aiming for a different class of customer, many of whom did not like to go into a shop and ask for an item, preferring instead to ask for, 'one like that one in the window'.

If you went below the class of trade that Greenwood's were striving for you were amongst the Army & Navy Stores, government surplus shops, and specialist workwear suppliers etc. who usually filled their windows to capacity and backed up a wider array of goods with an equally wide selection of big tickets.

Naturally, every multiple trader tried to establish his own identity so that one of his branches would be instantly recognisable whether you saw it in Bradford or Brighton.

Before the war Greenwood's branches had all kinds of shop front, usually the one installed by the previous occupier, but, from the mid-1930s onwards Father had decided to go for a specific design and colour scheme. He chose a pale green Vitriolite (a kind of hardened glass) with black bases to the window beds and the side pilasters and with black lettering on the facia. Father was taken with the way Montague Burton had dealt with signage at his vast chain. A scroll before the letter 'B' usually included, in small letters, the words, 'Sir Montague' and then with underlining, which continued from the base of the letter 'N', beneath the large letters of the word 'Burton'. In that tail, or underlining, were added the words, 'The Tailor of Taste' and thus a typical Burton's sign read, 'Sir Montague Burton, The Tailor of Taste'.

Father cheerfully cribbed the idea of having an underlining tail in which a slogan could be added. He simply chose the words, 'For Menswear' and for about thirty years, that is from the mid-1930s until the mid-1960s – a typical Greenwood's branch would have a green Vitriolite front carrying the name and slogan, 'Greenwoods for Menswear' and at each side of the name on the facia there would be the names of three other towns where we had major branches. Normally towns a long way from the shop front in question were so named in order to give the impression of a very widely spread chain.

Most Greenwood's branches had two windows. If they were of an unequal size, the larger one would be known as the outfitting window and would contain shirts, ties, socks, underwear, knitwear, etc. The other window was known, until the 1950s, as the hat and cap window and headwear took up most of the space. However, servicemen returning from the war who had been obliged to wear their forage caps or military headgear of some kind, turned against wearing the hats and caps which had been universal in pre-war days and the hat and cap trade went into steep decline. Consequently the second window was used increasingly for clothing.

Until the post war years Greenwood's were certainly not clothiers, but rather outfitters with a significant hat and cap trade. Indeed many of their early shop signs carried the words, 'Greenwoods Hatters & Hosiers' and the limited company which owned the business was known as, 'Green-woods Hosiers & Outfitters Ltd.'.

However, the decline of the hat and cap trade necessitated a significant move into outerwear. A clothing range which began with only sports jackets and trousers was gradually extended over the years to include all kinds of men's outerwear – suits, raincoats, overcoats and car coats, and an ever-widening range of trousers.

The type of merchandise stocked obviously affected both the window displays and the layout of each shop's interior. A typical Greenwood's branch of the 1950s would have been modest in size, perhaps seventeen or eighteen feet of frontage and a shop depth of forty or fifty feet. On the left-hand wall would be two or three quick-serving fixtures. These effectively were racks of trays containing shirts, socks, underwear, etc. The fixtures were so designed that a sliding glass door protected the merchandise from dust. Beyond the quick-servers a short run of open shelving would accommodate boxed goods – belts, braces, etc. In front of these fixtures there would be two or sometimes three brass-bound counters. Some of these were fitted with trays for ties, of which a large stock was always carried, and socks and other small items. Other counters would be for display purposes with a glass shelf for small items, cuff links, armbands, etc. Between the counters would be a wooden till-stand inside which was space for wrapping paper and bags. There was nothing elaborate about Greenwood's tills. They were quite simply just a cash drawer and it was many years before more sophisticated cash handling facilities were used. We must of course remember that in the 1950s virtually every transaction was for cash. There was no such thing as paying with plastic. Cheques were not acceptable (unless the customer was known personally to the manager) so a simple till-drawer was all that was necessary at that time.

On the other side of the shop would be the hat and cap fixtures, originally two or more of these in every shop but later reduced to just one so as to permit more hanging space for jackets and top coats.

The typical Greenwood's branch described above would have in those days an annual turnover of around only £10,000. Indeed, the 100-branch mark and the first ever £1,000,000 annual turnover year fell together in 1951. That figure does not sound much but, of course, today's equivalent would be around £20m or more.

Such was a typical Greenwood's branch but obviously there were exceptions in both directions. Some of the older, very small branches, were operated by just one person – the manager or manageress. There were also several larger branches with four or five staff.

The chain was sub-divided into areas, each comprising about twenty branches. Responsible for each of these groups was an area manager – invariably a successful branch manager who had been promoted to this new role. Weekly deliveries in the company's own vans kept the shops supplied and by 1949 larger headquarters had proved essential. The head office and warehouse were moved to a large building, which had apparently originally been built as a cigar factory, on Manningham Lane, Bradford.

Although we were operating on four floors, this new head office and warehouse was able to cope efficiently with the continuing growth of the business for a few years. However, by 1956, with 150 branches in existence and many more anticipated in the future, it was clear that the time had come for a purpose-built headquarters. A site at White Cross, Guiseley, near Leeds was chosen and the fine headquarters comprising a vast single-storey warehouse fronted by a two-storey office block was under construction and in full use the following year.

In the mid-1950s we opened the largest branch to date on the corner of Darley Street and Godwin Street, Bradford. This was a sufficiently large and imposing branch to justify requesting that the Lord Mayor and other Bradford dignitaries should attend the opening ceremony and the luncheon in the Midland Hotel immediately thereafter. The luncheon was going well until, during a lull in the conversation, Grandma Greenwood – Grandfather Willie's wife – who had obviously had too many glasses of sherry, spoke out in a loud voice, 'The trouble with these Greenwood men is that they are only interested in two things – brass and women!' My brother, Denis, stepped in at that point and called across the room, 'That's not right, Grandma – I've never cared about money!'

To end this chapter on a personal note as regards my own work, I can do no better than tell you a story which went down very well at staff conventions.

A young man was called into the office of the chairman who asked him, 'How long have you been with us now?'

The young man said, 'About four years.'

'Ah, that's right,' said the chairman. 'I remember now. You did a few months as an assistant and then we promoted you to branch manager.'

'That's right,' said the young man.

'Yes,' continued the chairman. 'Then after twelve months we made you an area manager and, if I remember rightly, it was only about a year after that that we made you sales manager?'

'Yes, that's quite right,' replied the young man.

'Now then,' said the chairman. 'I've some good news for you. We're going to give you the ultimate promotion. We're putting you on the board of directors. You'll be a director of the company from next Monday. Now, what have you got to say to that?'

'Thanks, Dad.'

I suppose that pretty well sums up my meteoric rise to responsibility in the business. In fact, from day one I had been very happy to be deeply immersed in the family business's affairs. Happily, my brother and I were interested in different parts of the business – he gradually took over from Father all the responsibility for buying merchandise and the control of its distribution to the branches. I was just like the young man in the story, I had worked as a shop assistant. I had done some relief management. I took charge of a group of branches in Lancashire and Cheshire and, before I was thirty, was running the sales side of the business and also becoming increasingly involved in securing, by purchase or lease, new branches in an ever-widening area.

Young men who are lucky enough to have serious responsibilities at an early age frequently need special guidance. I was lucky in that one man, who very easily could have totally resented my appearance in the business, chose instead to teach me a very great deal. His name was R.O. Bennett, one-time branch manager in Blackpool, later an area manager, then sales manager and finally a director. Ronnie Bennett got there the hard way. I had the easy path.

He took me under his wing and taught me a lot. I clearly remember sitting in his car outside the Oldham branch where business had not been too good. I was anticipating accompanying Ronnie as he went through the branch with his usual thoroughness, checking the window displays, studying the standard of stock keeping, looking at the records for evidence of poor salesmanship etc. Not so.

When I said, 'Aren't we going to go in there and try and sort things out then?' his answer was simple. 'No. You are. Whose name is on the sign?'

Ronnie Bennett, apart from being an excellent man-manager and a first class outfitter, was also a skilled display man and it was his ideas which established the difficult and complex display style that we struggled to standardise at all branches. People could very easily be critical of our window displays in those years because the windows looked very full. They were, but a great deal of thought had gone into the positioning and presentation of all the garments on display – down to such details as, if a line of shirts came in three colours and one was more popular than the other two, then it was that one which appeared on the shirt unit at eye level.

In any kind of shop front there are certain sections of the glass which are more valuable than others, they being the places where the eye of the passer-by would fall most naturally. The golden rule was that the best selling goods must always be in the best window positions.

Now let's leave the world of business for a chapter and think about a life – not on the ocean wave.

CHAPTER 7

A Dry Land Sailor

IN SEPTEMBER 1945 AC2 Greenwood G.B. received a letter from the Royal Air Force record office in Reading telling him that with the end of the war in the Far East the Air Force required no more aircrew recruits and I must either take up a ground trade in the RAF, transfer to the Royal Navy or to the Army. I soon discovered that the only trades or opportunities in any of the three services were for such jobs as a driver, a cook, or a clerk – not very appealing to someone who had been looking forward to training for his wings and ultimately being commissioned.

However, a careful study of all the literature sent to me showed what seemed to be an opportunity. There was one situation in the Royal Naval Air Service or as the RNAS was commonly known, the Fleet Air Arm, for which specific educational qualifications were required. The minimum qualification was a good Higher School Certificate and clearly the intention was to recruit as many graduates as possible. The opportunity was to train as a radar technician. The attractions included the fact that, if the training course was satisfactorily completed you would be automatically promoted to Leading Seaman level, the same level as a corporal in the Army. Furthermore, after a year's satisfactory service, there was again automatic promotion, this time to the rank of petty officer. Whilst this was still a far cry from being an RAF flier it seemed obvious that some costly technical training, in a subject which – in those days – was at the leading edge of military technology and in the company of young men who had had a good education, was not a bad alternative. I therefore transferred into the RNAS to follow that route.

There was a significant downside to my situation at that time. I was classified as being part of the Forces 'for the duration of the present emergency' and, whilst the war was over that situation still remained. Consequently, unlike many of my contemporaries who had not sought to get into the Forces early but had rather simply waited until they became liable for National Service a little later, I had no idea when I would get out of the services. National Servicemen did two years and that was that, but I was in the same position as somebody who had been in the

Forces for several years. I would simply have to wait until my demobilisation number came up and that might take quite a lot longer than two years.

On 4 February 1946 I was to report to HMS *Royal Arthur*. I need not be worried about sea sickness since *Royal Arthur* was, in fact, the former Butlin's holiday camp at Skegness. I spent a grim couple of weeks there being fitted out and doing some elementary square-bashing. I was very unimpressed with my sailor suit when it was issued to me. The outfit included various ancient features which were presumably instigated by Lord Nelson or the Admiralty of his day. Bell-bottom trousers served no particular useful purpose that I could see. Apart from the bell-bottoms they were unusual in that they had neither a zip nor a button fly but, instead, a flap of material at the front secured by a button on each side of your stomach, which could be lowered when nature called.

The short-sleeved, square-necked shirt, which was not very dissimilar to a modern T-shirt was all right. But on top of that you had to tie on your sailor's collar with tapes. The collar came in dark navy blue and, immediately these were issued recruits began trying to scrub and wash them to a lighter shade of blue with the intention that this would indicate time spent at sea in sunny climes. You then had to struggle into the tight-fitting jersey which was far more difficult to put on than a battle-dress top. The next piece of nonsense was the black silk issued to you in a strip four or five feet long and about six inches wide. You had to fold this laboriously into a strip about one-and-a-half inches wide which then went under your collar and down the front of your jersey. To this was added a white lanyard for which I never saw any use.

My clearest memory of HMS *Royal Arthur* is being part of a working party brushing the main road along the front of the camp. It didn't need brushing. There was not a speck of dirt on it which was perhaps as well, since the broom with which I had been issued had no bristles! The misery of those early days was somewhat lightened by the fact that I had made at least one good friend. I had met George Hopwood in the recruiting office in Leeds from whence we had been despatched to Skegness and we were together for much of the next two years.

We were posted from Skegness to HMS *Glendower* which perhaps I should describe as a sister ship to HMS *Royal Arthur* since it, too, was a former Butlin's holiday camp. This time at Pwllheli, North Wales.

HMS *Glendower* was a basic training establishment for all entrants into the Navy but my particular group was destined for the RNAS and we all had similar hopes of succeeding on the radar course.

George Hopwood and I shared one of the holiday chalets – which were certainly better than the Nissen huts – with a very tall young man from Nottingham who was known, not surprisingly as 'Lofty' Hudson. George, Lofty and I earned the reward of half a day outside the camp by winning the competition for the best kept billet. All the chalets were immaculate but we three went one better than all the others by polishing the threshold and sides of the door with boot polish until they shone like mirrors.

It was a tough and indeed harsh regime at Glendower. The morning parades – 'divisions' – were frequently held in bitter cold weather without greatcoats. In fact we were cold most of the time since spring came late in 1946. One of the recruits died whilst we were there and there was quite a fuss in the national newspapers on the question of whether conditions were too harsh at this particular naval establishment.

There were some – I think – damn silly situations such as the way in which we were taught to leave a ship. A round section wooden beam – about the thickness of a telegraph pole – jutted out from a platform meant to represent the deck of a naval vessel with the beam secured by a wire rope running at approximately 45° from a fixing six or eight feet above the 'deck' down to the end of the beam. Hanging on the end of the beam was the rope ladder which you were to descend. Below that was the frozen surface of Butlin's swimming pool which represented the sea.

Edging one's way along the beam was at first easy since the wire stay was above your head and you could hold it comfortably but after another pace or two, due to its angle, the rope was down near your knees and obviously the last pace or two were dodgy. We were supposed to get to the end, go down the ladder, climb up again and return. Not everyone made it and those recruits who went through the ice into the pool certainly did not enjoy the experience.

The whole concept made me very cross. How ridiculous was it that a group of young men about to be trained in advanced scientific technology should be learning how to use a technique originally applied to nimble, barefoot sailors in Nelson's – and earlier – fleets? A fourteen-year-old could easily have designed a hinged metal walkway with side rails to lead to the dangling rope ladder.

I cheered up a bit when George rushed up to me one day with the news that there was to be a camp cross-country race. 'Haven't you done a bit of running?' he asked. I confirmed that this was so and we went to check what would be the prize for success in this sporting contest. It proved to be a NAAFI voucher for 30/-, i.e. £1.50, which was almost as much as our weekly pay and therefore worth striving for.

The race was run in wet and windy conditions on a difficult course, over the hills and fields outside the camp. I came home a comfortable winner over a hundred or two other entrants and George and I blew the winnings on tea and cakes in the NAAFI. Incidentally, I should mention that NAAFI stands for Navy, Army and Air Force Institute and was basically a canteen with a few amenities such as table tennis, or a darts board.

There was a second cross-country race at *Glendower* before we left there and for that one the unofficial bookies – and there were some – had me as favourite. I am happy to say I did not disappoint those who had backed me and noted with interest that my success had given me some popularity with the Wrens (members of the WRNS, i.e. Women's Royal Naval Service) who were part of the permanent staff on the camp.

The letters I sent from *Glendower* were fairly few but besides writing home I wrote regularly to Renée Rhodes of whom I had grown very fond in the time I was working as a shop assistant after leaving school.

I had an extraordinary and I think amusing reaction to the letters I had sent, in which I moaned about the tough time we recruits were experiencing. The tough time was dramatically enlivened one day when, over the camp tannoy (loud speaker system), came the message, 'Ordinary Seaman Greenwood report to the guardhouse on the double.' I left my squad and doubled smartly through all the chalets up the main road to the guardhouse at the front gates of the camp – there to be met by a most surprising sight.

Parked outside the guardhouse was a magnificent Rolls Royce with chauffeur at the wheel. My jaw dropped for it was Father's Phantom III with his chauffeur, Arthur Lee at the wheel with my brother, Denis, beside him. Sitting in the back were Mother, Denis's fiancée and Renée Rhodes. Standing smartly alongside it were the duty petty officer and those ratings on duty in the guardhouse that day.

My mother, who clearly took the view that a Royal Navy recruit training establishment was not much different from boarding school had taken it into her head to visit her younger son and brought along family and his girlfriend for the ride.

The officer of the day was faced with a very unusual call from his duty petty officer which I think probably went something like this:

Sir,
There's a dirty great Rolls Royce with a chauffeur and a lady in the back here at the front gate. She wants to know if it's in order to take her son out for tea.

Probably the officer of the day feared that my mother might be related to an admiral and that his wisest move was to be helpful. In any event, I was given on the spot permission to leave the camp and drive into Pwllheli for a very pleasant afternoon tea.

In early April 1946 we were moved to HMS *Gosling*, a naval camp on the outskirts of Warrington. At that point in time nearly everyone at *Gosling* was in a similar position to me. They had hoped to fly with the RAF or the RNAS but the war's end had denied them their ambitions. Some of the young men on camp had been within weeks or even days of completing their flying training in, for example, Canada and, instead of finding themselves with wings and a commission in the Fleet Air Arm, perhaps on an aircraft carrier in sunny climes, they found themselves thrust back amongst a bunch of raw recruits. They were not best pleased and conditions at HMS *Gosling* were on occasions quite close to mutiny.

At least one hut somehow managed to catch fire and less serious but quite visible protests included flying a bedstead on the station flagpole.

I managed to avoid serious trouble but, nevertheless in the month I was there, I had punishments known, if I remember correctly, as number elevens or number sixteens. I can't remember which was the more serious but I do remember doubling round the parade ground carrying a rifle above my head until pretty close to exhaustion. I also remember the classical military and naval type of punishment involving painstakingly shoveling a mountain of coal twenty yards in one direction and then, having completed the task, shovelling it back to where it came from.

I recall that one or other of those punishments was the result of my leisurely approach to cleaning our hut. On that particular day we were all supposed to be polishing floors, cleaning sinks, light fittings etc. Very Ordinary Seaman Greenwood was reclining on his bunk, reading the *Daily Mirror*, and sucking an orange, when he sensed that the bustle and chatter around him had stilled. I slowly lowered the newspaper and there, only a foot in front of me, were the red beard and staring eyes of the fiery little commander of the camp. Number elevens – or was it sixteens? – inevitably followed.

Our time at *Gosling* was simply to wait for the commencement of our technical course. The good news was that on 20 May we were to travel to Guildford and become students at Guildford Technical College for a six-month course in radio theory. This was a very happy time. George and I managed to be billeted together in a private house only a leisurely walk away from the tech. We were allowed to wear civilian clothes at all times save for when we put on our uniforms to collect our pay, such as it was. The ritual was that you stepped up in front of the officer at the pay desk set up in one of the rooms at the college, gave him a smart salute, took off your hat, he put your pay on the top of it, you pocketed the pay, saluted him again, and off you went.

Up to this point pay had not mattered very much, but living in a civilian billet in as pleasant a place as Guildford and with London only a short train journey away, there was an awful lot on which you could spend your money. Fortunately my parents were generous in supplementing my meagre naval pay and a very happy time lay before me.

Absence is supposed to make the heart grow fonder. I found the opposite to be the case and I began to drift away from Renée. George Hopwood was a singularly bad influence. Although he had a supposedly steady and regular girlfriend back in Leeds, affairs with as many young Guildford women as possible seemed to be top of his list of priorities. We met a number of the local beauties with two of them remaining clear in my memory.

One girl was the daughter of the chemist in Guildford High Street, Pamela by name. I recall that she invited both George and me to have a meal with her parents. They viewed us with grave suspicion. Her mother enquired of George about his background and her eyes glazed a bit when George cheerfully told her that his family kept a fish and chip shop in Hunslet, Leeds.

'And what about you?' was the next question.

'My family's in the menswear trade,' was my reply and I would have been happy to leave it at that but Pamela's father pressed me further.

'Whereabouts is your shop?' he asked.

'Well, they're sort of all over the north of England,' I replied. We had about eighty branches at that time. The atmosphere lightened rapidly.

'Do have another piece of pie,' said Pamela's mother. Pamela was a well-educated girl and she encouraged me to take advantage of our proximity to London and to go to one or two concerts.

With another girl – I cannot recall her name – but I can certainly well remember how our happy little friendship came to an abrupt end. She was an amiable buxom lass who must have had a fancy for sailors, even including the dry land variety, since she cheerfully told me she was engaged to a stoker on a warship out of Portsmouth. I found myself in the Odeon Cinema at the top of Guildford High Street with an arm round her when I heard a shout from across the aisle.

'Oh, Lord!' said the girl. 'It's my fiancé!'

The burly-looking sailor, who had presumably unexpectedly got leave, and come out searching for his girl was clambering over cinema seats in his haste to get at me. Discretion was clearly the better part of valour and I took to my heels. Once again fleetness of foot stood me in good stead and I was out of the cinema and haring away down Guildford High Street long before he had a chance to get a good look at me, still less wreak his revenge.

The course at Guildford Tech. was fairly interesting but the trouble was that there were so many distractions that few of us worked as hard as we should. We were nevertheless very keen indeed to pass each interim exam as the course progressed since failure at any point meant you were out and destined for some lowly naval position.

George and I used to travel home to Leeds, frequently leaving Guildford on Friday evening and returning on overnight trains on Sunday night. There were problems with this travel. The late train out of Leeds deposited us at Kings Cross in the early hours of the morning. There were usually lots of other servicemen making similar journeys so a group of us, sometimes as many as ten, would share a taxi to Waterloo. There would then be three or four hours to kill before catching a morning train to Guildford. We would either try to sleep on a station bench or on occasion use the Salvation Army Hostel – or Red Shield Club – which was part of the Waterloo Station complex. That was a very busy place indeed on Sunday nights and it was also a very insecure place. The trick was to sleep with your head on your suitcase or kitbag and put the posts of your bunk bed into your boots or shoes. Without such precautions you were very likely to find that some of your belongings had gone missing when you woke up after an hour or two's sleep.

George and I would walk bleary-eyed from Guildford Station, call in our billet for a wash and a shave, and then go straight on to the tech. for the first Monday morning lecture. In that first lecture of the day a large part of the audience and certainly George and I were usually fast asleep.

During the Guildford course I had a brief but interesting experience as a 'groupie' – by which I mean I was a particularly enthusiastic fan of a particular band. As a boy at school I had come to enjoy jazz and swing music, especially big bands and the trumpet as an instrument. I had a small collection of 78 rpm records during my school days and this featured musicians such as Benny Goodman, Artie Shaw and, of course, Louis Armstrong. There was no chance of ever seeing Louis Armstrong in the flesh at that time, but Britain had its own Louis Armstrong in the shape of Nat Gonella, a good trumpet player who modelled himself on Armstrong. I learned that Nat Gonella and his band were playing at different theatres and dance halls around London that summer and there I was, attending as many performances as possible, appreciating Gonella's trumpet playing and particularly appreciating his vocalist, one Helen Mack. In a short period of time I attended so many of their concerts that when I found myself outside the theatre watching Nat Gonella and his men packing their kit into a bus I was able to speak with Helen. She promptly invited me – subject to Nat's approval – to go with them to their next show. They were playing two shows a night at that time and were headed for another theatre. Gonella had no objection to my climbing on the band bus. Helen Mack and I got on famously and when she came on stage later that night I was in the happy position of sitting in the front row of the stalls whilst a very pretty and quite competent lady vocalist sang to me and for me, 'Embraceable You'. Ah, happy days!

To pass the course at Guildford you had to reach the 65% pass mark. I scraped by with 69% and was then sent back to the Warrington area at the end of October to another dry land ship, HMS *Ariel*. This was the camp where we were to move from the theory of radio into the practicalities of servicing and operating the different kinds of radar equipment then in use with the Fleet Air Arm. We were of course back in uniform every day with normal naval discipline. However, we were allowed into Warrington fairly frequently and even a short, say thirty-six hour pass meant I could spend time at home.

Warrington in the early post-war years was still, as it had been during the war, almost a garrison town. It was surrounded by military and naval establishments. Not far away was the massive US air base at Burtonwood. Very close to Warrington town centre was Padgate, the entry point into the RAF for almost every recruit. On the Cheshire side of the town was Stretton Royal Naval Air Station. To the north were the several camps that constituted HMS *Gosling* and the two camps which made up HMS *Ariel*. There were therefore many thousands of servicemen and women based all around the town. The pubs, the dance halls, the cinemas and theatres in Warrington did very well indeed.

However, it was not all peace and tranquillity in Warrington town centre when the various different types of servicemen were filling the pubs and inter-service brawls were not uncommon. The most efficient at breaking up that kind of public disorder were the US military police from Burtonwood. These hefty, club-swinging, white-helmeted figures were an interesting sight – from a safe distance. Their techniques seemed to boil down – if any US personnel were involved in a disturbance – to bopping them on the head and slinging them in the back of the truck. All in all, however, it was remarkable how few serious problems arose despite this dense concentration of young service personnel.

George, Lofty and I and all the other survivors from the Guildford course, ground our way through the *Ariel* programme until March 1947 when we completed the course. From that point on we were known as Leading Radio Mechanics and sewed one anchor on to the left sleeve of our tunics and a radio mechanic's badge on to the right. We were ready for service.

I clearly recall standing in a group of about twenty who had passed the course and were now waiting to be posted. A petty officer with a clipboard in his hand stood in front of us and called out names and postings. It was like an exciting lottery. Two or three names would be called out, then their destination. HMS *Illustrious* – that is, they were off to an aircraft carrier. RNAS Evanton – they were off to a naval aerodrome in Scotland. RNAS Hong Kong – and so on. As the names were called, the people named were immediately dismissed, went to collect their gear and travel warrants and set off on what were for so many, fascinating journeys. After a few minutes there were only two of us left, wondering anxiously where we were to be sent.

'You two,' said the petty officer, 'HMS *Blackcap*.'

He didn't need to tell us where that was. *Blackcap* was the name of RNAS Stretton – an exciting bus journey to the other side of Warrington!

My friends George and Lofty had gone to other UK air stations. I didn't know particularly well the other man going to Stretton, so when I arrived at HMS *Blackcap* my spirits were pretty low since I had hoped to be posted to somewhere interesting abroad or, better still, to do a stint on a carrier. Or failing that at least to be in the company of one or other of my close friends.

My spirits began to lift soon after arriving at *Blackcap*. I was told I was to join a special unit known as NARIU. This stood for Naval Air Radar Installation Unit. It was a small and very specialised unit with its own hangar at one side of the Stretton airfield, which housed at least one example of all the planes then in service with the Fleet Air Arm. The unit's task was to work out how to install into the different aircraft types the different kinds of radio and particularly radar apparatus that were being introduced. The unit contained its own department for drawing up blue prints and plans showing precisely how, let's say, an 'Ash bomb' (that was a bomb-shaped forward scanning radar) might be fitted to, say, a Barracuda torpedo plane. The unit could not only work out how the thing was to be fitted, it could draw the plans, then print copies of them for circulation to every naval air station in the world and of course to every carrier – of which the Royal Navy still had several.

To back up all this technical work NARIU had a technical library housed in a Nissen hut adjoining the main hangar. This library contained the manuals for every aircraft used by, or ever likely to be used by the RNAS. These manuals were not unlike the handbook you get with a new car except that they were infinitely more detailed and far larger, frequently running to a number of volumes. Every piece of every aircraft was described and usually illustrated in the many hundreds of technical publications which lined the technical library's metal shelves.

On my first day I walked through the hangar, past all the very interesting aircraft therein, into the library to be greeted by three cheerful Wrens. Two were petty officers, Reggie and Sylvia, and there was a Leading Wren, ie. my rank, Margaret. My duties were simple. I was to assist the three of them in the not particularly onerous task of keeping all the manuals absolutely up-to-date. The situation was that every day amendments and revisions came into us and the appropriate manual had to be updated, usually by inserting fresh pages containing the revised information. The work was not difficult but one had to be careful, thorough and accurate. In fact we were significantly overmanned. I think any one of the four of us could have done the job alone if working hard and consistently. So, as it was, we had plenty of time for conversation, reading books, writing letters and generally idling away the days.

I took a fancy to Sylvia from the start, probably because she was a particularly cheerful girl with a wide and frequent smile. Altogether I realised that I had dropped into a very pleasant situation.

After my first few days with the three Wrens I was able to go home for the weekend and saw Renée for, what in fact proved to be, the last meeting of our teenage romance. We didn't quarrel but we were no longer at ease with each other. I had not seen enough of her during the last year to maintain our closeness and I had of course met a number of other girls particularly whilst in Guildford.

The following week Sylvia and Reggie insisted on my going with them on an organised trip from the camp to the ice rink in Liverpool. I couldn't skate but I still enjoyed the trip and especially Sylvia's company. In fact within a few days I had definitely fallen for her and to some extent my feelings were reciprocated. After a few more weeks working together during the day and going to the cinema and the occasional concert in Manchester or Liverpool I had come to the conclusion that I was going to marry Sylvia in due course. We both got leave at about the same time. My mother, who believed in helping things along, bullied Father into taking a trip to London for a day or two so that I might meet Sylvia Wisdom's parents. Her father was a headmaster and was both clever and shrewd. Her mother was a charming woman and I found that, like me, Sylvia had an older brother named Denis. My parents seemed to get on well with Sylvia, so much so that they invited her to spend the rest of her leave with us at Briaden.

After her leave she was due to go on an EVT (Educational and Vocational Training) course at HMS *Cabbala*, an RNAS station near Stafford. I drove her there and then reported back to Stretton. We were only apart for two or three weeks but I was daft enough to write as many as four letters a day to her. The fact is that I was quite infatuated with her, so much so that I did at least one rather silly thing. Father had spoiled me even further by replacing my pre-war MG sports car with a brand new model TC two-seater, black with red upholstery. I had a sign-writer write Sylvia's name in white paint down each side! I might say it cost me more to have the name removed when – as perhaps was inevitable – the infatuation wore off.

My brother got married in the middle of my infatuated period and I was to be his best man. I applied properly for a forty-eight hour pass on compassionate grounds to fulfil that function. My already not-very-high opinion of naval affairs and procedures went even lower when this modest request was flatly refused. Nothing daunted, on the wedding day, I simply sneaked out of camp, collected my Sylvia-inscribed car from the farm near the airfield where I kept it, and roared over the moors to Briaden. I changed into full wedding attire and duly performed my best man duties. I had hoped to take Sylvia to the wedding but she had been unwell that morning. However, there was to be a good party at Briaden that evening after Denis and his new bride, Marjorie, had departed and I would have liked very much for Sylvia to be there.

I was daft enough, therefore, to roar back over the moors still in full wedding kit, and drive to the requisitioned country house, known as the 'Wrennery', a mile or so from the airfield where Sylvia and forty or fifty of her fellow Wrens were billeted. I was taking a bit of a chance since, if any officer had recognised the smart young man in his morning suit and top hat who was enquiring after Petty Officer Wisdom, I would have been in very deep trouble. Fortunately no one other than Reggie and one or two others of Sylvia's friends realised that I was part of the crew of HMS *Blackcap*!

The bad news was that Sylvia's ailment had got worse and she was in the Wrennery sick bay in another ex-country mansion a little further away. Reggie and I drove there, found that she was quite ill – but not anything particularly serious – and obviously must miss the party.

I was now in something of a dilemma. I was only a mile away from the camp which of course I should never have left but I was dressed as for a wedding and my uniform was seventy miles away at Briaden. I therefore drove back again over the moors, enjoyed the party at Briaden and then, at the crack of the following dawn, yet again crossed the moors – this time in uniform – and sneaked back to camp. Thankfully I learned that I had not been missed.

I ran another cross-country race whilst at HMS *Blackcap*. The course was all around the airfield for several miles but with generally fairly easy terrain. Once more I had no difficulty in coming home first. The camp sports officer was impressed by this performance and immediately entered me for the RNAS annual cross-country championships which were to take place only a few days later. I travelled to an RNAS base in the

Midlands for the event but, once again, I had no training or coaching and this time I was running against a field of genuine athletes with some knowledge of cross-country techniques.

I remember that there was the usual mass start – I would think somewhere around a hundred of us. After the first two or three hundred yards we all had to pass through a farm gate. The knowledgeable ones who had looked at the course beforehand, and who knew the importance of getting off to a good start, raced away in the early part of the race and got through the gate in comfort. Having started at a modest pace I found myself struggling with sixty or seventy others to get through that bottleneck. The result was that I spent the rest of the race overtaking, one by one, all the knowledgeable and good runners who had not made my mistake. To my mild surprise I did not win. I still had three people in front of me when the finish line was upon us. I felt sure that if we had had perhaps another half mile to run I could have overtaken the other three, but I had to settle for fourth. To my surprise this was good enough to justify my immediate inclusion in the eight-man RNAS cross-country team which was to take part in the Royal Navy championships at Portsmouth a few weeks later.

Around this time I had contact with a family in Warrington, a Mr and Mrs R.F. Anderton and their niece, Enid Bennett. The connection was an odd one. Shortly after the end of the war, I had been given the address of a French girl who sought a 'pen-pal' in England. This girl, Renée Gozzi, had another British pen-pal in the form of Enid Bennett. When Miss Gozzi came to England in 1947 she stayed at Briaden first and was later to be turned over, as it were, to the Andertons. That hand over of Miss Gozzi actually took place at a Blackpool hotel where my family – and I, too, since I had some leave at the time – were on holiday. Enid Bennett chose not to bother even to get out of Mr Anderton's car on that occasion. So whilst I saw her it can hardly be classed as a first meeting. However, when I was stationed at Stretton airfield, that is to say HMS *Blackcap*, Mr and Mrs Anderton invited me to tea and agreed that I might bring Sylvia Wisdom with me.

At the Anderton's house in Winmarleigh Street, Warrington, 'Bob' Anderton, a keen amateur photographer, took Sylvia outside the house to take her photograph. I took that opportunity to tell Mrs Anderton, her niece Enid Bennett and another lady there present that it was my firm intention to marry the Wren who was being photographed. Enid has consistently said in the sixty years since then that the thought instantly came into her mind, 'Oh, no, you won't'.

Shortly afterwards Sylvia was posted away and my infatuation began to fade as absence certainly did not make my heart grow fonder.

My relationship with Sylvia finally came to an end when we both had leave and were able to accept my mother's and father's invitation to go with them to Belfast where some of Greenwood's principal suppliers of clothing and shirts were based. We were only there for two or three days but it was long enough for both Sylvia and me to agree – without any rancour – that we were not really suited to each other. I remember putting her on the train for London at Heysham Docks after we had got off the boat from Belfast. I gave her chocolates and an armful of magazines, put her on the train and never saw her again.

I then entered into a rather rough phase of my life. My work in the technical library on the airfield became boring. There was little or no supervision. Indeed the work of the whole NARIU unit almost ground to a halt. Everyone on the entire base other than a handful of regulars was interested in only one thing – when would their demob. number come up? Different groups in the Forces were given different classifications covering their length of service, the work they were doing and other factors, and this was translated into a group number. As and when the time came for people in that group to be demobilised that was it. Their number had come up and very quickly they would be through the demob. centre and back into civilian life – a prospect eagerly awaited by one and all.

I was obviously not going to be amongst the first to be demobbed but rather amongst the last and so, with a boring job and nothing to look forward to other than my automatic promotion to petty officer in a few months' time, I was very much at a loose end.

My friend, George Hopwood, (who had recently been posted to RNAS Stretton from his first posting in Scotland), and I spent much of our time either trying to make friends with the Wrens – there was really too much competition there – or trying to arrange blind dates with the girls who manned the Warrington telephone exchange. We got a lot of rebuffs but sometimes we managed to persuade one of the operators to meet us in town.

On one occasion we had arranged to meet two of the telephone girls outside Boots The Chemist shop in the middle of Warrington. That particular Boots branch was old fashioned in that it had two steps up to the front door. When George and I, two young men of modest size, in our sailor suits, walked up to meet our blind dates at this appointed spot that evening we were shattered to see that standing there – and towering above us – were two of the biggest girls in Lancashire. Their considerable height was made even more impressive by the fact that they were standing on the two steps and when we greeted them we were speaking at about the height of their waists.

We certainly looked a weird foursome as we walked off to the cinema but I did manage to raise a smile amongst other cinema-goers waiting at the box office when I enquired of my enormous blind date, 'Now don't forget, you promised to let me sit on your knee!'

I used to smoke in those days – thanks to the Navy's practice of the free issue of tobacco from which you could roll your own cigarettes. Or more likely turn over the sealed tin of excellent tobacco to one of the bright sparks on the camp who had obtained a hand-cranked cigarette-making machine and who would convert your tin of tobacco into some hundreds of cigarettes, subject of course to him taking a percentage of them.

I didn't drink very much but in a brief period during a cold spell in the autumn of 1947 I found that the best way to face a cold and miserable day on the camp was to start it with a slug of gin from a small bottle kept under my pillow. I wince now – as you will – at the thought of starting the day with a cigarette and a mouthful of neat gin.

It was during this rather bleak period that Bob Anderton saw me in town one evening and duly reported to his wife and his niece, Enid, 'I've just seen Brian Greenwood hanging about outside the telephone exchange with a cigarette in his mouth and looking a real scruff'.

It was probably a fair description but happily my bad time was shortly to end. Again I was asked to tea at the Andertons. This time Mr Anderton suggested I take his niece to the cinema and pressed money into my hand. Enid and I can still remember the film we saw – *Hungry Hill* with Margaret Lockwood. We began to go out whenever I could get away from the camp and an instant attraction, one for the other, very quickly deepened.

This was not the young love – sometimes people call it 'calf love' – that I had felt for Renée Rhodes as a schoolboy. Nor was it the short-lived infatuation which had left me with Sylvia's name written on the side of my car but certainly not on my heart. This was without doubt the real thing, and for the benefit of anybody unlucky enough not to have experienced it I will simply say that the old song words have got it right. 'True Love is a Many Splendoured Thing!'

Enid at seventeen was, as she always has been, very attractive. She was actually a quiet girl, probably as a result of her unusual upbringing. Her mother had died when she was born and so her aunt – her mother's significantly older sister – had cared for her since she was a baby. Auntie 'Pem' Anderton and Bob Anderton were effectively her parents but she always had affection for her father, Jim Bennett. He owned a garage and later a general contracting business in Warrington. When Enid was about five her father married again and in due course Enid had a half-brother, John, and a half-sister, Mary.

Bob Anderton was the best-known publican in Warrington, probably in Lancashire and possibly in the whole of the north of England. Apart from his tenancy of the White Hart, the largest and busiest pub in the town, shortly before I met Enid and the Andertons, he had been at various times a leading figure at Warrington Rugby League Club, and twice Chairman of the Rugby League itself. He had twice managed touring teams on pre-war tours of Australia. He was in fact frequently referred to as 'Mr Rugby League' and was very well known in sporting circles. Enid was therefore brought up in a pub and amongst her earliest memories are as a three- or four-year-old dancing on the bar in the vaults at the Crown & Sceptre, Bob Anderton's earlier pub tenancy.

During the war the White Hart in Sankey Street did a roaring trade with the personnel from all the camps round the town. So much so that no fewer than fourteen barmaids, all chosen by Bob Anderton for their good looks, were serving behind the bar. At the end of the bar, seated at the till, was Auntie Pem, no doubt exercising a very rigorous cash control.

The Americans from Burtonwood base were a major source of revenue for the White Hart and a large part of their generous pay passed through Auntie Pem's hands. However, some of them were occasionally hard up and Auntie was their unofficial banker. She had a boxful of rings, watches, etc. which the GIs had left with her as security for what they had borrowed.

Enid was still a schoolgirl in those war-time days – which is perhaps as well! I fear that if she had been a year or two older, she might have ended up as a GI bride as did some of the barmaids.

Shortly after the war's end Bob Anderton retired as a publican but remained very active in rugby league affairs. The family moved to a town house only a hundred yards away from the pub in the street opposite Warrington's famous park gates. These were magnificent wrought iron creations topped with the statuettes of four female angels. It was the joke of every camp around the town that 'there were only four virgins in Warrington and they were on the park gates'. It was that story, not the splendid workmanship that made the gates famous!

CHAPTER 8

Let Me Out!

THE WINTER OF 1947/48 was cold and bitter and that was how I was beginning to feel about my position in His Majesty's Senior Service. I was bored with my work. There no longer seemed any sensible purpose in what we were doing, the Russian threat had yet to materialise in any significant way and consequently, like just about every other serviceman and woman, all I wanted was for my demob. number to come up.

I was quite clear what I wanted to do. I most certainly intended to marry Enid but I appreciated that I would have to make some progress in business before that could happen.

I did in fact have one job offer. I received the letter below which was a pretty good indication of my father's sense of humour. Although my mentor of two years previously, Ronnie Bennett, Greenwood's Sales Director, had signed the letter, it was clearly Father's idea that I be invited to apply for an apprenticeship to Mr Berry, described in the letter as 'our packing room manager'. In truth Mr Berry was an amiable old bloke whose sole function was to open packing cases and cartons in the basement of the then head office at Drewton Street, Bradford.

Such was my eagerness to find out when I was to be demobbed that I found myself on a charge for asking about it. Some errand took me from my part of Stretton airfield to the other side thereof where the demob. office was situated. I got off my bike, put my head round the demob. office door to ask, 'Anyone got any idea when my number's coming up?'

Nobody had and the sundry clerks – known in the Navy as 'Writers' shooed me away. One of them was unkind enough to report me to an officer for interrupting their vital work.

Since it had only been a week or two previously that my own C.O. had told me that my demob. was probably two or three months away, my casual enquiry resulted in my being placed on a charge for: 'Conduct prejudicial to good order and naval discipline in that he did doubt his commanding officer's word'.

I was much aggrieved by this and by the pettiness of the whole incident and so when I was up before the Captain of HMS *Blackcap* on this charge

ALL COMMUNICATIONS TO BE ADDRESSED TO 17, DREWTON STREET, BRADFORD.

DIRECTORS :
W. H. GREENWOOD.
H. I. GREENWOOD.
W. GREENWOOD.

Greenwoods
(HOSIERS & OUTFITTERS) LTD

ESTABLISHED 1860.
TELEPHONE 6131.

OUR REF.

YOUR REF.

Registered Office and Warehouse :-
**17, DREWTON STREET,
BRADFORD.**
2.2.48.

BRANCHES AT :

BRADFORD, (14)

BLACKPOOL, (3)

BRIGHOUSE,

BINGLEY,

BARNOLDSWICK,

BATLEY,

BURY,

BARNSLEY,

COLNE,

CLECKHEATON,

CLITHEROE,

DEWSBURY,

GLOSSOP,

HALIFAX,

HECKMONDWIKE,

KEIGHLEY, (2)

LEEDS,

LANCASTER,

MALTON,

MORECAMBE, (2)

MIDDLESBROUGH,

NELSON,

OTLEY,

OLDHAM,

PRESTON,

RUNCORN,

SHIPLEY,

SKIPTON,

SOUTHPORT,

SCARBOROUGH,

WAKEFIELD, (2)

YORK,

ETC. ETC.

G.B. GReenwood,
R.N.A.S.
Stretton.

Dear Sir,

We have received your application, and cannot help wondering why we have been so favoured as to be preferred, by a man of your obvious abilities, to such progressive concerns as the N.C.B., B.O.T., C.W.S., etc.

Unfortunately, the position for which your qualifications appear most suitable is at present, adequately filled by a man who, although perhaps not quite up to your standard, we are bound to retain until his retirement. We have no wish at present, to accelerate this retirement owing to his long record of faithful service. The position to which we refer is, of course that of managing director.

However, it is not our policy to pass by such promising material, and have prevailed upon Mr. Berry, our packing room manager, to consider you as an articled apprentice on consideration that you are prepared to work under him for a period of 15 years. There will, of course, be a premium required of £150. This sum will be repaid over the period of your apprenticeship in the form of wages.

The prospects of advancement are excellent as Mr. Berry retires at the end of this period, and there is no reason why you should not, by then, have gained sufficient knowledge to make you proficient enough to take over his position.

Your early reply is requested as this position will not remain open for long, and Mr. Berry wishes to make it clear that the offer is subject to a personal interview.

Yours faithfully,

p.p. Greenwoods Ltd.,

I defended myself vigorously and vehemently. To my pleasant surprise, since very few were ever acquitted in that forum, the Captain took my point and pronounced that I was guilty of no offence.

The winter rolled on, brightened only by the occasions when I could get out of camp and see Enid, and by one particular evening – 5 February 1948 – when HMS *Blackcap* held, what the dance programme describes as, 'A Grand Dance in the Station Cinema'.

The programme for the evening was as set out below and as far as I can remember I danced every dance with Enid who in my eyes was the belle of the ball. She wore an emerald green dress with a gold chain serving as a belt round her trim waist.

PROGRAMME

1.   QUICK STEP
2.   WALTZ
3.   SLOW FOX TROT
4.   PAUL JONES
5.   WALTZ (LADIES' CHOICE)
6.   TANGO
7.   FOX TROT
8.   ST BERNARD WALTZ
9.   QUICK STEP
10. WALTZ (SPOT)
11. SLOW FOX TROT
12. WALTZ

INTERVAL :: REFRESHMENTS

13. QUICK STEP
14. WALTZ (SPOT)
15. FOX TROT
16. FOLLOW THE BAND (HOKEY-COKEY, ETC.)
17. WALTZ (ELIMINATION)
18. QUICK STEP
19. WALTZ (OLD FASHIONED)
20. SLOW FOX TROT
21. WALTZ (SPOT)
22. RHUMBA AND TANGO
23. QUICK STEP
24. LAST WALTZ

'THE KING'

The dance programme was typical for the late 1940s. Programmes were strictly adhered to and normally included all the dances shown. Each dance usually consisted of a set of three numbers so that, if you got up for a quickstep, you would dance to three different tunes before that one was over and the programme therefore consisted of some seventy-plus pieces of music rather than the twenty-four as shown on the programme suggested. There would always be a ladies' choice, normally a waltz. Then it was the men's turn to feel rather anxious and hope that someone was going to ask them to dance. Spot dances, again usually waltzes, were simply dances where the music stopped and the couple either caught in a certain spot or in the beam of a spot light were awarded a modest prize.

The last waltz was a very important dance in those distant days. A popular waltz tune frequently played at this point was 'Who's Taking You Home Tonight?' and that was, of course, a matter of great importance. The worst answer you could get to that question was, 'I'm going home with my friend.'

It is an interesting fact that a significant number, as many as one in three, of marriages resulted from couples meeting for the first time at a dance. Despite their semi-formal nature, the dances were usually hugely enjoyable. Everyone made an effort to look their best and standards of courtesy almost unheard of today were the norm. 'May I have this dance, miss?' was the normal approach and it was regarded as very rude for a girl to refuse without a good reason.

And that reminds me of an event, some years later, when the team with which I was touring decided to visit the local dance hall after the match. My good friend, Tom Horsfall – of whom more anon – saw a couple of very attractive women across the ballroom and decided he would ask the blonde one to dance. In his most polite tone of voice he greeted her, 'Good evening, miss, may I have this dance?' To which she replied, 'Nah. Dance with mi mate – I'm sweatin'.'

I occasionally had weekend leave and usually spent this at Briaden – with Enid either travelling with me or making her own way across into Yorkshire by train and bus. None of the behaviour which is regarded as pretty normal today between a young couple who intend to marry applied to us. Kisses and cuddles were as far as it went possibly, I suppose, for lack of opportunity. Certainly my mother made a practice of putting Enid into a spare bedroom as far as possible away from my own in the large house that was Briaden. On one occasion that gave me a seriously embarrassing moment.

The family and two or three house guests had all gone to bed. When silence reigned, I tiptoed furtively down the corridor into the small spare room which was Enid's usual billet. I slid gently into the bed and embraced the female figure lying there . . . only to be shattered when the figure sat up and said, 'You've got the wrong woman, Brian!' Unbeknown to me there had been a last minute switch of bedrooms and Enid's normal place was occupied by an old friend of my parents. I beat a hasty retreat back to my own room.

Interest was added to the final period of my time in the RNAS when the day dawned for the Royal Navy cross-country championships. I was sent down to Lee-on-Solent, the main base of the RNAS, to join up with the other seven members of the Fleet Air Arm team. Once again there was little or no training, but at least my fellow team members were all experienced cross-country runners and I was able to glean a few tips from them – such as the technique for running across ploughed land and the need to carry your arms high when trying to run fast downhill. The teams from all the other parts of the Royal Navy duly assembled and the race was run – over about ten miles, if I remember correctly – in the Ports Down Hills behind Portsmouth, early in 1948. The RNAS team won the event but personally I had a rather surprising setback.

Towards the end of the race I was running along a ridge with a fairly steep slope and was just about to pass a burly competitor. It would have been too much to hope that he would move to one side and give me room to pass but he had a technique all of his own. He simply thumped me off the track and I went head over heels down the steep slope at the side. By the time I had got up the hill and back on to the track any hope of winning the race, or even being amongst the leaders, had gone and I finished a very angry sixth.

This should have been good enough to include me in the Royal Navy team for the inter-Services race which was to follow shortly thereafter since the first six were supposedly picked automatically to run against the Army and Air Force. I was angrier still when I learned that I had been picked as reserve for the Navy team and an officer, who had finished behind me, had been given a place in preference to me.

There was nothing I could do about it and in any event there were some compensations. I was posted promptly to Lee-on-Solent to train for a week or two with the Royal Navy team. This was a very happy period of my Service life since we enjoyed a special – and good – diet and we were free of all duties other than training. My personal training consisted of running briskly out of the front gate of RNAS Lee-on-Solent, jogging along the promenade until out of everyone's sight and then settling down in a cafe for coffee, cigarettes and a thorough study of the *Daily Mirror*. After an appropriate length of time I would run back to camp trying to look as if I had just completed a ten- or twelve-mile training run.

Although I did not run in the inter-Services competition, at least a little later I did have a chance to run for the Royal Navy and by that time was in reasonably good condition and with the benefit of some serious cross-country experience. The Navy team was to run against the London Metropolitan Police on a course at Hayes, Middlesex. The RN team plus sundry supporters, including a group of Wrens, filled a coach and we drove up to the London area in good time for the race. We had learned that the Met. had one star runner who was expected to win the event and who we gathered was in line for selection as a distance runner in the 1948 Olympics.

The start and finish of the race were on the playing fields in front of a fine mansion which presumably served as the headquarters of the London Met.'s sporting activities. The day was bright and sunny, but since it was early in the year it was not too warm. In fact, conditions were ideal for long distance running. In due course the race got underway and after several miles the situation was that the Met.'s star was way out in front, but three of us from the Navy team were running shoulder to shoulder in joint second place with the intention of crossing the line in that same formation and thus earning more points for our team.

As we ran through woodland not far from the playing fields where the race would end, I told my two colleagues, 'I'm going to try and catch him'.

Neither of my team colleagues felt they had enough energy to go with me so I quickened my pace and began gradually to overhaul the Met.'s star runner. The final part of the long course was down through the woods parallel to the finishing line. At the bottom of the wood you turned left and left again into the finishing straight which ran up the playing fields to the front of the mansion.

The Met. star, who was running confidently, didn't realise he had any competition until we were within 100 yards or so of leaving the wood. He glanced over his shoulder and was, I think, amazed to find that a member of the Navy team was hot on his heels. He turned into the finishing straight up the playing fields with me gaining on him with every stride. I surged past him and burst the finishing tape to the accompaniment of much applause, particularly from the Royal Navy supporters.

Not only had I beaten the star of the Metropolitan Police but I was a long way ahead of several members of the Royal Navy team who had been selected – mistakenly in my view, of course – ahead of me in the recent inter-Services championships. Furthermore, I learned that my time for the course (which was fairly short at something just over five miles), was 28 min. 5 sec. and a record for that course. Altogether a very gratifying result.

I found myself the hero of the hour. At the party that followed the event I was on the receiving end of many slaps on the back, numerous kisses from the Wrens and a very large number of drinks. So many that for the second time in my young life I had much too much to drink and passed the journey back to 'Pompey' in a state of blissful oblivion.

That was the last time I ever ran a race. Shortly afterwards my demob. number finally came up. Had this not been so I am quite sure I would have been a regular choice for both the Navy's cross-country team and any other long distance running events. However, I couldn't wait to get out of the Service and, once out, I was too busy with my work, with other sports and, of course, with Enid to trouble to join an athletics club, which I suppose I should have done. I have always believed that last race proved conclusively that I had been gifted with all the attributes of a top-class long distance runner.

I learned that I was to be demobbed in April and a few weeks before that – on 1 March to be precise – my automatic promotion to petty officer came through. I immediately enjoyed a significant improvement in my quarters with a room to myself and regular use of the petty officers' mess. Thus my last few weeks in the Service were quite enjoyable. I had little or no work to do in the technical library which was my official duty, the sports officer thought I was lovely and soon had me playing on the wing for the station rugby team whilst I was ticking off the days to my release.

I got into a bit of bother in one match for the station rugby side. We went to play an RAF team not far from Preston and when we changed and trotted out on to the field we found the opposition only had eleven players and that the field was a soccer pitch. The respective sports officers had clearly got their wires crossed. However, eleven of us offered to take on the RAF boys at soccer and an unusual and entertaining match followed. I think we lost about 12–1 and I got sent off. I had never played organised soccer but had always understood that shouldering your opponent is quite permissible. Consequently when my opposite number came dribbling down the wing I made no attempt to play the ball but simply hit him as hard as I could with a shoulder charge which deposited him neatly into touch. I thought I had done well until the referee accused me of dangerous play and sent me off. As far as I can remember this was the only time in my life I have been so disciplined at any form of sport.

The day came. I got my railway warrant and set off to HMS *Daedalus*, the RNAS main base at Lee-on-Solent where I had recently spent some time as a member of the cross-country team. This time I was able to check into the petty officers' quarters and was enjoying a drink in the mess that evening when someone said to me, 'Is your name Greenwood?' He went on to tell me that if I looked at the noticeboard I would find that I was Duty Petty Officer for the following day. Shock and horror was my reaction. 'What am I supposed to do?' I asked and learned that the day would start with the morning parade – 'divisions' as it was known in the Navy.

I didn't sleep that night as I tried to remember all the commands that I would have to shout to get hundreds of men marching on to the parade ground into the right places and generally, 'All present and correct.' The last time I had done or seen any organised drill had been at Pwllheli over two years previously.

Another petty officer gave me a lot of helpful instructions and then on the following morning, almost paralysed with anxiety, I somehow managed to get the parade on to the central parade ground, all lined up and in good order. I marched briskly up to the officer of the day, saluted him smartly and told him his parade was as it should be. He presumably repeated that message to the commander, then came back to me and instructed me to dismiss the parade, which I did with great relief.

I went back to the POs' mess to recover and to ask advice as to what other duties the petty officer of the day had to fulfil. Even more shock horror followed when I learned that for the rest of the day my duties were confined to my own trade. I was supposed to be a fully trained radar technician which is what my papers showed. What did not appear was the fact that I had spent the last several weeks on athletics and that for more than a year prior to that I had never so much as picked up a screwdriver, still less serviced or repaired any kind of radar or radio equipment.

I made further enquiries and learned that my trade duty for the day was to ensure that the radio altimeters in a squadron of Seafires (Spitfires adapted for landing on aircraft carriers) were all in good and working order. I urgently sought the advice of a real radar technician and happily his instructions were simple. He told me that, by the headrest for the pilot of a Seafire, there was a panel which could be opened by removing only one screw. If I reached therein I would find a black box. If I shook it and it didn't rattle all was well. Armed with this hi-tech information I spent an hour putting my hand into the back of the cockpits of an entire squadron and then, with my heart beating mightily, I signed that all was in order with their radio altimeters.

I have to say that, when the Seafires took off for a flying exercise a little later in the day, I anxiously counted them out and counted them in. Thank heavens none of them had any altitude problems! That was in fact the only time a year's training, first in radio theory and then on specific pieces of equipment, was ever put into use.

I very soon forgot all I had been taught about radio and radar and, from my early married life onwards, mending a domestic fuse was for me, a significant accomplishment. When I look back into old notebooks from my training days and I see paragraphs such as that below, I have to confess that I can't understand a word of it.

A.G.S. in A.B.K.

The −ve output signal from V.B.A. (diode) is applied via a pulse amplifier, G24 and R20 to the grid of the A.G.S. amplifier V8. A +ve voltage pulse is caused in the T.C. at the anode of this amplifier (300kc/s). The output signal of this amp is applied through the 2^{ary} of the transformer to the A.G.S. diode V6A whence it is applied to the grid of the D.C. amplifier (−ve pulses). A +ve potential from the cathode load of V9 R27 and is applied to the grid of the Rx tube V_2.

On the day after my anxious time with the Seafires I went through the demob. procedure, handing in my Navy kit and receiving in exchange a quite reasonable civilian suit, shirt, tie etc. topped by a grey felt hat. Thus attired I travelled home to Briaden to begin the next part of my life.

Those last few words would obviously seem to be an appropriate chapter ending, but there was one other incident during my time in the Forces that must go into this book somewhere, so I shall recount it here. Sometime in 1947 I was home on leave and Father took me for a walk in the woods near Briaden to explain to me his plans for a flotation of the family business as a public company. His plans were well advanced. Indeed, a first draft of the prospectus had already been produced. This showed that Greenwood's at that time was a successful medium-sized business with an ever-increasing branch list, a similarly increasing turnover and a good level of profitability which could confidently be expected to improve still further when the post war economy fully recovered.

Father had obviously been thinking deeply about this question of 'going public'. The intention would have been to sell about a third of the shares in the business to the general public and thus family control would not have been affected. Such a transaction would certainly have resulted in a very large cheque for Father – and a smaller one for Mother – since they were the only shareholders at that time. That fact, together perhaps with the anticipation that running a public company would bring him a certain kudos, were what was motivating my father. However, he had not finally committed himself and wanted to know what I thought of the plan. After a moment's thought I told him that, whilst obviously I knew very little about flotations, I could not think that that point in time was the right one for such a major step. Both my brother, Denis, and I were anticipating coming into the business. Denis would be out of the RAF very shortly and I would certainly be out of the RNAS sometime in the first half of 1948.

'Surely,' I said, 'it would be more sensible to let Denis and me have a year or two in the business and see how it developed rather than parting with a third of it now.'

I was very glad indeed that Father took the advice and he cancelled the flotation. Such thoughts never entered our heads for the next decade during which time the business developed quite dramatically with all the advantages accruing only to the family rather than a third of them going to outside shareholders.

I suppose that was my first significant business decision and, unlike some at the latter part of my career, that was a good one.

CHAPTER 9

A Young Executive

> I am a young executive
> My cuffs could not be cleaner
> I drive up and down the motorways
> In the company's Cortina
>> (with apologies to John Betjeman)

I DID INDEED BEGIN MY WORK in the family business as a young executive but in Greenwood's at that time executives turned their hand to whatever was required. For example, I often found myself driving a van rather than a Cortina or any other kind of car. In those early post war years just about the most economical form of transport was a Jowett utility van and it was these that the firm's area managers – at that time known as branch inspectors – used to visit the branches under their control. From the company's point of view these vehicles were fine. It meant the area manager not only visited the shops under his control to supervise their operation but also frequently took their weekly delivery of goods with him. Those little Jowetts were usually packed so full of menswear that it was stacked high on the passenger seat as well as in the back. I drove many miles one-handed since my left hand was needed to prevent a pile of shirt boxes falling into my lap.

A good example of the way the family and executives would turn to was the re-opening of Oldham branch after a complete refit. The manager and his assistant had been sent home to get some rest before the anticipated rush at the re-opening the following morning. At ten o'clock at night the lights in the shop were blazing. The company's Chairman – my father – was finishing a counter display. Ronnie Bennett, the Sales Director, was putting the finishing touches to the window displays. My brother, Denis, was displaying merchandise along the fixture tops and I had my head in a glass counter polishing the interior. The Area Manager, who was helping with these opening preparations, had just been sent out in order to bring back a fish and chip supper. There was a rattling on the shop door and a large Oldham policeman wanted to enter.

'What's going on?' he enquired having first – I suppose – satisfied himself that we were not there to burgle the shop but were, rather, working hard at its appearance. We explained the situation and confirmed that we would shortly be going back to Bradford having finalised the shop ready for its opening in the morning. The policeman pondered our explanation and then observed, 'Your bosses must be a bloody hard lot if they have you working at this time of night so far from home.'

I contrived to have responsibility for the Greenwood branches in Lancashire and Cheshire for the very good reason that this meant I could call on and sometimes stay overnight with Enid at the Andertons. I worked hard to ensure that the shops in my area did well. I think that the time and effort I put in gradually earned the respect of the managers and manageresses for whom I had responsibility, despite the inevitable initial resentment by people, many of whom were old enough to be my mother or father, having to take instructions from the young man whose chief claim to fame was that he was the boss's son.

I began a custom which I kept on for very many years: whichever branch I was in at the end of the trading day I stayed there until the shop closed. That was fine if, for example, I was in Northwich branch and going to stay with the Andertons less than twenty miles away. It was not so good if I was in Runcorn or Widnes and had to drive some eighty or ninety miles back over the Pennine moors – motorways had not yet appeared – in the little Jowett van. I can fairly claim to have put in some long hours both in my early days and also much later.

In 1948 Greenwood's had eighty-seven branches open and trading. Incredibly no fewer than seventeen of these were in Bradford where there was a branch in every main shopping street and also most of the suburbs. Business was good – one could almost say booming were it not for the fact that all kinds of garments were still in very short supply. Although it was three years since the end of the war a delivery of men's shirts, for example, and a notice to that effect in the shop window would produce a small queue and the shirts would be sold out within a few hours.

Father, now assisted by my brother, Denis, who had been demobbed from his role in the RAF as a PT instructor in 1947, struggled hard to find suitable merchandise for the chain. We even dabbled in government surplus goods. I remember one purchase of 100,000 ex-US Army collar-attached shirts sold extraordinarily well.

Denis had been made a director of the company and shortly after my twenty-first birthday I was in the position of the young man in the story

I recounted earlier and, on being told that I was to have a seat on the board, I was able to reply, 'Thanks, Dad.' However, something better than that happened to me on my twenty-first birthday, 20 August 1948. Enid and I got engaged. There was a good party at Briaden to make the announcement and celebrate the event. Enid was only just turned eighteen and from all sides we were pressured to wait at least a year before we married. With some reluctance we agreed.

The year of our engagement was a very busy one for the family business. Twenty-four of the existing branches were refitted and five new shops were opened. Most of the branches now had the green Vitriolite shop front and, as the branch list moved up into the nineties, 'Greenwood's for Menswear' became an ever more familiar sight in northern counties. The new head office and warehouse building on Manningham Lane, Bradford, was in the process of conversion. The stone facade's leaded light windows each bore a new company logo – a shield with an oak tree surmounted by a boar's head symbolising Bradford and with the motto 'Sturdy as the Oak' in a scroll beneath – to all the ground floor offices. These made the corner building look rather like a large hotel or pub. So much so that people began to refer to it as the Greenwood Arms.

Enid and I were married at Guiseley Parish Church on 31 August 1949. The sun shone and everything about the day was a success. My brother, Denis, acted as my best man and three of my other groomsmen were friends from schooldays. Happily, the same three and their wives have been our closest friends ever since. Not surprisingly, the eight of us are known to our children and grandchildren as 'the golden oldies'.

Nineteen-year-old Enid looked what she was – a very attractive and happy young woman. After quite a large function at the Midland Hotel in Bradford following the wedding ceremony, the family and closest friends moved on to Briaden and it was from there that Enid and I set off on our honeymoon.

Happily we were not going in a Jowett van. The business was certainly now prosperous enough to buy its youngest executive a handsome Riley car. We set off with the usual trail of tin cans – and a little later learned that we were cooking kippers on the cylinder head – and drove down to London. I hadn't much money of my own at this point but the first night of our honeymoon seemed to be an opportunity to spend it and I had booked a suite – no less – at the Grosvenor House Hotel in London's Park Lane. I remember clearly the fitted wardrobe units in that palatial accommodation. They would have accommodated at least a hundred garments and the seven or eight coat hangers that were all our clothes required looked rather forlorn. However, they didn't look as forlorn as Enid did a little later. There she was, on the first night of our married life, in a pretty new nightdress and where was I? – in the bath!

I was afflicted with the most ghastly cramp in my left leg, a consequence of driving over 200 miles down the old Great North Road which was a very long way short of modern motorway standards. The dozens – make that hundreds – of gear changes had tired me and, of course, it had been a long and exciting day. In any event, the fact was I really had agonising cramp for virtually all of our first night and spent it in a hot bath.

The following day we drove leisurely down to Dover where we had booked to stay at the White Cliffs Hotel with a view to catching the early trans-channel ferry the following morning. We spent the afternoon in a cinema and when we went back to the White Cliffs I was shocked to see my brother and sister-in-law just checking in. I knew they were taking a holiday at the same time as our honeymoon but I certainly hadn't expected to see them whilst we were on it.

After a happily cramp-free night we got up early and crossed on the morning boat to Boulogne. After a leisurely drive and a very good dinner in its restaurant, Enid and I were sitting at a table just outside the Hotel de la Poste in Rouen. I remember clearly that I was enjoying a Benedictine with my coffee when, in a puff of dust, Denis's Triumph sports car braked to a halt in front of us.

No one was supposed to know where we were touring on our honeymoon and I was certainly suspicious as to why it was turning into a family outing. Denis assured me it was pure coincidence so I asked him where his next stop was. Incredibly enough he had booked into the same hotel as us at Mont St Michel. We gave up the struggle at that point and spent our next day with them. They were going, as we were, south to the Riviera. Denis and Majorie who had already learned where to find the better things in life were staying in a smart hotel in Juan les Pins. We were staying in a second-grade hotel in Nice.

These were the days when the amount of foreign currency you could obtain was very strictly controlled. I believe the amount we were allowed to take was only £35 each. Of course, everyone tried to find a way round this. The simplest and most basic arrangement was that British ladies touring abroad stuffed pound notes into their underwear. My sister-in-law, Majorie, had certainly followed this practice, but for Denis's and Majorie's rate of expenditure the amount of cash so secreted was proving inadequate. We therefore had to fall back on our emergency plan for dealing with a shortage of foreign currency when abroad.

A rather disreputable business contact had told us of a totally illegal arrangement for getting around the exchange control regulations. It involved mentioning someone's name to the right person in France and then, at a later date, settling the account in cash at an address in Manchester. In view of Denis's needs we followed this advice and went to an address in Nice. It was an office over a shop and, when we climbed the stairs, a steel door at the top had one of those slide-to-open peepholes through which we explained we had come to see Monsieur X on the instructions of Mr. Y of Manchester. The door was opened and we entered an office containing three or four very tough looking characters. The man who was clearly the boss was seated behind a large desk. In our schoolboy French we confirmed that we wanted some French francs and would be happy to repay the debt with English pounds in Manchester two weeks hence. We queried the exchange rate and whilst we were doing sums in our heads the Boss told us that all was in order and suggested how much we might like to have.

All we wanted was perhaps £100 or so but to our horror we realised that he was talking in terms of thousands, indeed tens of thousands, and we were meeting with a major figure in the post war currency black market. We assured him that we would consider the exchange rate he had quoted and would return the following day to confirm precisely how many French francs we required. With that assurance the steel door was unbolted and we made our exit vowing, of course, never to go near the place again.

We had got out of an awkward situation, but we were no nearer solving Denis's shortage of cash problem. Naturally he suggested that I should lend him money. Equally naturally I told him that I was not going to be desperately short of funds on my honeymoon in order to let him stay at a posh hotel. The outcome was that Denis and Majorie came to stay in our hotel and our honeymoon did indeed end up as a family holiday.

We returned after the two weeks' break and moved in to Littlecroft, the house which Father had given us as a wedding present.

Our first married home was less than a mile from Briaden and only a few hundred yards from Woodhouse Grove School. It was an unusual property in that, although it had three bedrooms, there was only one living-room/dining-room downstairs. Nevertheless, built on top of the garage at the side of the house was a sun lounge with access from the principal bedroom. Small though it was, this became the scene of many a happy party with dancing to gramophone records in a smoke-filled atmosphere – nearly everyone smoked cigarettes in those days – which meant we had to have all our bedroom windows open for half an hour after each party to let the smoke clear.

This handsome detached house standing in half an acre of garden in a very desirable location cost, in 1949, £3,400 and its insured rebuilding cost was a mere £2,000. Such have been the ravages of inflation and the boom in house prices, that the same property today would cost a hundred times as much as Father then generously paid.

Enid and I were a blissfully happy young couple in our first years at Littlecroft. The bliss was dented on two occasions. The first time was the occasion that we always laughed about later as an example of flaming passion! Described briefly and leaving you to use your imagination . . . let's just say Enid was in bed and I was happy to join her as quickly as possible. I tore off my pyjamas and threw them over my shoulder. What I did not know at first was that they had come to rest on the electric fire. A minute or two later they were ablaze!

There's nothing like a small fire just behind you to dampen your ardour!

The other blow to our marital bliss might have been tragic. In the autumn of 1950 Enid was expecting our first child. Littlecroft was heated by a gas-fired boiler which could be temperamental. It had gone out and when Enid went to re-light it there had been a build up of gas which exploded. Fortunately she was not hurt, although badly shocked.

From day one of our marriage there was a third important figure involved. This was Wilfred – the third of a trio Pip, Squeak and Wilfred – of puppies which my mother's well-bred Scotch terrier had produced after, presumably, meeting a sheepdog. With that parentage Wilfred was a rather unusual-looking crossbreed but he was a highly intelligent dog and an excellent companion for Enid during the working week when I usually left home quite early and almost invariably got home late.

Although we were indeed very happy Enid did occasionally have a moment of doubt. She recalls sitting alone one lunchtime, still only a few months after her twentieth birthday but pregnant, and with a house and a husband to care for. She cried a little and said out loud, 'What am I doing here? I want to go home.' Happily that was only a passing thought and, as we moved into 1951, our impending new arrival was foremost in our thoughts.

Our daughter Patricia was born at home on 16 March 1951. My knowledge of childbirth was limited to what I had seen on the films, which boiled down to the father pacing up and down the living-room while a succession of females scurried about shouting for 'more hot water'. Then, after a little while, a smiling doctor would call the father upstairs so that he might hold for a moment or two the little bundle of joy which his smiling wife had in her arms.

In real life it's not like that at all! The first thing is that childbirth is, or can be, significantly more painful than old movies might lead you to believe. Consequently the expectant father is sitting downstairs listening to his suffering wife screaming blue murder in the room above. Then the job can sometimes take much longer than anticipated and things may not go smoothly. The anxiety of the midwife and doctor communicates itself very quickly to the expectant father. In our case Patricia's birth took long enough to require another cylinder of oxygen . . . or was it gas? All I know is that I was despatched in the middle of the night to collect another cylinder of something from the midwife's house two or three miles away.

When it was all over and done with, and the complications resolved, we had a super baby who was a quiet and well-behaved infant, a quick-learning toddler and a bright little girl in what seemed to be very quick time.

By the time Tricia was born, the Greenwood's business had moved into its new headquarters and rapid expansion of the business continued. The post war supply problems were now pretty well eliminated and business was as it should be – a question of competing efficiently and effectively with all the other firms selling similar goods.

Nineteen fifty-one was a significant year for the business. We opened the 100th branch in Victoria Lane, Huddersfield, and total sales passed the £1,000,000 mark for the first time. Of course a million pounds sounds very little today but 1951 prices were very different. Our best selling line of shirts were 19/6d. each – that is, 97½p. A variety of items, socks underwear, ties, braces, etc. were all available at 2/11d., i.e. 14p. Our prices were always very competitive and just about everything we sold was of British manufacture.

We had become a reasonably well-organised multiple firm which ran smoothly but in a pretty exciting way since there was always a new branch to be worked on somewhere or a private business to be taken over, or major refits sometimes involving temporary premises followed by a full-blown re-opening.

We used to open and re-open branches with some razzamatazz. Adverts in the local newspapers played their part, but the old technique of a sprat to catch a mackerel was better. Special opening offers invariably did the trick and an opening or a re-opening meant a queue of customers waiting for ten o'clock, usually on a Thursday morning.

Like all retailers we had problems with shoplifting and also staff dishonesty. I managed to come up with a good scheme which helped a lot to combat these problems. We called it 'the stocktaking bonus scheme'.

Every branch had its stock physically checked at least twice a year either by one of the two men we employed as full-time stocktakers or by the area managers. The normal outcome for a stocktake should, in theory, be a small deficiency since it is impossible to prevent some minor shoplifting. Therefore, a deficiency of a few pounds was entirely acceptable. We decided that we would allow a penny in every pound of turnover to be written off for stock losses. If the stocktaking showed a smaller deficit or perhaps a surplus, the manager received the amount as a bonus. If his deficit exceeded the stocktaking bonus figure by a modest amount, that part of the deficit above the bonus level was carried forward into the next period together with a 'Bad luck – please try harder' letter. If the deficit was seriously outside the bonus level, then obviously the manager's competence or his honesty came into question. Some managers made sure they never had a deficit by overcharging customers. This was impossible to prevent since the overcharging was usually impossible to prove. A fairly sure sign that a manager was thinking on those lines would be if the garment tickets on clothing – which indicated the size and the price were *not*, as they should be, stitched on to the garment but were, rather, in the pocket.

Of course, the majority of managers and assistants were entirely honest and reliable people but sadly there were always a few bad apples in the barrel. Some of the 'fiddlers', as we called them, were really very efficient. They would, for example, overcharge steadily at every opportunity and then, when they guessed they were about due for a stocktaking, would take their own stock, confirm that they had indeed generated a substantial surplus which they would then promptly steal from the next few weeks' takings.

There were others who were really sad cases. They would get into trouble gambling or perhaps get into an extra-marital affair and they would simply supplement their wage and commission by stealing every week from the till. If the stocktakers did their job correctly their next stocktaking would show a thumping great deficit which would mark the end of that fiddler's career in the retail trade.

Several dyed-in-the-wool fiddlers were pretty cute. I remember the manager of one of our Leeds branches whose stocktakings always showed a modest surplus. But there was something unusual about him that made me suspicious. I therefore had his stock taken again and supervised this extra and particularly careful stocktaking myself. In his waistcoat pockets he had not one or two pens, but umpteen! There were ink pens both black and blue, biros in two or three colours, and also an assortment of pencils. His closely supervised extra stocktaking produced a very large deficiency. The explanation for his previous satisfactory results lay in his assortment of pens and pencils. He had made sure that whatever writing implement the stocktaker used, he had a very similar one ready to hand. Stocktaking was carried out on sheets with many vertical columns, each headed with a price – for example, £5. If a stocktaker working his way round the shop came across two – shall we say – raincoats priced at £5, he entered two in the £5 column. At some stage the stocktaker would break off for a few minutes and that was the fiddling manager's chance. All he had to do was put a figure one in front of the two and he had added £50 to the stocktaking total. Using this technique and with a rough idea of how much he needed to increase the stocktaking total, this particular fiddler had managed to cover up a very large deficit for a very long time. Thereafter, of course, the stocktakers were instructed never to let the stocktaking sheets out of their own hands.

Turning from such unpleasant topics to the happier side of operating a menswear shop in the fifties you might be interested to learn that there was a significant difference in the capabilities of men and women. Without doubt men were better window dressers but women always seemed to have the edge in salesmanship. Furthermore, manageresses were found generally to be better stock keepers and their shops were neater and cleaner than that of the typical manager.

I suppose if we had taken that thought to its logical conclusion we would have ended up with an all female staff and that might not have been such a bad idea except that there might have been some embarrassing moments when it became necessary to measure a man for a bespoke garment.

CHAPTER 10

Grim Time and Big Time

I N 1953 WE HAD ENJOYED a holiday in Austria, spent mostly in the charming mountain village of Igls, not far from Innsbruck. Enid was expecting our second child. Business continued to be good with constant expansion. We had almost completed the building of an extension to Littlecroft which transformed it into a quite substantial house. We had our first resident domestic help, a young girl from a Durham mining village and altogether life was good.

When Enid was at about the six months stage, she woke me one night to complain of pain in her side and back. The following day she was quite ill and I called the doctor. After a further day in bed, Enid's condition was worse so our family doctor called in the obstetrician who was to take charge of her confinement. He – Mr Craig – was a large, quiet, usually reassuring man. After he had examined her, he told me he was not happy at all since Enid had appendicitis and must go into hospital immediately. Naturally this frightened Enid – and me, too – but we got her comfortably settled in a private room in the maternity department at the Duke of York Nursing Home which was then the private wing of the Bradford Royal Infirmary. Once she was settled, I left her to go and get something to eat. I returned an hour or so later and was shattered to find her room empty.

At first I could not find anyone to tell me what had happened. Then I heard that she had been taken up to the operating theatre for the removal of her appendix. During the following day all was well, but on the succeeding days the doctors began to be increasingly anxious about her. The trouble was apparently some paralysis of, or stoppage in, the bowels. Our doctor told me this was a not-infrequent complication and there was nothing to worry about yet.

They then had Enid swallow the first of several tubes. This was connected to what seemed to me a Heath Robinson-like set of flasks, bottles and connecting tubes which apparently exerted a constant suction to drain waste products from her stomach. The next move was the first of several intravenous drips. Her condition began to deteriorate and our doctor, Bill Smart, made no secret of the fact that things were getting really serious. One week after she had first gone into hospital, I was with her. I had stayed in the maternity wing all night in a spare room and during the next several days only left the hospital to go home for a shower and shave and then straight back. On that particular Sunday the hospital seemed short staffed. Indeed at that time, it seemed to be perpetually short staffed – so much so that I had to help to get Enid on to a trolley and then a nurse and I set off pushing Enid down the long draughty corridors to the X-ray department in the main hospital.

Enid was very ill and I was desperate with anxiety so that when we entered into the X-ray department and I saw no one whom I recognised I panicked and asked them to wait until Mr Craig, the obstetrician, arrived. I think my face probably showed that I doubted their competence. They gave me the impression they were no more concerned than if they were about to wash a car.

A youngish man in a rubber apron, whom I took for an assistant in the department, was on the verge of having a scene when he asked me to go out into the corridor. There he explained that he was a specialist radiologist by the name of Reginald Carr and that he was fully aware of what he was doing and what was needed. He told me that time was important, that Enid's condition could grow worse very rapidly and he made it plain that he was just as alive as I was to the cold and unpleasant situation she was in.

First Mr Craig and then Dr Smart arrived on the scene and explained to me that what they were attempting was to pass a tube down her throat, through the stomach and into the intestine. Apparently such a tube would clear the waste that was, I supposed, slowly poisoning her. I gathered the tube had, on its end, a small inflatable bag or bulb which would press against the side of the intestines and be moved along by their normal movement. They were using X-rays so they could see to manipulate the tube into the small opening from the stomach.

To give some idea how difficult this was, I can only say that Enid was there for something like two hours being pushed and pulled into all sorts of positions. She looked dreadful as they wheeled her out and back into the Duke of York's wing but this time not into the maternity ward but on to the top floor where the majority of the cases were men under the care of Mr Stewart, a well-known local surgeon.

Enid had hardly been settled in the bed when they wheeled in a portable X-ray machine for the first picture which was to record the progress – or lack of it – of the blasted tube. Each such X-ray was hard on Enid, as plates were slid under her and her condition was such that she suffered real pain each time she was moved. The tube was again connected to another suction device and I gathered that the question was now fairly simple – would the tube move fast enough to clear the blockage in her intestines – or would she die first?

There was no doubt about the seriousness of her condition. Everyone made that clear to me. I was practically living at the hospital, spending, I suppose, at least twenty hours out of every twenty-four there. Most nights I simply sat in a chair in her room. She could eat nothing and now had two more drips into her legs, one for some sort of glucose and the other a salt solution. I became adept at changing these bottles to help the nurses. Occasionally, if she was sleeping fitfully I managed a brief walk in the hospital gardens, thinking deeply – yes, and praying, too.

My father was in America at this time on his first ever visit there, having crossed on the *Queen Mary*. At first no one had told him of Enid's condition but when it became desperate, my mother let him know. To his enormous credit – he was terrified of heights – he flew back immediately, via the Azores in those days. I know Enid was very glad to see him.

She didn't talk much at this stage. I tried to talk to her to encourage her to hang on and fight. Only one thing she said sticks in my memory. It was very late one night. She was pretty bad. We were both frightened. She said, 'I don't want to die,' and cried a little. It was a bad moment.

The doctors were looking increasingly worried. I understand the snag was that the bag on the end of the tube was unfortunately perforated and it did not grip the sides of the intestines as it should. Consequently the progress towards clearing the stoppage was slow. It was a race against time and we were losing. They were taking X-rays twice a day with the portable machine to check the progress of the tube. I would speak to the radiographer and occasionally went with him into his dark room, which was only down the corridor to see him develop the plates. It was in that room that I realised that Enid was carrying twins. The outlines of their back bones and ribs made that perfectly clear. The doctors had not told me this. Having one baby was enough with all her troubles and presumably they wished to avoid adding to my anxiety.

The situation reached a critical point. The family was all in the hospital. Enid's auntie and uncle had come over from Warrington to join my father, mother and brother and I well remember their anxious faces when I told them how bad things were.

I was with Enid when the radiographer and his assistant trundled in the portable X-ray machine for the last time. Enid must have been within hours of dying. I know nothing about these things, but her colour was dreadful, she could hardly speak and was just moaning as they moved her to get the X-ray plate under her. Her stomach was dreadfully distended. Immediately after that X-ray, they prepared her for the theatre. Mr Stewart, who was to operate, came to see her but said very little. And then it was time to wheel her into the theatre.

Again the hospital seemed short staffed since I actually pushed her trolley into the theatre ante-room myself with a nurse attending to all her tubes.

I don't know how long the operation – which was quite obviously kill or cure – took. I simply stood in the corridor, outside the theatre looking at the doors, wondering how I would react if someone came out to say, 'I'm sorry Mr Greenwood –'

Fate seemed so much against us. Whilst taking Enid back to her room, the young nurse knocked over the metal stand with the various bottles which dripped into Enid's legs. I managed to catch it just before it hit her in the face. Then, back in her room, an equally inexperienced young nurse knocked the screen over and almost hit Enid with it.

I stayed with her throughout the night and as the hours passed, I grew more hopeful. When she first came from the theatre she had looked pretty dreadful.

I sat watching the bed from a hard and uncomfortable armchair throughout the night. I was so tired, that when Enid cried out, I could not get out of the chair. But then, as I sat and watched her closely she began to come round from the anaesthetic and it was soon clear to me that the operation to clear the stoppage had been successful. Her colour was better and she seemed to feel better. With each succeeding day the improvement continued until she was well enough to be discharged from hospital.

She obviously needed a careful convalescence during that autumn before going back into the maternity department of the Duke of York to have the twins. It would have been impossible for us to cope at home, so she convalesced at Briaden and when the time for her confinement drew closer we were again a happy couple. It had been a very close call indeed but now it seemed we could look forward to the birth of two babies and have the three children which had always been our wish.

Fate had two more vicious tricks to play upon us.

In late December Enid was back in the maternity department and on 20th of that month she gave birth to two bonny babies, a boy who we decided to call John, and a girl to be called Gillian. We were delighted.

And then the first blow fell. Little baby Gillian died. Not, as I understood it, for any reason to do with Enid's illness or all the X-rays etc. which had happened – but just one of those post-natal problems that can affect a newly born baby's breathing. On 23 December I looked for the last time at the body which would have been my second daughter and then I stepped out into the corridor to return to Enid's room.

Mr Craig, the obstetrician, was in the corridor and he stopped me. He had apparently decided, that if we had to have two hard blows, it would be better if we had them at the same time. The blow he then delivered was to tell me that Johnny, the surviving twin, was destined to be spastic. Neither Enid nor I knew what the term meant, but we soon learned all the circumstances. Our blood groups were different. I am apparently rhesus positive and Enid rhesus negative. In such circumstances, the first child of the union is all right but with subsequent children severe jaundice and brain damage will apparently inevitably follow unless there is a prompt exchange blood transfusion. It was now too late for Johnny to have such a transfusion. The damage was done. All the problems of Enid's illness had meant no one had taken the, I understand routine, precaution of checking our blood before the confinement.

It was very hard to take. A twist of the knife in the wound came when our two and a half year old little girl, Patricia, came to see Mummy and her babies in the hospital and wanted to know where the other one was.

In due course we took Johnny home and at first he seemed a normal bonny little blue-eyed, fair-haired infant. But his spastic condition became increasingly evident and we suffered more than two years of the pain that only parents of grossly handicapped children can appreciate.

Johnny was hospitalised several times during his short life and there were many days and nights when we suffered with him at Littlecroft. It was heart-breaking to see he was suffering severe pain as his back arched and his limbs writhed. I must confess that there was a time when I thought – very seriously – how easy and sensible it would be to take his pillow and hold it firmly over his face.

He died in our arms in February 1956.

Enid and I made a sad couple. She was only twenty-five but had had three children and seen two of them die. It took us quite a while to get over the trauma that we had experienced over almost three years.

The middle and latter part of the 1950s were otherwise good times. The business continued its growth and began to move into the big time. The branch list was expanding all the time and by the end of the decade it totalled 170 units of which more than 100 were owned, thus making a very substantial property portfolio. The increasing number of shops generated an ever-increasing turnover and by the end of the fifties, sales totalled £2.3m which, in today's terms would be somewhere between £35 and £40m.

The business continued to be profitable with net profits comfortably exceeding £200,000, the equivalent today of more than £3m. Naturally some of the benefits from these steadily improving figures reached the family. By the mid-1950s both Enid and I were running Jaguar cars. Mine was one of which I was very proud – a two-seater Jaguar XK140. For its time it was one of the fastest cars in the world. Enid had a 2.4 litre saloon in the same shade of pale green.

Nineteen fifty-seven saw the completion of the new head office and warehouse at Guiseley which at last gave the business a purpose-built headquarters. The building was rather like a human body. The office block fronting on to Leeds Road, Guiseley was like the head. To the left of the double entrance doors was a single-storey wing with offices for my father and brother and their secretaries, and their helpers on the buying and merchandising side. To the right of the entrance hall was a two-storey building with the ground floor devoted to the general office, company secretary, etc. and on the first floor was my office and the sales department together with a handsome board room.

The neck of the building linked this office block to the warehouse space and included staff entrance, canteen, directors' dining-room, toilet facilities, etc. and then the body of the new headquarters was the single-storey building with a barrel-vaulted, stressed concrete roof covering thousands of square feet of storage space for fixture after fixture and rack after rack of menswear. At the rear there was a loading bay which could accommodate more than a dozen vans at any one time.

It was in the autumn of 1955 that we had the opportunity to take a big step towards big time business. We learned that Bunney's departmental store on the corner of Church Street and Whitechapel in Liverpool could be bought. Bunney's Corner had been a household name in Liverpool for over eighty years. It was a large five-storey building at the junction of these two busy streets. Indeed it was one of the best sites in the city. The Victorian elevation included two large towers and a ten-foot high statue of a goddess standing in state between them, looking out towards Liverpool's famous Pier Head. Not only did Bunney's own this prestigious, but now very old-fashioned, Liverpool store, but also it had a smaller branch store in an excellent position in Llandudno.

We were able to negotiate the acquisition of Bunney's for what we thought was a very favourable price, not least because the vendors had given their local agent unusual instructions as regards the sale of the company. He had been told to obtain the best price he could, but he was not to let it be known generally that the two stores were on the market. The retiring directors were apparently afraid that if their staff knew of a possible sale, it might cause them problems which they were afraid to tackle. Obviously the agent's task of finding a purchaser without anyone knowing about it was a difficult one.

We had a very valuable input to the whole Bunney's deal from our accountant, Harry W. Clough. We had been his principal clients since he first started his own practice. He had a flair for pointing out advantageous solutions to sometimes complex problems and the happy situation at Liverpool owed much to him. Although it was Greenwoods Limited which bought the Bunney's shares, in due course the building lease from the local authority was allotted to Investments White Cross Ltd. which company had only three shareholders, my father, my brother and I. In due course Investments White Cross Ltd. was re-named Shop & Store Developments Ltd.

We therefore had a personal involvement in the later flotation of Shop & Store Developments Ltd. which resulted in the three of us — for the first time, it must be said — receiving a very substantial tax-free sum in those happy days when capital gains tax had not been introduced.

A lot of pre-planning went into the time that followed our agreement to buy Bunney's. The store was old-fashioned enough to close on Saturday afternoons so, at 1 p.m. on Saturday 31 March 1956 all Greenwood's directors and their wives, together with all the area managers (still known in those days as inspectors), together with several display staff, congregated at the store. Each director took stock in an appointed department with the directors' wives assisting in taking stock in the cosmetics department.

The team of branch inspectors and the window dressers emptied every window of the store and began at once to redress them sales-style. Our own ticket writer worked flat out producing hundreds of compelling hand-written showcards and sales tickets.

The windows and facias were plastered with posters advising that this was indeed a closing down sale and that it would begin on 5 April, that is to say with only four and a half days from start to finish on which to check the stock of twenty or more departments including jewellery, cosmetics, fancy goods, toys, crockery, gardening, brassware, stationery, silver plate, drapery, linens, hardware and carpets. Every price in the store was drastically reduced and every window and interior display was changed. The work went on all Saturday afternoon, all Sunday, Monday, Tuesday and Wednesday, from 8.30 a.m. until midnight on each day.

On the Thursday morning the customers began arriving just after 6 a.m. and by 10 o'clock a huge queue stretched away down Whitechapel and through several other streets as far as Williamson Square.

The reason this sale generated so much interest lay in the fact that it was quite obviously a genuine closing down sale and there were literally tens of thousands of bargains to be had. Since we had no intention of running the business as a departmental store, we cheerfully reduced all the branded merchandise. This was regardless of the fact that, in those days, a situation known as 'retail price maintenance' applied, whereby shops promised the suppliers of such famous branded goods as, shall we say, Chanel perfume or Parker pens, that they would sell those products at a fixed price. We were offering such items at less than half the fixed price and the same applied to everything from Dinky cars in the toy department to lawn mowers in the garden section. Scant wonder then that the good people of Liverpool turned out in their thousands.

Our plan had been to keep the doors closed until 10.30 a.m. for a last hour or two of preparation but the weight of the queue outside had already broken one of the store's windows. People in the queue were fainting and there was an ambulance cruising up and down it for the benefit of those shoppers not up to all the pushing and shoving. A senior policeman hammered on the door and insisted that we let the sale begin before the planned start time.

From then until the evening the store was packed. The mainly elderly but quite competent Bunney's staff were supplemented by all Greenwood's directors and executives and somehow we managed to take all the money that was being thrust at us.

There were snags with this. The store was so old-fashioned that, rather than one of the Lamson Paragon vacuum tube systems which were common in stores in those days, and which whizzed a container of money and the bill up into a cash office from whence it returned quickly down the tube with the change and a receipt, here at Bunney's the Victorian Lamson system was still in place. This consisted of overhead wires with little travelling carriages which would hold the container with the money and bill but which required a firm pull on a dangling chain, rather like an old-fashioned lavatory chain, to send it on its way.

As that first hectic day wore on the overhead wires began to sag. I well remember the frustration of trying to despatch a container along the wire up to the cash desk a long way from the toy department where I had chosen to work. The container would travel most of the way and then just when the cashier was leaning out of the cash desk to grasp it, the thing would run out of steam and gradually trundle back towards you. All round the store, Bunney's staff and Greenwood's executives were heaving mightily on the dangling chains to try and keep the cash containers moving.

The queue was still there at the end of the day's trading when all the doors were locked save for one exit through which we had to drive the reluctant shoppers still in the store back into the street.

The queue was there again the following morning and in fact continued for more than a week until we finally decided the store must close for a day in order to reorganise everything.

A similar situation, but on a smaller scale, followed a week later at Bunney's Llandudno branch.

Our intention was to demolish the Liverpool store and replace it with a handsome block of shop property. However, sorting out all the planning and details of that major move was certainly going to take time. Therefore, as the last remnants of the Bunney's stocks were being cleared, we filled the ground floor with menswear and the first floor with ladieswear, much of which came from Ernest Wilson & Son who were well known in the north for ladieswear and drapery. Indeed, Frank Wilson, their Chairman was a long-time friend of my father and very often Greenwood's and Wilson's branches in a north country town were in adjoining premises usually, I might add, owned by Greenwood's.

Demolition and rebuilding took some time and it was the autumn of 1959 before the scheme was complete. The building was fully let with the principal tenant being a substantial store with frontages to both Church Street and Whitechapel for Boots The Chemist. Greenwood's took the corner unit for what was to be by far the busiest and most valuable Greenwood's branch.

The Bunney's deal gave us the opportunity to create a separate property business. Investments White Cross Limited was renamed 'Shop & Store Developments Limited'. A number of Greenwood's shops and other units owned by Greenwood's, but leased to other firms, were all moved into Shop & Store and then, on 2 November 1959 it was floated as a public company with a capital of £1m (today's equivalent would be c. £16/20m), composed of 4m 5/- (25p) ordinary shares; 1.2m of those shares were offered to the general public at 6/9d. per share. The offer was well received and the share price moved up to around 10/- per share during the first few months of the company's life. They later settled back a little but remained at above the initial offer price throughout their comparatively short life.

Father took the chairmanship of the company and my brother and I were directors. R.S. Newiss, an expert in shop property and R.M. Priestley, the senior partner in Lee & Priestley the solicitors who did all our work, joined us as directors of Shop & Store.

I can truthfully say that I knew quite a lot about retail property even before the Bunney's deal. I would have to have been pretty thick not to have learned something when during the late forties and early fifties our two professional advisers were, as estate agent, Sam Chippindale and, as solicitor, Ralph Yablon. Sam Chippindale went on to become the founder of the Arndale Property Trust whose Arndale Centres are still a feature of the shopping in many towns and cities. As a matter of mild interest, let me explain that the name Arndale came from the first name of Sam's first partner, one Arnold Hagenbach, proprietor of a chain of confectioners and tea shops in the north and Dale came from the end of Sam's surname.

Actually, there were three partners when that enterprise began. Arnold Hagenbach, Sam Chippindale and my father. They did the first deal of what was to become the Arndale property empire in Carlton Street, Castleford, with the three of them acting as equal partners. After that first deal, which might have resulted in Arndale Centres being called Arngrendale Centres, Father decided that he was happier working with his own business rather than sharing with someone else and he backed out of the partnership.

Ralph Yablon was a leading Bradford solicitor who went on to become chairman of two significant PLCs – Caravans International and Town & Commercial Properties.

Working frequently with people of the calibre of Sam Chippindale and Ralph Yablon at an early age most certainly brightened my ideas as regards property matters.

R.S. Newiss, known to his close friends as Reg and in his later years to the wide world as Stewart Newiss, began his property career as Sam's junior assistant. In due course he started his own practice and we were his principal clients with Ernest Wilson & Co. probably being the second most important to him as he began to build up a significant reputation in the retail property world.

In Shop & Store's early days the seeking for properties and much of the work other than admin went on in Reg Newiss's office with Lee & Priestley doing all the legal work. Father and I were effectively part-timers in Shop & Store's early days and Denis, my brother, was not closely involved other than expressing his views at board meetings. Despite this part-time approach to what was potentially an immensely lucrative business, Shop & Store made progress, as we shall see later. In its first full year it produced a net profit which was the equivalent of about £1.5m today. Since that profit was less than half of what the parent company menswear chain was producing at that time, I think it is fair to say that the combined enterprise had reached a scale that could be reasonably described as Big Time, when the family business celebrated its centenary in 1960.

19. A recruit at HMS Royal Arthur i.e. Butlins, Skegness 1946

20. A leading radio mechanic 1947

22. Royal Navy Cross Country Championships 1948 Winners – R.N.A.S. G.B.G. number 32

21. Wren P.O. Sylvia Wisdom

23. Tom and Cynthia Whitfield, Enid and G.B.G. at Otley Show 1948

24. R.F. ('Bob') Anderton and 'Auntie Pem', who brought up Enid from birth, on their Golden Wedding 1965

25. Enid with her father Jim Bennett and bridesmaids – 31 August 1949

26. Groom and Groomsmen. L to R Dick Atkinson, Tom Whitfield, G.B.G.,
Denis Greenwood, Fred Ayers

27. L to R Cynthia and Tom Whitfield, Cousins Joan Greenwood and Susan Lister, Walter, Fred Ayers, Anne, Brian and Enid, Denis and Marjorie, Dick Atkinson and Barbara Broadhurst at Briaden post the Wedding ceremony 31 August 1949

28. Crown Street, Halifax a major West Riding branch

29. Another corner position with the blue pearl granite frontage – Freeman Street, Grimsby

30. A particularly successful corner unit in Altrincham

31. Hodges Aberystwyth branch shows clearly its similarity to Greenwoods units in the North

Chairman's Report

The year which ended on 31st October, 1964, has seen further steady progress by the Company. Gross income has increased to £250,804 and, with the consequent improvement in net profits, your Directors are pleased to recommend a further increase in dividend to 9%.

It is now five years since our flotation and you will be interested to note that, in view of the size of our issued capital and the fact that dividends have been paid for five years without interruption, the Company's shares now enjoy Trustee status.

In accordance with the recent recommendations of the Stock Exchange Council the brochure, of which this report and our accounts are part, contains full information on the Company's affairs. We are happy to implement these recommendations since your Directors are anxious that Shareholders are always kept fully informed. In fact, only small changes have been necessary in the information given to satisfy the new requirements.

MANAGEMENT. Our former Chairman, Mr. W. H. Greenwood, who remains a valued member of the Board, was also the Managing Director. He has now relinquished this office and you will be glad to know that Mr. R. S. Newiss, F.A.I., has accepted the position of Managing Director of the Company. Mr. Newiss has played a leading part in the Company's affairs and the additional responsibilities which he now takes on are in very capable hands.

FINANCE. The mortgage arrangement with the Friends' Provident and Century Insurance Offices arranged towards the end of 1963 is proceeding smoothly and the second instalment of this will shortly be received. Apart from this arrangement, we continue to enjoy excellent and much appreciated support from our Bankers. We have agreed special arrangements for the financing of our major project in Carlisle and thus we anticipate no financial problems in the foreseeable future.

PROFESSIONAL ADVISERS. I should like to place on record the Board's appreciation of the excellent support which the Company enjoys from its professional advisers. The advice and assistance that we have received is of the highest order and has contributed materially to the Company's progress.

VALUATION OF PROPERTIES. I feel I should draw Shareholders' attention to the fact that it is now our policy to revalue our portfolio on a triennial basis. The last revaluation was on 31st October, 1962, consequently, the many properties dealt with during the last two years remain in our books at their cost and we have not yet taken credit for their development and improvement, nor have we taken credit for the increasing value of those properties where substantial reversions are to be expected at the end of the present leases. Shareholders must bear in mind that, considering current share prices, which are at the time of writing below the net asset value and thus there is no good-will element whatsoever in the market's valuation of the Company but rather this represents a discounted valuation of bricks and mortar.

GUISELEY PROPERTIES LIMITED. The function of this wholly owned subsidiary company is dealing in property. During the year a number of shops have been bought and re-sold profitably and a worthwhile contribution to the Group's profit has resulted. Several similar transactions are in progress at the moment and we are anticipating that these activities will continue at an increasing tempo in the current financial year.

INVESTMENTS AND DEVELOPMENTS

Blackpool—Abingdon Street. It has now been decided to lease the whole site as existing and satisfactory terms have now been agreed.

Bradford—North Parade. Planning difficulties as regards this property, mentioned in the half-yearly statement, have proved to be insuperable and this project has been abandoned.

Bury. Here the opposite has proved to be the case and planning difficulties which we thought incapable of solution have now largely been resolved and we anticipate carrying out our scheme for a five shop development with a restaurant on the floors above during the coming year.

Carlisle. Our site acquisition programme here is proceeding very satisfactorily and only a few buildings are still to be acquired. Due to existing tenancies we do not anticipate commencing the redevelopment scheme for approximately two years but, in the meantime, the site is largely self-financing.

Cheadle. The building of three shops and a Public House on this site is proceeding satisfactorily and will be completed during the current year.

Harrogate. The reconstruction of this block is now almost complete, it is fully let and the project has proved to be a very satisfactory investment.

Kendal. If plans at present under consideration by the Local Authority are acceptable we anticipate commencing work on the first phase on this scheme in the next few months. Apart from our large site in this town we acquired recently a smaller property which, when rebuilt, will provide two units and an office block. We hope to commence building on this site very shortly.

Leeds. Our second site in Albion Street is the subject of a planning appeal which will be resolved in the near future. We are hopeful that it will be possible to demolish the existing buildings and complete the new block during the current financial year.

Preston. Plans for the rebuilding of these premises are agreed and work will commence early in the New Year.

Scarborough. We recently acquired a valuable site in this town and hope to commence building a Supermarket, together with three units and showrooms over, in the Spring.

Skipton. This site has been cleared but the redevelopment is held up pending a planning enquiry in the New Year.

Several individual shop units, including Brecon, Ilkley and Morecambe have been acquired and several larger projects are in hand with site acquisitions proceeding satisfactorily. Our joint scheme with the Hammerson Group of Companies for Wokingham is also proceeding satisfactorily. My colleagues and I are therefore satisfied that the Company's steady and unbroken growth will continue.

There is one further item of the Company's affairs on which I should like to comment in order to clear up the misapprehension which I believe exists in some Shareholders' minds. It is the relationship between this company and Greenwoods (Hosiers and Outfitters) Limited. At the time of the flotation more than 50% of our revenue was derived from Greenwoods. These circumstances are now completely changed. In the current year the proportion of our total income from that source will only be in the order of 25% and this percentage will decline steadily since most of our activities today have no connection with Greenwoods. However, Shareholders should not disregard the great value which the Board finds in this relationship with an active multiple retail concern. This provides us with extensive knowledge of local trading conditions, provides contact with other multiple concerns and is a most useful facility in such matters as temporary lettings.

As regards the future. It seems likely that the tempo of commercial development in the country as a whole will slow down but we have sufficient work on hand and we anticipate no major problems for a considerable time. Similarly, in view of the almost complete absence from our portfolio of domestic accommodation, impending legislation as regards the Rent Act is of no concern to us. Possible changes in the taxation of distributed profits will, of course, affect us but until the Government's intentions in this direction are fully known I cannot comment upon them.

With the projects in hand and under consideration together with the very substantial reversions to which we can look forward, I am confident of the Company's continued progress.

GEOFFREY BRIAN GREENWOOD.

32. *This Chairman's report which formed part of the 1964 accounts for Shop & Store Developments Ltd was the last for that company in its Plc form*

33. *Greenwoods Head Office and Warehouse at White Cross, Guisley, Leeds built 1957 and later twice extended. On the left are Shop and Store's first offices*

34. *Bunney's store on the corner of Church Street and Whitechapel, Liverpool, was re-built as this building, which housed Greenwood's busiest branch*

35. *Yorkshire v. Cheshire 10.3.1962. A close but disappointing result for me!*
Cheshire 8, Yorkshire 7

CHAPTER 11

Happy Days Are Here Again

THE LATE FIFTIES and early sixties were probably the happiest times of my life. I was very busy. Our business affairs were going ahead at full speed. I had a very active social and sporting life and was taking on an increasing number of responsibilities outside our own business.

However, all of those paled into insignificance in comparison with October 1956 when we adopted our son, David. He was only four months old but Enid and I knew from the moment we saw him that he was meant to be a part of our family. His presence made our family life complete and gave us massive and continuing happiness.

In that same year – 1956 – I did something good which I hope the recording angel will accept as a counter-balance for numerous bad deeds. It was the time of the Hungarian Revolution. I had always loathed Soviet Communism beginning, I suppose, with the Russian invasion of Finland when I was a thirteen-year-old boy. I certainly remember that, when there was a popular clamour to, 'open a second front,' in order to help the Red Army in its fight against the Nazi invaders, my view was to wait as long as we could and let the Nazis and the Reds destroy each other. When the Hungarians fought for their freedom in 1956, my sympathies were with them and when they were – as was sadly inevitable – crushed, my sympathy moved to the Hungarians who had managed to escape and some of whom had come to England as penniless refugees.

I decided to help at least one couple and so went to the refugee camp and chose a man and wife, who had nothing and who could not speak a word of English, to come to Yorkshire. I took a flat over one of our Bradford branches, partly furnished it, bullied all my friends and relatives into giving everything else that was needed to establish the couple in a fully equipped new home and then gave the husband a job in Greenwood's warehouse.

The good deed had a happy ending. After a few years working for us and mastering the English language, the couple emigrated to Australia. Oddly enough, history repeated itself in that, after the Americans withdrew from Vietnam two decades later, I was also able to do the same for a South Vietnamese couple. He had been a helicopter pilot with the South Vietnamese forces. He and his wife had managed to escape. Just as with the Hungarians, I was able to find them a comfortable house and a starting job from which they could re-launch their lives.

It was towards the end of the fifties that I became deeply involved in the affairs of my old school, Woodhouse Grove. In 1957, the Old Grovian Association appointed me as its Chairman, which office I took over from my former headmaster, C.W. Towlson. I recall that when, at the AGM, he offered me the chair I observed that having regard to our earlier relationship I did not know whether to sit on it or to bend over it!

Two years later – in November 1959 to be precise – I was invited to become a governor at the school and in 1964 was appointed Vice-Chairman.

Sport continued to be a large part of my life. Apart from sport in the Navy, my first involvement in club rugby was when I played for the AVRO Works XV. I never had anything to do with AVRO Ltd. who, in those distant days had a large aircraft factory adjoining what is now the Leeds/Bradford airport, but on one afternoon I was passing a field at Apperley Bridge where a rugby match was about to begin.

I asked one of the players who was trotting out on to the field if there was any objection to my coming to watch them, to which he replied, 'You can bloody well play, if you like – we're one short!' Having confirmed that he was serious I dashed off home, got my kit and was able to join them early in the first half. Naturally, they put me on the wing with no intention of involving me unless it were absolutely necessary. Such a moment occurred and someone flung me a long pass. To their surprise, I tore up the field, beat my opposite number and scored a pretty good try. Consequently I was invited to play with them for the next few weeks which was quite an experience.

For the AVRO Works team an afternoon's rugby had to include two other elements: first of all, a serious punch-up on the field and, secondly, a prodigious amount of drinking after the final whistle. It was all good fun for a while, but I decided to take my rugby a little more seriously and joined the now-long defunct Headingley Old Boys Club. I played mostly on the wing where I could use my speed to good effect. Three memories remain clear in my mind.

The first was during a home game when I threw in the ball to a line-out on about the halfway mark on the left-hand side of the field (wing three-quarters took throw-ins in those days). We gained the ball and, as it was moved along our backline, I followed it, increasing my pace so that, much to his surprise, the right winger found me – the left winger – outside him. I duly aimed for the corner flag for what would be a most spectacular try and woke up staring at the roof of the changing room! One of the visitors had 'corner-flagged' so effectively that he took me, the corner flag and the ball well and truly out and some part of his anatomy, or perhaps it was the flag post, gave me such a crack on the head that I was apparently out completely for quite some time. Fortunately there was no lasting damage.

The second moment of glory, on a small scale, happened when we were playing Castleford on their ground. I fielded a kick ahead deep in our own twenty-five (it was a twenty-five yard line then, not twenty-two metres) and decided to counter-attack. I kicked a high punt up ahead, chased through the Castleford ranks, and caught my own kick. Now there was only the odd three-quarter and a full-back in front of me. For some reason I decided to repeat the performance and to my surprise as much as that of everyone else it came off beautifully. Up went the kick over their heads, round them I dashed, caught the ball on the full and covered the last thirty or forty yards in a flash for a try under the posts. That was a happy moment!

My third memory of club rugby days was not so happy. We were due to play Cleckheaton away. At that distant point in time, rather late in the chronology of these memoirs – the autumn of 1952 – I was captain of my club's first team (we were fielding three sides at that time) and had the freedom to pick my position in the backs.

Cleckheaton in the early fifties had a centre three-quarter who also filled that berth for Yorkshire and England – one Geoff Butterfield. Being the cocky young man that I was, I picked myself to play opposite him so that I might learn just how good a full-blown international was. The moment came when, with ball in hand, I tried to go through him – not a wise decision. I might have been quick, but I was light and slight. Butterfield's crash tackle, in which he was assisted by a loose forward hitting me almost simultaneously, did my right shoulder a great deal of no good.

Unlike my schoolboy injury, this was not something with which one could carry on playing. The shoulder was certainly dislocated and from the grinding of bone ends and some pretty severe pain I knew I was fairly badly broken. I was carted off to the casualty department at Bradford Royal Infirmary where a Pakistani doctor – believe it or not quite a rarity in those days in Bradford – said to me, 'Oh, dear me! What a very bad mess we have here.' He then proceeded to put my dislocated shoulder back in, and was then apparently so pleased with his handiwork that he gave my arm a fairly vigorous twirl and promptly dislocated it once more!

The upshot of all that was that my rugby career was over. The orthopaedic surgeon who saw me later warned me that further damage to my right shoulder might cripple me for life.

I did, in fact, play one further game of rugby, that being for the Old Boys versus Woodhouse Grove. To protect my damaged shoulder I bought a large quantity of cotton wool and stuffed it all up my jersey appearing on the field looking a bit like the Hunchback of Notre Dame. However, I did not dare to take similar risks again and my rugby playing career had come to an abrupt stop. Then, to my great surprise, I was invited to join the Yorkshire Rugby Union county committee representing Leeds which, for someone only in his mid-twenties, was a signal honour.

I duly attended committee meetings and found myself spending Saturday afternoons watching other people play and making notes on their performance. This was not a role I enjoyed. I shocked my Yorkshire Committee colleagues by resigning in order to play another sport.

What else could I play without undue risk to the suspect shoulder? The answer was clear to me.

Until the middle of the war Woodhouse Grove had played lacrosse in the spring term. Indeed it was one of the first schools in Britain to take up the game way back in the 1880s. Some Old Grovians were still playing lacrosse, mostly with the thriving men's lacrosse clubs in the South Manchester and Stockport areas. However, my brother was playing with the Leeds Men's Lacrosse Club, which was the only Yorkshire men's club not to have folded during the war, when not only were fixtures difficult, but equipment (mostly of American or Canadian origin) could not be obtained. I therefore joined Denis at Leeds Lacrosse Club, but very quickly decided that it would be a better bet if the club could be moved from Leeds to a field at Apperley Bridge close to Woodhouse Grove and thereafter be known as the Old Grovians Lacrosse Club. This duly happened. We recruited a few other Old Grovians, agreed that our membership was open to lacrosse players who had not been educated at the school, and we were away.

The Old Grovians went on to enjoy many years playing in the North of England Lacrosse League which initially comprised three divisions, later expanded to five, and the club later earned the reputation of being the most social club in the north. We made our headquarters the Stansfield Arms, then and now a popular hostelry.

For season 1953/54 the Old Grovians Lacrosse Club entered the North of England League in the third of the then four divisions. We promptly won promotion to the second division and then for the next few years the club fluctuated between the first and second division, twice earning promotion to top league level – but on each occasion soon suffering relegation back to the second.

Some readers may have little or no knowledge of this minority sport, but men's lacrosse most certainly should not be underestimated. Rules have changed in recent years, but back in the fifties and sixties the game was played twelve a side on a field without boundaries – a throw-back to the game's historical origins amongst North American Indians who, centuries ago, played a version of the game on wide open spaces.

In the UK lacrosse is more frequently thought of as a girls' game, since it is certainly a major sport at many girls' schools, particularly the posher ones. In ladies' lacrosse there is less fierce checking – i.e. hitting your opponent's stick with yours – and no body checking – i.e. a defence man bouncing an opponent off his chest. Ladies passing the ball normally do so fairly gently, with the ball describing a smooth parabola. In the men's game, passes are hard, fast and flat with the solid rubber ball at a high enough speed to do you serious damage if you are unlucky enough to be hit by one. The six-foot square goals, around a hundred yards apart, are defended by well-padded goal-keepers. It is the task of five defence men to subdue five attackers by dispossessing them of the ball either with a stick check – theoretically always to be aimed at the attacker's stick – but in practice frequently connecting with hands, arms and other parts of the body or the aforementioned body check. The twelfth player on each side is the centre who is – as you might expect – both defender and attacker.

The men's game is now played very widely in places as far apart as Canada and Australia, sundry European countries, and is a major college sport in the USA. In the UK, most leading universities now have men's lacrosse teams and the North of England League continues to flourish with numerous clubs mostly in the Greater Manchester area. There is a southern league with rather fewer clubs than in the north and most of the clubs, north and south, run several sides, including juniors.

My part in all this was threefold. First, I was appointed secretary of the Old Grovians Club and, later, when we resurrected the Yorkshire County Association, I had that responsibility also. Lastly, as a player the wing was obviously the natural place for me and I think that for the first few seasons I was probably the fastest man in the North of England League. The passing years inevitably took their toll over a playing career which spanned some twenty years.

From the outset we opened the membership of our club to players who had not been pupils at The Grove – of whom the best remembered was Tom Horsfall. Tom played first home which meant that he was the attacker nearest the opponents' goal. Each goal was surrounded by a marked circle which was the goalkeeper's territory and was known as 'the crease'. Tom's technique was to hover on the edge of the crease and depend on his prodigious handling skills to convert accurate passes into spectacular goals. He was a big, heavy man and five or ten yards was about as far as he was prepared to run, but what he lacked in mobility was more than made up for by the way he could handle a 'crosse stick. For twenty years he and I worked in close partnership. Our club's attacking game was based on Tom's ability to convert passes and whilst all our team tried to lay on the right sort of pass for him, I can immodestly say that no one gave him more than me. In the twenty years we played together, I see that between us we scored some thirteen hundred goals of which over a thousand were by Tom.

A typical Horsfall goal would happen like this. My brother, playing in the centre, would win the ball and send a pass up field. The receiver would send the ball out to me on the right wing. My task was to get close enough to Tom to give him the pass he wanted. From many years of playing together I would know from his position, and sometimes a hand signal, whether he wanted the ball on his left side or his right, at his ankle, at waist height or higher. I would shake off the attentions of the defender marking me and then belt in a flat, hard pass – let's say, low down to his right hand side – perhaps six feet wide of his feet. Tom would have been standing with his back to the opponents' goal, with his defence man right alongside him or behind him, ready to check him hard.

With exquisite timing, he would bump off his man, move one pace to the right, stretch out his stick and take the pass. As quick as light he would turn his stick over and shoot backwards into the top corner of the goal.

Tom Horsfall was not the only significant figure in the Old Grovians XII. Over the years we had numerous other very good players, but none of them earned the fear and respect of our opponents as much as Tony Facer. Tony was very much what would nowadays be called a 'a hard man' – he was credited with a succinct description of men's lacrosse as he felt it should be played. On one occasion an opponent, who Tony had just whacked with a particularly vicious stick check, turned and remonstrated with him. To this Tony replied in a long-remembered phrase, 'Shut up and get stuck in, lad, it's not a tart's game'.

Tony spent a fair part of most matches watching from the side, having been sent off and ultimately he suffered the dubious distinction of being the only 'crosse player in the north of England to be banned permanently from the game. However, before that time, his fearsome reputation frequently gave me the opportunity for some mild amusement. When a visiting team arrived at Apperley Bridge and descended from their coach, I was often the first to welcome them in my capacity as Club Secretary and also for a season or two when I captained our side. The visitors would look at our players and would often say to me, 'Which is Tony Facer?'

Keeping my face straight, I would usually point to Fred Ayers or Tom Whitfield, both of whom were sound and capable defence men but neither of them was anything other than a good and courteous player. I suppose this white lie was quite a valuable ploy since it effectively gave Tony licence to kill whilst surrounding Fred or Tom with an aura of danger which curbed their opposite number's aggression.

Throughout the later fifties and the whole of the sixties 'crosse played an ever-increasing part in my life. We resurrected the old Yorkshire County Lacrosse Association and I served as YCLA Secretary for many years. At first we had only three teams to choose from if we wished to raise a county side. Apart from the Old Grovians, Leeds University had taken up the game, followed a little later by Sheffield University. Three sides was too small a pool from which to draw a representative side, so I had the bright idea of inviting two other universities which had taken up the game – Nottingham and Birmingham – to become affiliated to the YCLA.

The Yorkshire XII, drawn mainly from the Old Grovians but with some Leeds University players, played the first post war county match against Cheshire in 1955. Not surprisingly we were well beaten and this continued to be the case until 1961 when, to our great joy and most people's surprise, Yorkshire beat Lancashire 9–5.

In the following year, I was chosen to captain the Yorkshire XII in a team consisting of seven Old Grovians, four from Leeds University and one player from Sheffield University. To my great disappointment we lost 8–7 to Cheshire.

It was in 1965 that the Yorkshire Ladies' Lacrosse side challenged us to play a match under their rules. This caused us much anxiety as it meant that we had to give up the heavy gauntlets which were essential to protect hands in the men's game. Similarly we had to give up the face masks and padded caps that represented protective headgear (nowadays US football-style helmets are worn by all male players).

Feeling rather naked without those items, I found myself playing centre for the first draw. (In the men's game the ball is on the ground and the two centres have their sticks against it and then draw for the ball and push and shove, as necessary, until one of them obtains possession. In the ladies' game the draw takes place with the two centres standing, the ball placed between the strings of their sticks and whoever pulls most powerfully has the ball flying out in her preferred direction.)

On that day in 1965, the ball came out my way and I was able to gather it. A couple of quotes from the *Yorkshire Post* for 5 April 1965 are interesting.

> Did I say the weaker sex? In the first few minutes a man was taken off the field spitting teeth! One of the women's sticks had caught him fairly and squarely in the mouth. (That was me!)

The newspaper report on the match ended with:

> Perhaps the best comment came from a small boy who, after seeing the injured man helped off the field clutching his mouth, asked innocently, 'What are they trying to do, Daddy, kill each other?'

I took no further part in that match but certainly decided I was never again going to play 'crosse against anyone, be it man woman or child, without the usual protective gear.

In 1960 I re-introduced the game to Woodhouse Grove School and for two or three seasons I suppose I was the school coach and instructor and the school continued to play 'crosse for a few years. But then, just as in the war years when the game was abandoned at WGS largely due to the absence of any fixtures other than those across the Pennines and the problem of having some member of staff able to coach the boys, the school dropped lacrosse and reverted to playing rugby in the spring term.

I continued playing for the Old Grovians' side until well into my forties. Most of the club's members who had actually been pupils at WGS had retired one by one and the club was first re-named Leeds/Grovians and moved to a ground on the Leeds Ring Road, and then later its core members re-established themselves in Sheffield where the game continues to flourish.

We had immense enjoyment from the game – and the proceedings afterwards – for some twenty years. Apart from playing regularly in the North of England League we had one or two tours including a visit to Oxford where we duly defeated the university side on the weekend that J.F. Kennedy was assassinated.

We had a southern tour where we convincingly beat two representative county sides.

A team composed mainly of thirty-odd year old respectable (?) married men could not be expected to enjoy a cup of tea after the match and then promptly return home. The Old Grovians' reputation for sociability meant that post-match celebrations after away games were long and varied. These were the days before the trans-Pennine motorway – the M62 – had opened. Nevertheless, it required a fair degree of naiveté for wives of team members to accept that the journey home from south Manchester or Stockport meant a return to the Leeds and Bradford areas after midnight. Certainly, at least one club member's wife remained convinced, until long after we had all given up the game, that it was indeed a good six-hour journey and that for her husband to get home at one or two o'clock in the morning, was not unreasonable. My Lancashire-born wife was not so easily deceived. I remember getting home at such an hour after visiting some of the Manchester nightspots – Manchester was the first provincial city as far as I know to have a significant nightlife – and finding my pyjamas lying on the wet path outside our front door. There was no breathalyser in those days and I confess that, like all my fellow players, I had in the course of the post-match drinking and visit to a nightclub which I had discovered, drunk rather too much. So much so that I was only mildly surprised to find my pyjamas in that strange place and was content to stagger into the house, undressing as I went, before putting my pyjamas on, wet though they were, and collapsing into bed – only to be woken with a severe shock since my pillow contained an encyclopaedia on which I had thumped my head. Enid turned on the lights and, not unreasonably, enquired, 'Where the hell have you been?'

Just one more story from the lacrosse era and then we'll move on. We had arranged a friendly fixture with Nottingham University and in anticipation of a happy evening thereafter, we had chartered a bus rather than travelling in our own cars as we usually did. We were well aware that Nottingham was then – and I wonder if it still is? – famous as the city with the prettiest girls in England. That being the case it was agreed that, after the match, we would go into the city centre and await the opening of the Mecca Ballroom. Some went off to nearby pubs, but I set off accompanied by two friends for the main shopping street and managed to get into Marks & Spencers just before they closed for the evening. A wicked plan was in my mind.

I marched into the ladies' lingerie section and with the help of a rather surprised shop assistant, purchased what could be described with alliteration as, 'A pretty pair of pale pink panties.'

'What are you up to now, Greenwood?' asked my friends as we returned to the bus. 'Watch,' said I and dropped the panties on to the gravel, ground a little bit of dirt and dust into them with my heel, picked them up and tore them slightly. I then reached into the luggage compartment of the coach, found Tom Horsfall's kitbag and thrust the panties deep therein.

My anticipation was that, come Monday, when Tom's wife would be doing a weekly wash which would include her husband's lacrosse kit, there would be dramatic scenes in the Horsfall household. I was not disappointed. It took Tom a long time to convince his wife, Pat, that he was guilty of nothing more than being on the receiving end of a practical joke.

In the early sixties I tried my hand at another sport. My brother, Denis, and his wife, Marjorie, had taken up skiing and had settled on Grindelwald in Switzerland as an ideal location. They suggested that Enid and I should join them and we duly did. We found ourselves on the nursery slopes in the usual Swiss ski school under the direction of a German instructor who I suspect had received some early instruction himself from either the Gestapo or the SS. He was certainly a hard man who drove his class hard. Indeed, the only enjoyment to be had from his instruction came when he shouted at me and others, 'No, no, no – you must stand on your balls!' I suppose I hardly need to confirm that he had in mind the balls of our feet.

I found that I progressed quite rapidly with elementary skiing – so much so that while Enid was prepared to go back to the village on the tramway,

I suggested to a young American lady that we should try to ski down. We were going quite well for most of the way, but then she took an almighty tumble into a snowdrift from which she emerged exclaiming, 'Oh, hell! I've popped my goddam contact lens!' She had indeed lost one of her contact lenses but, extraordinary though it may sound, we found it in a search which theoretically would have made looking for a needle in a haystack child's play.

I enjoyed my first skiing holiday sufficiently to repeat it the following year. Enid had another brief struggle in class 1, but finally wrote off skiing as a sport in favour of après-ski activities. The last straw for her came when, after a hard day on the nursery slopes with the German instructor and in a snow storm, she staggered – covered with snowflakes – into a bar in the village to be welcomed with the unkind remark (not from me!), 'Here comes Eskimo Nell!'

For my part I found myself promoted to class 2 with an instructor known, if I remember correctly, as Beezy Hans. We were about twenty strong on the first day of our class 2 instruction, but after a couple of days Beezy promoted us to class 3 and took us down ever more difficult routes. Falls were frequent and members of the class began to fall out from same speedily. I managed another day or two, by which time I think Beezy had promoted us to class 5. At that point I decided this artificial rate of progress was becoming dangerous and I, too, left the class. I saw what was left of it – Beezy and three others – heading for black routes (normally only tackled by really experienced and competent skiers) a few days later. Whether or not he managed to kill any of his remaining pupils, I don't know but it looked to me as if he was trying hard enough.

Having abandoned winter sports, most of our holidays throughout the fifties and sixties concentrated on cruises during the summer months. In those years, cruising had still to find its present massive popularity. Cruise ships were fewer in number and much smaller in size. Perhaps most enjoyable was the RMS *Andes*, which I believe had started life making scheduled trips to South America before being converted first into a two-class cruise liner and finally into an extremely comfortable first-class only ship.

We cruised on the *Andes* and other ships to all the usual destinations – around the Mediterranean, the Canary Isles, West Indies and the northern capitals. In those happy and prosperous days the costs involved were of little or no consequence and we always had the best state rooms or suites that were available. For example, I remember that the *Canberra* in its early days only had four suites despite its size, so I promptly booked two of them for our trip. Our children, Patricia and David, frequently joined us.

I had, in fact, begun my cruising career as a nine- or ten-year-old boy on pre-war cruises on the ill-fated *Lancastria* which was sunk with a heavy loss of life during the war. With all these sea-going trips in the fifties and sixties, and with what later became regular voyages to and from South Africa on the Union Castle liners, I calculated later that, by the time I was in my mid-fifties, I had spent more than a year of my life at sea.

Holidays never lasted longer than three weeks until the late sixties when I began trips to South Africa. There was too much to do back home. The business continued to thrive with the ever-lengthening chain of Greenwood's shops turning over in, say, 1955 the equivalent of £30-odd million today with profits to match.

Retailing was so different fifty years ago. Shops were normally open for only five and a half days a week. Sunday trading was unheard of. An early closing day in the middle of the week, when the whole town centre closed down at one o'clock was normal. The overwhelming majority of shop staff were full-time workers. Large scale part-time work, flexi-time, etc. was still a long way in the future.

Work was hard in the menswear trade, but the rewards were there since most retail businesses paid their staff with different kinds of incentives. Commission on sales made up a large part of the Greenwood's manager's pay, and bonuses could be earned for a variety of sales incentive schemes.

Very common in the retail trade in those days were what were known as, 'spiffs'. Different companies had slightly different arrangements but the idea was quite simply that, if you sold one particular garment there was a reward for so doing. If you sold another type of garment, either the reward was less or there was no reward at all. At Greenwood's we accomplished this by having small stamps – spiff tickets – which were applied to the lines that we were particularly anxious to move. Different coloured stamps had different values with, of course, the higher value stamps going on the higher value merchandise and garments that were going to be difficult to sell.

If the buyers had bought some 'pups', the first step in trying to move them was to put them on the spiff list and hope the really able salesman would concentrate on them and get them sold. If that failed, the obvious step was for a garment to be included in the next sale. Greenwood's generally held two sales a year. The usual New Year sale dragged on as long as we dared from immediately after Christmas until well into February or even beyond, February being the worst month in the year for clothing retailers.

The other sale came towards the end of the summer season with a fluctuating start date. If we were enjoying an excellent summer we were in no hurry to start cutting prices on summer merchandise but if the weather had been poor and stocks of summer lines – lightweight clothing, half sleeve sports shirts, etc. – were too high then an early start with drastic reductions was needed.

Apart from the motivation provided by cash incentives, ambitious staff were very well aware that our policy was always for internal promotion if possible. Thus every shop assistant knew that he or she could hope to earn a manager or manageress's position. Similarly, those who were managing branches knew full well that the team of area managers was composed entirely of former branch managers who had been particularly successful in that role – and that, at director level, first Ronnie Bennett, and later George Eley, had followed the path from behind the counter to the boardroom table.

The early sixties found the business in very good shape and the founding family happily enjoying the proceeds of the firm's success. The flotation of Shop & Store Developments Ltd. in November 1959 had put me – for the first time – very much in funds. My share of the flotation proceeds was sufficient for me to buy a splendid new home – Hillcourt, Cliff Drive, Rawdon, near Leeds. It was a fine stone-built house with two acres of immaculate garden just half a mile away from our first married home and a similar distance from Woodhouse Grove School where I was, by then, already a very active Governor.

We bought Hillcourt in unusual circumstances. Enid had heard that the house might be for sale and in a move contrary to her usual quiet and reserved nature (that was then!), she contacted Mr Park Guild, the owner, and asked if it were true that he was contemplating selling the house. Her move was well-timed, for he had just decided so to do. One look inside the house was sufficient to convince us both that it was ideal for us and we very much wanted it.

Neither I nor Park Guild wanted a lengthy haggle over price. I suggested to him that he should choose a reliable and reputable estate agent to value the house and he would accept and I would pay whatever price the valuer put on it. Mr Guild liked the idea and immediately said, 'Agreed. I'd like us to use Kenneth Hanson.' Ken Hanson was, at that time, the senior partner of Dacre Son & Hartley – then and still one of the north of England's leading firms of estate agents, particularly as regards residential property.

I immediately said to the prospective vendor, 'I'm not so sure you'll want Ken Hanson. I think you should know that he and I have been friends for a long time. In fact we were at school together.'

'No problem,' came the reply. 'I know Ken Hanson to be as straight as a die and the fact that he's a friend of yours won't make a bit of difference.'

We therefore asked Ken Hanson to name a fair price for the property – the figure seems laughable today when the house would command a price of around £1.5m or perhaps even more. But Ken gave us a price of (I think it was), £24,000 and that was that. We shortly moved into that very fine property.

By this time our daughter Patricia was away at boarding school – the now defunct Lowther College for girls in North Wales. My morning trips taking son David to school at Rossefield, Heaton, Bradford, soon came to an end and he followed in my footsteps as a small boy at Brontë House, the junior department of Woodhouse Grove, which was only a few hundred yards down the hill of Apperley Lane below us.

I used another piece of my Shop & Store proceeds for a purchase which gave the rest of my life an added dimension. I bought a farm in glorious Wensleydale.

We had a friend, John Watson, who was the third son of a family of farmers and therefore with dubious future prospects. It seemed to me that he would be an ideal tenant if I could find a suitable farm, and from his point of view I would be an ideal landlord. I had dreamt up this scheme in, of all places, the first class lounge of the *Queen Mary* on our way back from an interesting visit to the USA in the autumn of 1961. John Watson had been delighted with the idea but it had taken us some time to find the right farm. My chief requirement was that it was located somewhere attractive and with the chance of a cottage as a weekend retreat for us. Naturally John's first requirement was that it could be a successful and productive farm.

We looked at two others. One was in a beautiful location, but in John's view there was little hope of it ever being a profitable farming operation. Another failed the tests because the accommodation was far too large for

John and his wife. I finally decided to stop merely hoping for something to turn up and I put an advertisement in the *Yorkshire Post* describing briefly what I was looking for. I received just one reply. However, that one reply was the right one.

The farm in question, Hutton Hill near Leyburn, was a mixed farm of some 200-plus acres and with it was a most attractive cottage, Rose Cottage, in the nearby Fingall village. The retiring owner and I agreed a mutually satisfactory deal and John began a happy and successful tenancy which lasted for some thirty-two years.

With the farm and the cottage I took up two serious interests which became a major part of my life – namely shooting and fishing. My days were now full. There was lots of work during the week, sometimes tennis parties on the first class court which I laid in Hillcourt's kitchen gardens, and now shooting on my own farm and adjoining farms in Wensleydale, and fishing on the Dales rivers, particularly the Nidd and the Ure.

I'll end this chapter with a fishing story – of which, be warned, there will be more later.

Another old school friend from Woodhouse Grove was Denis (Dick) Atkinson, a Harrogate dental surgeon. He had for years been a member of the Harrogate Fly Fishers' Club into which, in due course, he enrolled me. It was hearing him speak of the joys of fly fishing that prompted me to take up the sport, now that I had a base in Wensleydale.

I obtained a copy of Hardy's (the well-known fishing tackle suppliers) catalogue and from their Manchester branch ordered everything that a well-equipped fly fisher should have, including a fine split-cane rod and Hardy's patent wading staff/landing net. This was a clever device with a rubber hand grip at one end, a point and a hook at the other. Hinged from the top of the handle there was a landing net which could be flipped open and, with the use of the long staff this would enable one to reach several feet away and into the water to any hooked fish.

We had a few practice casts on the lawn and then away we went to the point on the River Ure where the River Cover joins it. In those happy days a ten shilling (50p) ticket from a local pub was all you needed for access to some splendid trout water.

Dick put me in the pool in what he deemed to be a likely spot and then went off a hundred yards or so upstream and we began fishing. I was in the middle of the river wearing my brand new thigh waders, casting rather clumsily with my shiny new rod and leaning when necessary on my wading staff/landing net. I was beginning to get the hang of it, casting with increasing confidence, when my concentration was disturbed.

Out of the corner of my eye I saw a movement on the opposite bank. I turned to look and there was a rabbit at the water's edge looking, I suppose, rather like the White Rabbit in *Alice in Wonderland*, i.e. anxious and worried. I looked at him and he looked at me and then, to my complete amazement, he jumped into the river and began swimming strongly towards me.

Until then I did not know that rabbits could swim but, indeed, they can manage a very impressive doggy-paddle. A few feet in front of me was a part-submerged boulder with the top few inches just above the surface of the water. The rabbit struck out bravely towards it, scrambled on top and then sat looking at me – wet and bedraggled but perhaps less anxious than earlier.

I realised that something – almost certainly a stoat – had been close to him when he reached the water's edge and his choice was stark, swim or be killed. I immediately wondered how I might assist him. The answer was obvious, my shiny new combination wading staff/landing net was flicked open in an instant and with one, I think I might say dextrous, sweep, I had him in the net.

I shouted to my instructor. Dick looked downstream and could see his angling pupil with a landing net, which clearly contained something large and lively, perhaps a really large brown trout? He splashed rapidly towards me anticipating, I suppose, giving me another lesson – this time in how to despatch the fish. His face was a picture when I thrust the net at him and enquired: 'What about that then?' I waded back to the near bank and tipped my furry friend out of the net. He made off smartly and we resumed fishing.

After that highly unusual start to my fly-fishing career I took the sport very seriously – so much so that it was not long before I had bought the fishing rights on a half mile stretch of the River Nidd, leased the rights to almost a mile of the best water on the River Ure and a little later, during my Whittington days (about which more later), I managed a series of purchases of the River Lune. Also as a family, we later became part proprietors of what I believe to be the best salmon river in Scotland – the Lower Oykel.

Therefore my friend introducing me to the sport caused me to spend an awful lot of money in the ensuing years, but I did have an awful lot of pleasure.

CHAPTER 12

The Good Life

FROM THE MID-1950s through to the early 1970s I led and very much enjoyed a good life. Continuing business successes – see later chapters – supported a wide variety of interests and activities. Living at Hillcourt and with the farm and cottage only an hour away in Wensleydale was a joy.

The nearest – and ultimately the most significant of my outside interests and activities – was an ever-increasing involvement with Woodhouse Grove School. I attended my first Governors' meeting there in October 1959. Five years later the then Chairman of Governors – the very forceful Sir George Martin – informed the board that, having reached the age of eighty, he needed a young Vice-Chairman and as far as he was concerned, Greenwood was the man for the job. Such was the power of Sir George's personality that no other suggestions were forthcoming and I became his Vice-Chairman working with him closely for the next five years. Then at the age of eighty-five dear old Sir George gave us another example of his interpretation of democratic procedures. He told the assembled board that the time had come for his retirement. Sotto voce murmurings of, 'About time!' were covered by rather insincere expressions of regret.

The fact was that Sir George was still an extremely able and effective administrator who continued the active chairmanship of a major business in Leeds well past his ninetieth birthday. However, he had decided that the time was right for a lessening of responsibilities.

He addressed the board. 'It's quite clear to me there's only one man for this position. I take it you're all agreed that Greenwood succeeds me as chairman?' With that phraseology and the force of Sir George's personality behind it, it would have been a very brave Governor indeed who might have had the temerity to suggest that perhaps there really should be some form of election. In the event I was immediately appointed by what the minutes described as a unanimous decision.

From 1950 until 1972 The Grove was under the headship of Dr Cyril Pritchard who – oddly enough – had been the youthful master in charge of Brontë House, the junior department of the school all those years previously when I had been the smallest boy therein. Thus Dr Pritchard was in the rare position of having a former pupil as his Chairman of Governors.

We got on well together and the school grew steadily in numbers, in the quality of its facilities and its standing in the local community. In those days it was primarily a boarding school. Indeed, it was not until 1976 that the number of day boys exceeded the number of boarders. For example, in 1965, of a total school population of 428, 264 were full-time boarders. In those days there was no such thing as part-time boarding or occasional boarding – you were either a boarder or a day boy and that was it. The question of co-education never arose in those days. It was not until 1985 that girls were first admitted to the sixth form and later throughout the school.

The big decision of the Governors in the late 1960s was that WGS would become an independent school. The Grove had flourished as a direct grant school which meant that in return for substantial cash grants, the school would take an agreed number of successful 11 + pupils from neighbouring local authorities. In practice this had come to mean pupils from both Bradford and Leeds and occasionally from the Lancashire Education Committee's area.

Part of the direct grant regulations was that the local authorities so served by the school would be entitled to representation on the governing body. Thus it was that, in my early years as Chairman, we had councillors from both Leeds and Bradford serving as Governors and at one time the Lord Mayors of both cities sat on opposite sides of the board table wasting rather more of the meeting's time scoring municipal points than the comparatively inexperienced Chairman should have allowed.

It was not easy chairing a board which contained some members – Labour councillors – who were dedicated to the closure of schools like ours. Attitudes tended to mellow when they realised what a fine job the school did with children from a wide variety of parental backgrounds. I well remember one Labour councillor from Leeds standing with me on the lawn in front of the school at the end of a useful and effective Governors' meeting.

He looked around at the old and the new buildings, at the boys playing cricket on the fields in front of him and then said, 'Anybody who wants to close a place like this must be mad.' Then he hastily added, 'Please don't quote me!' He must therefore remain nameless.

I put a great deal of time into the school's affairs, but this was not difficult for me since I lived so close to it. During this period the school population slowly increased from below 400 to just over 500 – which is only half of the present day school population.

Dr Pritchard's fine twenty-two year headship ended with his retirement in 1972. Naturally I was very much involved in the selection and appointment of his successor, David Miller.

It is sometimes said that governing bodies only ever have to take one decision that really matters and that is when they come to appoint a head. Whilst that is obviously not entirely true there is certainly a great deal of truth in it. If a competent governing body can secure the services of an able and hopefully long-serving head, then the result is likely to be a successful school.

David Miller's headship continued the practice of lengthy tenure of the headmaster's office which had begun with the thirty-one-year headship of Arthur Vinter up to the outbreak of the First World War. The custom continued with my old headmaster, Clifford Towlson, who was in charge of The Grove for twenty-eight years and after Cyril Pritchard's twenty-two-year term David Miller served for nineteen years.

Sport still played a big part in my life. In the winter months The Old Grovians Lacrosse Club and the Yorkshire County Lacrosse Association took a lot of time but gave a lot of pleasure, particularly of course, the post-match partying which I have already mentioned. There was one post-match incident, after I had been appointed a Governor at The Grove – in fact I think I was Vice-Chairman at the time. We were in the Stansfield Arms opposite Woodhouse Grove School. The visiting team had set off back to Manchester and the twelve of us were enjoying a quiet drink and a chat. Into this peaceful scene came five young men clearly much the worse for drink. Their singing and shouting was a real annoyance and so one of our team, Tom Whitfield, went over and remonstrated with them. He was polite, but they were not, and an ugly scene began to develop. I went at once to help Tom in his argument and it was clear that we were close to coming to blows. At that point the Swiss manager of the Stansfield, which was both a pub and restaurant, came into the bar, took in the scene at a glance, and immediately swept the five intruders out through the door. It was a skilful manoeuvre, but I realised that the manager was now out on the car park with the five of them and they were almost certainly going to attack him.

'Come on!' said I, 'we must go and help him,' and I rushed for the door secure, so I thought, in the knowledge that there were twelve of us and the rest of my team would sally forth to support the manager and me – not so! As I reached the outer door of the pub the manager burst back through it warding off blows from all five of the attackers. I joined in to help him and for a few ridiculous moments seven of us were jammed between the inner and outer doors of the pub trying hard to hit each other. In fact we were jammed so tightly together that it was physically impossible to land a meaningful blow and the potentially serious battle fizzled out and the five departed. The manager and I returned to the bar where my eleven friends (?) were sitting quietly sipping their drinks and reading their papers, thus proving conclusively that you cannot always depend on others to fight your battles for you. It was only after I had sat down and let my aggressive spirit subside that I began to wonder what the local papers might have made of it if there had indeed been a major brawl with the Vice-Chairman of Governors of WGS as a leading participant.

Besides lacrosse and tennis which I played regularly, albeit on a friendly basis, and fly fishing, I became seriously interested in shooting. My first gun was a 12-bore Webley & Scott, box-lock, a very sound workmanlike weapon which served me well. But my second gun was much more interesting.

I learned that there was to be an auction sale of fishing tackle and other sporting goods, including Hardy rods and reels which sounded very attractive. It seemed that they were likely to come up for sale in the early afternoon and, since I was very busy at that time, I asked Enid to go to the auction rooms and secure me a good seat during the lunchtime period and I would join her in time for the afternoon session. I got there to find her looking very excited and to be greeted by the surprising remark, 'I've bought you a gun.'

Enid had absolutely no knowledge of guns of any kind so to say I was surprised is putting it mildly. I was even more surprised when in answer to my question, 'What sort of a gun?' She told me, 'a Purdey'.

If you have not heard of Purdey shotguns let me tell you they are effectively the Rolls Royce of sporting weapons. If you want to buy a new one today you could expect to pay something over £60,000 for it and probably have to wait many months, perhaps even years, for it to be hand-made to your order.

'What have you paid for it?' I asked.

When Enid said, '£350,' my heart sank since, for at that kind of figure even in those far distant days (the late sixties) the only sort of Purdey you could expect would be an ancient hammer gun or one that was damaged or almost worn out.

My initial sorrow at what seemed a very rash and foolish decision changed to delight and appreciation when I examined the gun which was still there on the side table in the auction room, handsomely cased and, as far as I could see, in perfect condition. The following day I took the gun to Linsleys who were then well-known gun-makers and dealers in Leeds and asked them to examine it thoroughly in case there was some latent fault.

'We don't need to examine it,' said their manager, 'we know the gun. In fact we put it into the sale. Would you mind telling us what you paid for it?'

When I told them, there were gales of laughter. Apparently the auction firm had decided to improve the look of their advertising by stressing that their sale of sporting goods would include guns by Purdey and others as well as Hardy's fishing tackle etc. This gun was the star lot at the auction, but no one had told the auctioneer that and he had put it up for sale during the lunch period when there was only a handful of people in the room and only one – my wife – had bid for it. All of which is to say that I became the owner of a splendid top quality gun for a fraction of its real value.

A little later I went to Purdey's handsome showrooms in London and ordered a twin to be made. You have to be fitted for a hand-made gun just as carefully as for a Saville Row suit. The elderly expert who fitted me had fitted members of the Royal family as far back as King George V and he had even – surprisingly – fitted members of the Politbureau in Moscow. Since then I have been the proud possessor of a matched pair of Purdeys with which I have shot pheasants, partridges, duck and grouse all over the north of England and in parts of Scotland.

From quite early on in my shooting life I have kept accurate game books recording not only every bird I have shot but every cartridge fired. Shooting men – and ladies – may be interested to know that keeping such records is not difficult. I simply carried a card in my shooting jacket pocket and at the end of every drive, be it a pheasant shoot or a grouse moor, or wherever, I jotted down what I had shot and how many cartridges I had used. Then in the evening of a shooting day, it became a pleasant ritual to write up the game book to include these figures.

In fact, I only began keeping these very accurate records when I began to shoot regularly. In the early days, casual shooting on farms in Wensleydale only arose on two or three occasions each season and therefore my detailed figures cover the last thirty-five years, and not my early days in the shooting field.

I am gratified to see that, in thirty-five years I fired 41,640 cartridges, mostly through my pair of Purdeys. Those shots produced 15,877 head of game of which something over 80% would be pheasants, the remainder being split between grouse, wildfowl and partridge, with an occasional woodcock or snipe. Thus I managed to average a bird for every 2.6 bangs, which is probably quite a bit better than an average performance. On a normal pheasant shoot with average to good pheasants – that is in terms of height and general difficulty – throughout my forties, fifties and sixties I expected to have around forty-five pheasants gathered for every 100 shots fired. Driven grouse were, of course, more difficult and my average over many years was thirty to pick up per 100 shots.

We shall return to shooting a little later and cover the days when I ran my own pheasant shoot on the Whittington Estate near Kirkby Lonsdale and was shooting more than thirty days each season. To conclude these statistical details I note that my best-ever shooting season was 1989/90 when I shot 1,012 birds with 2,201 bangs and since the venues included, besides Whittington, such significant shoots as Rievaulx, Studley Royal, Barbon Manor, Longside, Ramsgill, Stockeld Park, Wemmergill, and the Langbar and Denton moors, I had by the peak of my shooting career reached a pretty high standard. There are of course many forms of shooting and long before I hit good form with a shotgun, I had tried my hand with a rifle.

Deerstalking had always appealed to me. The idea of pitting your skill together with your strength and endurance against a very wild animal in beautiful and remote surroundings seemed, from what I read, to be something I had to try. I visited Rigbys, who I understood to be amongst the best British rifle makers and soon found that they had indeed a distinguished clientele. Having handled various rifles in their showroom I said, 'This one seems fine, can you make me one just like it?'

The answer came, 'It certainly is a fine one – it belongs to the Prince of Wales – and yes, we can make you one exactly like it.'

In due course I took delivery of my Rigby .270 inch Winchester (that's the calibre) complete with a high quality telescopic sight. Stalking rifles are powerful weapons. This Rigby would punch a hole through the steel plate almost half an inch thick which I obtained, shaped in the outline of a deer, for practice shooting. Now I was ready for my first excursion.

In October 1972 my friend, Dick Atkinson, joined Enid and I on a trip to Scotland where we stayed in the Glengarry Hotel and where we were due to meet the stalker from the adjoining estate the following morning.

Dick and I awaited the arrival of Jock McGaskell with some trepidation. We knew professional stalkers were tough, hard men and we were afraid that too brisk a walk over ten or fifteen miles up and down the hills might be too much for us. We were relieved to see that McGaskell was quite a bit older than we were and with a build best described as short and tubby. He took us in his Landrover halfway up the glen and stopped the vehicle. He took from the back a cardboard box about eighteen inches high and a foot across which we assumed to be the target on which he would test us. He went to a rock about 100 yards away and put the box on top of it. Our anticipation that we would have no difficulty in putting a few shots in to a target that size quickly turned to alarm when from his pocket he produced an empty cigarette packet and fixed it with a drawing pin on to the middle of the box. Older readers will know this was a long time ago when I tell you that the cigarettes were Gold Flake and the packet was for ten.

Back he came to the vehicle and cheerfully said, 'Now gentlemen, will you just put a shot into the wee packet there.'

Leaning across the bonnet of the Landrover I struggled desperately to keep the cross-hairs of the telescopic sight steady on the little yellow packet and finally squeezed the trigger. McGaskell was looking at the target through his stalking telescope and said, 'Och, you just nicked the corner but it will do.' Dick managed similarly to satisfy him and we were away.

We met the pony man at the foot of the steeper hills and after a few words with Jock he led the pony – which was to carry the dead beast should all go according to plan – away around the shoulder of the hill to our right.

Jock McGaskell took the rifle and slung it across his back, checked that we had remembered to bring our 'piece' –i.e. a snack for lunch – and then staffs in our hands we set off up the hill.

Within five minutes we realised that short, tubby McGaskell had a level of fitness that was far beyond ours. It was only later that we learned that, during the war, he had served in a super-tough outfit known as the Lovat

Scouts to whom mere commandos and paratroopers were feeble sissies. He had Dick and I panting in his wake and wondering if we might have heart attacks before he let us take a breather. We finally reached the tops and from then on the going was easy, a wonderful walk with fairly good going punctuated by occasional stops to 'tak a spee', which is stalker-talk for spying for suitable deer.

It should be remembered there is no way that deerstalking consists of going up in the hills and shooting at the first stag you see. The object is to cull as humanely as possible – i.e. with a clean accurate shot – such beasts as may be near the end of their days or which were poor specimens as regards the horns on their heads.

We got lucky. We found a party of stags and, a little way from them was an old grey beast with what had clearly once been a handsome set of antlers, but he was now, as stalkers say, 'going back'. The set of antlers he had grown this year would not be of the quality of those when he was a year or two younger. Also, as a stag ages, it loses its teeth and chewing enough food becomes an increasing problem. This old chap was the perfect target.

The problem was – as always in deerstalking – how to get close enough to have an accurate shot. We were several hundred feet above him where he lay in the heather chewing the cud. There was very little cover on the hillside, but there was a stream running down a gully to a small plateau not so far away from the beast. We began a long, slow, flat crawl. The soles of McGaskell's boots were the main object in my vision for the next half hour or more. I followed him as we crossed an open area and then into the gully of the stream. With a complete disregard for the water we crawled slowly downhill, the tinkling of the water probably obscuring any small sounds we may have made dislodging the stones in the stream bed.

In due course, we emerged from the stream onto the small plateau which was rather like a large shelf above where the stag lay. Now was the time to prepare for the shot.

Very quietly the rifle was removed from its canvas carrying sleeve. Even more quietly a round was slid into the breech and the bolt closed. After gesturing to Dick and me to keep still and keep back, McGaskell crawled very carefully to the edge of the plateau and looked down. He gestured to me to crawl up on his right-hand side and, when I got to the edge and peered over, the old grey stag was clearly visible lying in the heather a hundred and odd yards away. McGaskell silently passed the rifle to me and

I slid it forwards slowly through a clump of heather. Through its telescope I could see the beast quite clearly. I gently released the safety catch.

McGaskell whispered into my ear, 'You dinna shoot till he gets up and only when I say so.' From my reading I knew the normal practice was to wait until a lying stag got to his feet and then wait until he was more or less broadside and try to kill him cleanly with a heart shot.

We waited – and waited. Flies crawled over us. My arms began to ache. Still the stag continued lying there chewing the cud peacefully. Minutes passed and silence reigned until it was broken by an extraordinary noise. Dick Atkinson, twenty yards behind us and having fallen fast asleep, was snoring. The sound had the beast's attention but did not alarm him particularly so he got up slowly. At first he stood with his backside towards us. Then he turned slightly to the left and was broadside on to us. I had already slid the crosshairs of the telescopic sight up his foreleg to the shoulder, then moved it back a few inches to where I knew his heart lay.

When McGaskell whispered urgently, 'Tak him!' I only had to squeeze the trigger.

Boom! Thwack! That is the sound of a successful end to the stalk of a stag. The boom of the rifle shot reverberates around the hills and the thwack is the bullet striking home. The expanding bullet knocked the stag over. His legs thrashed for a second and then were still.

'Well done!' said McGaskell and set off rapidly downhill.

I followed carefully behind having first ejected the spent cartridge and put another round up the spout and then put on the safety catch. My reading had told me that you must always be ready to give a stag a second shot since more than one apparently dead beast had got to its feet and bounded away over a ridge leaving the stalking team to follow, sometimes for hours since there is no worse stalking crime than failing to kill humanely a wounded beast.

The old grey stag was not wounded he was very dead.

McGaskell had his jacket off, his shirt sleeves rolled up and a sharp knife in his hand before I came up to him. Within a couple of minutes he had gralloched the stag by cutting a long slit along its belly and then reaching in and pulling out the whole of the stomach and intestines which, incidentally, look like so many pale grey sausages.

I asked him what happened to the gralloch and the answer came, 'That's for the ravens and the eagle'. From around his waist he uncoiled a length of rope with a broad canvas strap at one end. He hitched the rope around the stag's antlers which had no less than eleven points (a twelve-point stag is a sought-after trophy known as a 'Royal'). Better than twelve points on Scottish stags is very rare indeed. This animal had clearly, in his prime at least twelve points but he was now going back and no doubt, had he lived the next year's set of antlers would have been worse than those he was now carrying.

'Will ye tak a hind leg each?' McGaskell asked Dick and me whilst he put the strap of the towing rope round his chest, having already gathered up the rifle. Then he set off at a gallop down the hill dragging the stag behind him, bumping over the lumps and clumps whilst my friend and I did our best to keep it steady and on track. Way below us we could see the pony man who had heard the shot, and with an intimate knowledge of the terrain, was already on his way to meet us.

I was impressed with the procedure when it was time to hoist the dead stag on to the special saddle on the pony's back. Incidentally, 'pony' is something of a misnomer for these Scottish stag carriers. They are usually stocky, sturdy, sure-footed horses.

Scott, the pony man, took off his jacket and, to my surprise, put it over the pony's head wrapping the sleeves above its ears before we lifted the dead beast on to the saddle. I was about to ask why, when of course, it dawned on me. With his jacket over its head the pony was effectively blindfolded and all it could smell were the familiar scents of its master.

Once the stag was aboard, the jacket was removed and we set off at a very brisk walk down to the deer larder. There I was amazed to see the pony man give an example of sheer strength. He took hold of the dead beast in both hands and carried it as you or I might carry a small puppy and, with no help from the other three of us, walked twenty or thirty yards into the larder and strung it up.

We did not stay to see him begin the butchery process since McGaskell, as we learned later from the landlord of the hotel, had only one thought in his mind once his guests had got their stag. And that was to get into the hotel bar as quickly as possible and take all the drinks that the gratified client was happy to provide for him.

That was a good start to a deerstalking career that was to go on for many years and it was not until I was in my late seventies and had the pleasure of going stalking with both my son and my grandson that I retired from stalking in the Scottish hills. I may yet do a little more woodland and low ground stalking before my time is up but in any event the above account of my first day of this fascinating sport will hopefully have given you some idea of what it is all about.

I enjoyed an exciting first trip to the USA in November 1959. A wool merchant friend of mine – Fred Ayers, with whom I had been at school – had to go to Boston on business and he persuaded me to accompany him. We crossed from Liverpool in an interesting liner – the MV *Britannic*. I believe this ship was in fact the last still afloat of the old White Star Line, owners of the ill-fated *Titanic* and various other Atlantic liners whose names all ended in 'ic' – for example, the *Olympic*.

The voyage seemed to put the clock back many years since, from Liverpool we crossed the Irish Sea, anchored outside Cork in southern Ireland and tenders brought a hundred or two Irish emigrants, just as had been the case for the last hundred years. We then set sail for Boston in rough November weather which meant that it took eight days for the crossing.

Despite the rough seas, Fred and I enjoyed the voyage – not least because the handful of first-class passengers were probably outnumbered by the stewards who were there to serve us and consequently we had splendid food, fine wines and impeccable service throughout the voyage. It should be remembered that the late 1950s and early 1960s marked the beginning of the end of the scheduled transatlantic liner runs with such ships as the *Queen Mary* and *Queen Elizabeth* from the Cunard Line, and the *Normandie* from France plus sundry other fine ships. The reason for the end of transatlantic scheduled voyages lay, of course, in the rapid growth of flying. Once the jet engine had been perfected and planes such as the Boeing 707 came into service, there was going to be no future for a mode of travel which, however luxurious it might have been, still meant that the journey took at least four days longer than the flight.

We spent an interesting few days in Boston which became even more interesting after one particular evening. I was sitting opposite Fred at a table for two in the hotel dining-room when I pointed out to him that we were both getting somewhat bored with each other's company. I had noticed in the hotel lobby a sign advertising an 'Over Twenty-Fives' dance in the basement ballroom. We agreed it was time to enjoy some entertainment and duly attended the dance where we made quite a hit. English accents were quite rare at that time as were English manners and English ballroom dancing (shades of Woodhouse Grove School's dancing classes!). We made such a hit with two young ladies that they volunteered to take the following day off work and drive us around various Massachusetts tourist spots.

It must be said that our motives were of the purest. For my part I had not only promised Enid that I would behave myself, but I had sworn to myself that it would be so. Therefore, when I suggested to Marjie, the attractive fair-haired secretary with whom I had danced and who had been my guide on the tour, that she might join us for a weekend in New York, the aim was for nothing more than a happy and interesting weekend with lots of laughs. Not unnaturally, Marjie said she would like to think about it and would ring me at our New York hotel to which we were moving the following day. We checked into the old Commodore Hotel which was built immediately above Grand Central Station and which later became an office block.

I was delighted when the phone rang in my room and Marjie from Boston confirmed that she was willing to come down to New York for the weekend. When I booked a room for her, the not-too-helpful receptionist thought it appropriate to put Miss M. Hurley in a room twenty floors above mine. We had a memorable forty-eight hours in the 'Big Apple' seeing all the obvious sights during the day and staying up very late at night enjoying the night spots. Those were the happy days when you could drop into a late night bar on Forty-Second Street and find Benny Goodman appearing live or, if you pushed the boat out a bit further, and went to the Copacabana, Nat King Cole was the entertainer.

When we returned to our hotel very late after our second and – as regards Marjie – last night, she and I were saddened to think that I would be putting her on the train the following morning and would probably never see her again. I got out of the lift on my floor and she proceeded upwards a further twenty floors. I was just nicely settled into bed, pondering the wisdom of my decision to behave myself, when the telephone rang.

Marjie said, 'I've got an awful headache. Have you anything that might help?'

'Yes,' said I, 'I'll be up in a minute'.

I got out of bed, clad in my striped, winceyette, Greenwoods pyjamas, and an elderly woollen dressing gown. In my hand I had a bottle of aspirin. I pressed the button for the lift and when it stopped to collect me, I was mightily impressed to see its two passengers. She was a glamorous blonde, dripping with fur and diamonds. He was a particularly elegant-looking man – I especially remember the diamond shirt studs in his dress shirt. They looked at me with some wonder and he enquired, 'Where's the fire?'

I went to Marjie's room, delivered the aspirin, gave her a chaste kiss goodnight, returned to my room and have, I suppose, regretted my attack of righteousness ever since.

Perhaps rather oddly Enid began a correspondence with Marjie which has continued to the present day. She and her husband have stayed with us and we visited them in Vermont many years after our New York weekend.

I was sore tempted yet again in New York after Marjie had returned to Boston. Fred and I had another very late night on the town and we finally drifted into a dimly lit bar. Within seconds two young women had attached themselves to us and invited us to buy them a drink. We found ourselves plying them with New York State 'champagne' until I noticed that the one I'd thought of as mine was frequently emptying her glass on the floor. So I asked her how much of that rubbish we had to buy before she could have a drink she would enjoy. They were, of course, hostesses and their task was to boost the takings.

We reached the point where they could have a drink they were happy with and we were enjoying an interesting conversation when mine said, 'Excuse me fellas, it's time for my act'. To my significant amazement she walked across the bar on to a small stage and promptly began taking her clothes off. Both girls were, in fact, strippers with an act to perform two or three times each night. We stayed on, talking and dancing with the girls until the bar closed at some ludicrous time – probably about 4 a.m.

I asked mine if there was anywhere still open at that time where I could get a cup of tea. This, of course, greatly amused them, but they invited us to meet them at the stage door. We waited there but in the event the girl Fred had been with decided not to turn up so he pushed off back to our hotel whilst mine led me to the toughest-looking late night bar I've ever seen. Despite the time, it was packed, thick with cigarette smoke and a crowd of New Yorkers drinking hard and seemingly enjoying themselves.

When I was introduced as, 'This guy's from England and he reckons he just has to have a cup of tea,' the crowd were highly amused. All business stopped while the bar tender and his assistant, with some difficulty, found tea, a teapot and a cup and saucer and then with due ceremony served me a cup of tea, 'On the house.'

All was going well until the girl's minder, protector, or call-him-what-you-will arrived. I realised I was facing an anxious moment. He was dressed exactly as if for an old-time gangster film. Dark suit, black shirt, plain white tie and his hat remaining on his head throughout. He came to sit opposite the two of us in the side booth where I was enjoying my tea. As his jacket swung open I noticed with both interest and some alarm that he had a nasty-looking automatic pistol in a shoulder holster.

At first the conversation was stilted, but somehow we began to talk about cars and, when he learned that I was at that time the proud owner of a Jaguar XK140, a vehicle for which he had enormous enthusiasm and covetousness, he and I then got on famously. So much so that he raised no objection when I set off to see the girl home. She was as surprised as Marjie had been when I got out of the taxi for only a moment to shake her hand, thank her for a very interesting night and then depart.

I had a very interesting business appointment in New York which in fact produced a job offer. I had made arrangements to visit the headquarters of a firm called National Shirt Shops. I knew from the British trade press that this firm had somewhere between one and two hundred shops – or stores as they would say – from coast to coast and I thought I might learn something from them.

I found myself in their New York offices speaking to their CEO, a man named Ed Marks. He was fascinated to learn how few staff we had to administer over 150 shops and was very interested in some of my simple approaches to stock control, sales incentives etc. So much so that, with a dramatic gesture, he pressed all the switches on the intercom which sat on the end of his desk and called out to his various underlings, 'Bill, Sam, Joe, etc. etc. – come up to my office right now. There's a guy here you've got to meet.'

Consequently I found myself giving something of a talk to all his senior people. At the end of it he shooed them out of his office and turned to me and said quite seriously, 'I want you to come and work for us. Within reason you can name your own price.' Naturally I was somewhat flattered but of course, declined.

A little later I met the President of the National Shirt Company and he was a long-distance friend for a good number of years. His name was Sylvan Cole. Sylvan had started that company in San Francisco when he was a very young man and it was the San Francisco earthquake of 1906 that caused him to move the first branches of his company elsewhere and ultimately to establish his headquarters in New York. Sylvan ended his days in Palm Beach, Florida, and when – as I hope you will shortly read – I had some business interests in Florida I would make a point of visiting Sylvan even if it meant hiring a plane to get from one side of the state to the other.

Fred and I returned from New York in even greater style than on our crossing on the *Britannic*. We travelled first-class on the old *Queen Mary*. I was something of a party animal in those days and I am quite sure that the band and the staff in the liner's Verandah Grill were very glad to see the back of us since, with one or two like-minded passengers, we had very late night parties at the end of each day of the trip. So much so that Enid and Fred's wife, Margaret, were somewhat shocked at our rather haggard and sleep-deprived appearance when they met us off the ship in Southampton.

Back at work it was the mixture as before. Lots of travelling visiting the branches, frequently interviewing staff at the shops or in some provincial hotel. Big mileages to drive, a constant search for potential new shops. Negotiation with prospective vendors and so on.

I made a second trip to the US in 1961 and this time Enid went with me. We went out on the *Queen Mary*, again, a luxurious trip. First-class on the *Mary* was indeed first-class travel. Anyone who sailed in that ship and dined in the magnificent first-class dining-room will not easily forget it. That room was three decks high and a beautiful example of Art Deco design. An enormous wall map was mounted high up at one end of the room showing Europe and America and with two tracks leading from Southampton to New York and back. Along those tracks 'steamed' two little illuminated 'ships' representing the *Queen Mary* and its sister ship, the *Queen Elizabeth*. In the middle of each voyage, the two lights would converge as the great liners crossed each other in the middle of the Atlantic.

This trip was primarily for pleasure, but there was a business element in that I intended to go and meet the family who manufactured jeans for Greenwood's at that time. Their family-run business – Cowden Jeans – was based in Kentucky.

Enid and I were puzzled when Bill Cowden picked us up at our hotel, told us he had a surprise for us, and rather than taking us to one of their factories, he headed for the state capitol and the Governor's mansion. There, to my very great surprise, the Governor of Kentucky granted me the honour of being commissioned as a Kentucky Colonel. The reasons were two-fold. First the fact that Kentucky as a state had hardly any overseas exports other than perhaps racehorses. Therefore an export customer present in the state was quite a rarity. The second reason clearly lay in the fact that the Governor at that time was Bill Cowden's brother-in-law. Whatever the reason, since 1961 I have been entitled to call myself a Colonel and I assume that should the war between the states ever break out again I would be expected to don a grey uniform.

It is good to see different aspects of a country's life and it was interesting to visit both a Governor's mansion and then a little later in that trip a company-owned town, Steelton, Pennsylvania, where one of the American former customers of Enid's family's pub in Warrington then lived. I found it particularly interesting to have a few drinks in the Veterans of Foreign Wars Club where English was the second language to Polish. Another company-owned town nearby was the home of the Hershey chocolate makers.

While we were in New York during this trip we stayed in the Plaza Hotel which was most certainly then a very fine hostelry. I distinguished myself there by creating a serious scene and getting, I think, the best of the argument. Enid and I were sitting in the Palm Court and I had been trying unsuccessfully for several minutes to attract a waiter's attention. The head waiter noticed me signalling for help and deliberately chose to ignore me – not once, but twice. He was one of those tall, haughty figures you sometimes find in world famous restaurants or hotels who appear to think that they are doing their clients a favour by serving them. I suspect this man had a reputation for that kind of behaviour and of course in New York there is nothing a head waiter likes more than telling you his restaurant is full. This man was the epitome of the haughty head waiter and it was clear to me that his come-uppance was long overdue. To the considerable surprise of all the other clients I marched up to him, forced him to turn and speak to me and then proceeded to tell him he was a disgrace to his profession, a liability to what was otherwise an excellent hotel and a rude and ill-mannered boor to boot. As Enid and I swept out, I was delighted to hear a round of applause from all the clientele who clearly thought I had said what they had all often wanted to say.

We had an interesting return journey from that US trip in that we crossed on the liner *United States*. This ship had been designed with two objects in mind. It would be very fast and would win the then coveted

36. Whittington Hall south front seen from the park

37. Whittington Hall from the East. Estate cottages, stables and clock tower

38. Whittington Hall from the croquet lawn. The swimming pool was built at the end of the colonnade on the left

39. One of my third homes. Brook Cottage near Leyburn, the second of the two cottages we enjoyed, near Hutton Hill Farm

40. *The family in the drawing room at Whittington 8 August 1969. L to R: G.B.G., Mrs H Bussey, Diane, Stephen and Denise Rawson, Denis, Melissa, Marjorie, Walter, Enid, Patricia, David and Anne Greenwood*

41. Enid. Happy to hit 40! in 1970

42. Brian content to be a bit older

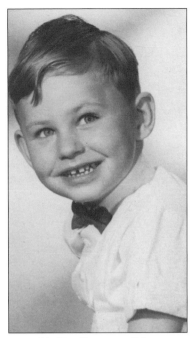

43. 'Tricia as a little girl

44. David as a small boy

45. Four generations. December 1966. L to R David, Walter, Willie and Brian Greenwood

46. G.B.G., David, 'Tricia and Enid in the garden at Hillcourt, Rawdon 1971

47. 'Tricia's 21st at Hillcourt in 1972

48. Lowes of Wigan at the time of our purchase of the store in 1962

49. Lowes after various alterations, including the extension to the right

50. Pentre in the Rhondda Valley. This branch had traded for over 100 years in the same location

51. Hodges fine, large Taunton branch, one of the best of the South Western shops

52. Frome, Somerset with window poster advising – 'Buy British at Hodges'

53. Chippenham branch

blue ribbon for the fastest Atlantic crossing – but it was also capable of quick transformation into a troop ship. The idea was that the *United States* could lift a whole army division and rush them across the Atlantic if the threat from the Soviet Union demanded it. With that purpose in mind the ship had been designed to be fireproof. No timber was used in its construction. Everything was steel and plastic. Indeed, the crew would quiz the passengers to see if they could guess where there was any wood to be found on the liner. One answer was, 'The only wood is in the grand piano in the first class lounge'.

The *United States* was indeed very fast. Sitting in a deck chair on the stern watching the wake bubbling away in an arrow-straight line felt rather like sitting in a speed boat. However, whilst comfortable and efficient, the *United States* was never in the same class as the *Queen Mary*.

I had an interesting excursion into liberal politics during the early 1960s. Whilst I have always voted Conservative in Parliamentary elections – on the basis that the Conservative Party is generally more sensible, less prejudiced and less corrupt than Labour – I have always tried to have a liberal (small 'l') outlook. With Harold Macmillan telling us we had 'never had it so good', I felt I could afford an interest in the Liberal Party's affairs. I therefore joined the local Liberal Party and, after only one meeting found myself, first, on its committee, and then invited to act as its chairman. Our local authority needed a shake up and, after considerable efforts which I took pride in leading – lo and behold! – the Liberals succeeded in capturing Aireborough which was my then local authority.

I might well have stayed with and in the Liberal Party were it not for the position which they took on immigration. Forty-odd years ago there were a few places where immigration looked as if it might one day be a serious question. Bradford was one of them. I have never forgotten the manageress of one of our Bradford suburban branches insisting that I come and look at where she lived. Almost everything she had in the world was a house in a pleasant terrace in the Girlington district of Bradford. Even then, houses all around her were being occupied by Pakistani immigrants and their families. Few of them spoke English and attempts at integration were minimal.

The Liberal Party nationally seemed to favour unrestricted immigration. I most certainly did not and nothing that has happened in the last forty-odd years in that field has done other than convince me that my original thoughts were right. Carefully controlled and limited immigration with real efforts towards integration were what was needed then and what is needed even more today.

I therefore resigned from the Liberals, cancelled my subscription to the then *Manchester Guardian* and returned wholeheartedly to the Tory fold.

Chapter 13

Highland Flings

SIGHTSEEING, FISHING AND SHOOTING in the Scottish Highlands have been such a big part of my life that I think they deserve a special chapter.

I suppose my interest in the Highlands began in the early 1960s when, following the flotation of Shop & Store, I had received a substantial tax free sum and besides buying Hillcourt as a new home and also Hutton Hill Farm I had surplus cash to spend. I saw an advertisement – I think it was in *The Field* magazine for the Durness Estate in the far north of Scotland. I sent for the particulars and was amazed to learn that most of the Durness peninsular, totalling around 10,000 acres and including the small village of Durness itself was available for sale at a price of only £8,000! In those days that was no more than the price of a semi-detached house, so I thought I must go and see this apparent bargain property.

If you look at a map of Scotland, Durness is just to the right of Cape Wrath which is the absolute end of the Scottish mainland at its north-west point. To get there in those days before the many road improvements which have since been made took more than two solid days of driving. When we finally reached Durness, Enid and I and the two friends who had accompanied us for the journey were fascinated with what we found. The northern shoreline of the peninsular has beautiful sandy beaches beyond which is the island of Eilean Hoan which was part of the property on offer. There were numerous typical Scottish crofts scattered over the lower ground beneath substantial hills. There was a large house in need of some renovation but solidly built and the estate also included the well-known Scottish landmark – Smoo Cave.

Seeing the property and studying the particulars very carefully, it soon became clear why it was available for what at first sight was a ludicrously small price. The first snag was of course the remote location. I might have been prepared to put up with that in the knowledge that the roads would improve as years passed but the second and most important snag lay with all the crofts.

The crofters enjoyed what was effectively a perpetual tenancy at a token rental. Each crofter was only paying a pound or two a year and the rental income from the whole estate was therefore negligible. However, the owner of the estate was responsible for all the repairs and maintenance of all those crofting households and effectively, therefore, you were considering an estate with a trivial income but significant and constant outgoings. So, with some reluctance as I was so taken with the beauty of the coastline, I decided not to buy it. However, that journey gave me an interest in the Highlands which has continued for forty years.

We made the odd tourist visit to the Highlands, but it was in 1973 that I had the opportunity to enjoy some of the best of Highland life. By that time I was seriously involved with shooting and fishing, both at Whittington and in Yorkshire where I had found a friend and very useful contact in the shape of Tom Waite, who for many years was Estate Manager or Factor to the late Lord Richard Bolton. In 1967 I had negotiated a lease with Tom in respect of nearly a mile of the Bolton Estate's fishing on the River Ure. He was an expert angler and a leading light in the Salmon and Trout Association, as well as being a good and keen hand with a shotgun. We had shot and fished together on several occasions prior to him inviting Enid and me to join a party at Glencalvie Lodge, which is an hour's drive beyond Inverness.

The situation was that Lord Bolton had taken a lease on the Glencalvie Estate and towards the end of each sporting season, he was happy for Tom to have the use of the estate for a couple of weeks. Consequently, Tom put together a house party of like-minded sportsmen and their wives and in 1973 and the three succeeding years about twelve of us would assemble at Glencalvie where there was salmon fishing in the River Carron, trout fishing in a large loch on the high ground, grouse to be walked-up on the lower ground, red deer to be stalked all over the estate and even ptarmigan to be attempted on the mountain tops.

After four annual visits – usually towards the end of August or early September, Lord Bolton's lease ran out and a new lessee took over the estate. I immediately arranged to rent the estate from him for a similar couple of weeks for the next several years. Then came the time that the actual freeholders of the property – they were, I believe, two elderly ladies – decided that it should be sold. I was certainly ready to buy the whole estate and at that time could view the sort of cost that would be involved as being of very little consequence. Unfortunately the new lessee of the estate also wanted to buy it and it seemed only right that, as the sitting tenant, he should have the first opportunity. Therefore – to, I am sure, his great advantage – I agreed to withdraw my interest in purchasing against his promise that my future requests for an annual sub-letting would have priority.

Most members of my family have happy memories of Glencalvie. Mine include such high-spots as catching my first salmon on a fly. I had caught the odd salmon on a spinning lure from the Lune at Whittington, but salmon fishing is really about fly fishing. During our 1974 stay as part of one of Tom Waite's house parties we had all flogged the river hard without success. The river was low, days were bright and sunny and towards the end of the season most of the fish had already run up the falls at the top of the Glencalvie stretch, so they were very few and very difficult.

As a last fling I went back to the river in the semi-darkness after we had all enjoyed the usual boisterous dinner in the lodge. I fished quietly and steadily in the pool and at last my efforts were rewarded. It was a good solid 13 lb fish which took some handling in the semi-dark, but finally I had him on the bank and was able to march past the lodge's brightly lit drawing-room windows carrying my prize, much to the surprise of the other anglers who had agreed that there was absolutely no chance.

The deerstalking and other sporting activities at Glencalvie were under the direction of the stalker John Gordon, a particularly fit and tough Highlander with a shaggy mop of jet black hair, a broad smile and a lifetime's experience of the estate. He would appear outside the lodge at about half past nine in a Land Rover towing a trailer which carried a Haflinger – a very useful all terrain vehicle. They no longer used ponies to bring back deer that had been shot, although one of the well-worn paths up to the high tops was still known as the pony path.

I would have had some practice shots on the lawn outside the lodge the previous day and was therefore ready to go.

The usual stalking day at Glencalvie started with a drive up the beautiful glen at the back of the house, down which ran one of the feeder streams into the River Carron which then flowed ultimately into the Dornoch Firth. About halfway up the glen was a convenient small hill from which one could spy the face of the main corrie at the head of the glen and usually there were deer to be seen. We would drive a little further on and then park the Land Rover. A large hinged flap at the rear of the trailer would permit the little Haflinger to be driven from it and then off we would go in the little machine higher and higher up one of the shoulders of the corrie. With a careful and skilful driver, and John Gordon was certainly that, the machine would go almost anywhere, up steep slopes and over damp patches.

The Haflinger and similar machines certainly took some of the pain out of deerstalking since it was so easy to make the first thousand or two feet of height, which in earlier days would have meant a strenuous walk or perhaps a ride on a sure-footed pony. Obviously, you could not try and get too close to the deer in a machine since, with their splendid vision, acute hearing and quite remarkable sense of smell, they would have been disturbed and away. Therefore, until the stalk was over, the ATV (the all terrain vehicle) was simply left in a convenient place and genuine stalking which involved careful walking, crouching, crawling and even flat, slow wriggling would begin.

Sometimes all would go well. We would get within a few hundred yards of the stags and, after a careful study through John's telescope and my binoculars, would select the particular beast which we deemed a suitable cull, then would follow crawl, and wriggle to a suitable firing point and in due time – sometimes after a quite lengthy wait – the chosen stag would stand broadside to us and so provide the opportunity for a clean heart shot. You move the cross hairs of the rifle's telescopic sight up the stag's front leg to the point of its shoulder then move them back a few inches and you are aiming at the animal's heart. A gentle squeeze on the trigger and you will have the 'boom' of the rifle reverberating around the hills followed by the 'thwack' of the bullet's strike. Sometimes the animal would go straight over and lie still. Occasionally it would run a few yards before keeling over. Sadly, there were occasions when a shot was not perfect and you had to work the bolt quickly and hit him again. The golden rule of stalking was that, if you wounded a deer, you must at all costs follow him and administer the *coup-de-grâce*.

When you take a Highland lodge for a sporting holiday, the deal normally includes the right to take so many stags per week. At Glencalvie our 'ration' was eight for our usual two-week stay and, since sometimes son David and son-in-law Stewart as well as other of my guests wanted to stalk, we sometimes arranged additional days on other nearby estates. I remember one such day when the stalk went very badly wrong.

We had taken some additional days on the Duchally Estate, which was several miles away from Glencalvie, being at the top end of the valley of the River Cassley. I went out on that day armed with a brand new and very expensive rifle. This was a hand-made weapon made by David Lloyd, who in those days was well known as a deerstalker as well as for his special hand-made rifles. The special feature of Lloyd rifles was that the telescopic sight was an integral part of the weapon rather than being something that was clamped or screwed on to the top of the barrel. His theory was that no matter how much the rifle was bumped or shaken the sight would never lose its zero. That is, it would always remain firmly fixed whereas normally telescopic sights are frequently knocked or bumped loose and consequently, at the moment of truth, the rifle does not shoot accurately.

As it happened the theory was only partially correct and it did not work well for higher calibre rifles where the bigger bang of larger cartridges sooner or later could shake even the supposedly permanently mounted sight off zero.

I took my brand new, particularly powerful – it was a 7mm. magnum Lloyd rifle – out on the Duchally Estate and for several hours the stalker and I looked in vain for any deer. He finally told me the truth. There had recently been some major construction works not far from the property and the workmen on that job had between them poached just about all the deer on the property. Quite obviously the ground should not have been let, but rather left for a few years for the stock of deer to recover.

We continued tramping over the hills and valleys and finally we did in fact come across a stag, but it was a small puny beast which normally one would have left in the hope that in time it would grow bigger and stronger. In this case the stalker wanted me to shoot it so that he could at least report that one of the stalking tenants had had some success. We managed to get in to reasonable range and I aimed at the beast in the usual manner. Just as I pulled the trigger he turned away from being more or less broadside on and the result was that my shot raked him and whilst it was certainly fatal, it was not going to be a quick clean kill. He ran over a low ridge out of our sight and when we breasted the ridge, he was lying at the foot of it but still – sadly – very much alive and kicking. From further away than was necessary I fired a hasty shot at his neck to end his misery as quickly as I could. My shot was too low and rather than breaking the vertebrae in his neck it simply passed through his throat. I was upset and angry and hit the handle of the bolt of the rifle hard so as to eject the spent cartridge quickly. To my horror the bolt handle sheared off completely and we were left with a useless rifle and a suffering stag.

I had no idea what to do, but fortunately the stalker had. He went up close to the poor, kicking, slowly dying beast and, picked up with both hands a large rock which he then dropped on the back of the stag's head whilst taking care to avoid the thrashing legs and moving antlers. The beast was stunned and in a second the stalker had cut its throat and it was all over.

The odd part about the incident was that in order to get back to Glencalvie from Duchally we had to drive all the way down Glen Cassley and past the handsome, albeit quite small castle which was in fact the property of David Lloyd's wife and which served as his base for Highland deerstalking. I was, therefore, able to call in and show Britain's leading expert on deerstalking rifles that one of his very best models had failed very badly indeed. He was appalled to see that the quality of the steel in the bolt of one of his rifles was such that part of it could just sheer off. In due course he was kind enough to replace the weapon and I learned what was the probable cause of the fault.

The action of stalking rifles, that is the moving parts, has been unchanged in its design since 1898 and many of the makers of hand-built rifles have bought the actions for same from Germany for many years. Pre-war Mauser (to give them their proper name) actions were known in the trade as Imperials, since they had come from military rifles destined for the Imperial German army before the First World War. They were of the highest quality steel. During the Second World War the same rifle action was still being produced, but the Nazi actions used inferior metal and clearly the rifle that let me down had been built around a Nazi rather than an Imperial action.

Turning back to the Glencalvie estate, I had some interesting times stalking there with John Gordon. I remember on one occasion being up on the high tops when cloud came down and completely enveloped us. Whilst we sat tight waiting for it to lift, a whole party of stags came through the cloud and literally surrounded us. Why they did not smell us I shall never know since we certainly smelled them. Perhaps it was because there were so many, but in any event we sat tight in the thick cloud with perhaps a hundred stags moving slowly around us, then, as the cloud began to lift, they moved away and we never even got a shot.

On one occasion John Gordon could not go out with me since he had to deal with some estate problem and he asked if I would be willing to go out with his assistant Robert. I was perfectly happy to try my luck with someone else, but I had expected my replacement stalker would have some idea of what he was doing. Robert did not!

He turned up in black trousers and a white shirt without anything on his head, which of course meant that he stuck out like a sore thumb on every hillside that we tackled. As if that were not enough, he was a chain smoker and our progress towards deer was clearly marked throughout the day by a gentle plume of cigarette smoke floating above us. However, what he lacked in knowledge and skill he certainly made up for in enthusiasm.

We got to the top of the glen and he advised me that we would 'creep up the burn' and get close to those stags up above. We could see the stags before we started and without doubt they could see us and were probably mildly amused to see us scrambling up the bottom of the burn with Robert's black trousers and white shirt clearly visible. To make things even worse, the strong wind was blowing his cigarette smoke towards them.

That party of stags had probably never seen such an inept attempt to stalk them and I like to think they watched us with interest and amusement before, at the psychological moment, moving out over the shoulder of the corrie and into the next one. Whereupon, Robert advised me that we must go down to the bottom and go up the burn in the next corrie. Three times we attempted this manoeuvre and three times the stags simply moved on long before we were near enough to even think of a shot. Finally Robert changed his technique and when the stags started to move out of the third corrie, he invited me to follow him as he ran after them! I promise you, running after stags from shoulder to shoulder of successive corries is a pretty silly thing to do.

Finally, the beasts disappeared and we wandered on a little further and then sat down to rest and recover. Then, by an extraordinary quirk of fate, I saw that there was one stag a long way beneath us which for some reason had not gone with the rest of them. It was a long, long way and I was weighing up our chances of crawling downhill for perhaps a couple of hundred yards to have a better chance, when Robert cheerfully said, 'Take him from here Mr Greenwood'. It was, by a considerable margin, the longest shot at deer which I have ever attempted. I got lucky. Even at that extreme range the beast went over dead as the proverbial nit. Robert was delighted and no doubt the story as he told it in the pubs at Ardgay or Bonar Bridge was rather different and described how his cunning and careful stalking had provided the 'rifle' he was taking out with a splendid opportunity.

Robert features in another of my Highland memories. Again at Glencalvie, John Gordon and I were chugging back down the glen with the trailer and Haflinger behind the Land Rover carrying a dead stag at the end of a successful day's stalking. On our right-hand side as we drove slowly down the glen was the small feeder stream up which many salmon ran to spawn. Halfway up the glen the feeder stream, which was only a few feet wide opened out into a small pool which was no larger than a typical living-room. This was known as the Poachers' Pool since, in low water conditions sometimes dozens or even hundreds of salmon would be lying there waiting for a bit more water to come down off the tops so that they could run a little further up stream to their preferred spawning grounds. .

On that particular day, John looked across the area of the Poachers' Pool and was shocked to see that Robert had climbed up a tree adjoining the pool, wriggled out along a branch and was lying on that branch smoking his inevitable cigarette and making a variety of signals with his left hand. John and I left the Land Rover and walked across towards them. Robert and one of my guests were happily engaged in deliberately foul-hooking salmon! My guest who I thought was a purist fly fisher had a very large hook – or was it two or three? – dangling from the end of his salmon rod and Robert on the branch above was directing him so as to get the hooks immediately below one of the dozens of fish lying there patiently in the small pool. At the appropriate signal from Robert, all that the guest had to do was jerk the rod upwards and, lo and behold a salmon was hooked, albeit most certainly not in its mouth.

John Gordon was shocked, I was both surprised and amused. Catching my friend in this utterly compromising situation was going to enable me to pull his leg for many years to come – and I have done so. However, the fun and games most certainly had to stop since I was the official tenant of the estate and that kind of activity was most certainly not permissible.

Robert reluctantly came down from his branch, the guest cheerfully picked up the – I think it was three salmon – he had already taken and I gave them a bit of a lecture. I remember telling them first of all that, if they had tried long enough, they probably could have caught a fish in that pool legitimately on a fly and, secondly, that there were so many fish in there that you could have probably caught them with your hands, never mind using the foul-hooking technique. They were sceptical about my views and the following day we went back to the Poachers' Pool and I actually caught one salmon quite legitimately on the fly. Other members of the party assembled later for what I proposed to do next, which was to wade into the Poachers' Pool and catch a salmon with my bare hands.

The pool might have been small, but it was quite deep and I had to wear chest waders to get into the middle of it. Once there I had the extraordinary sensation of having dozens of salmon swimming slowly and happily all around me and literally between my legs. It seemed to me quite likely that in those circumstances you could tickle salmon much as countrymen sometimes tickle trout. I still think my theory was basically sound but, in practice, it did not work out too well. I had to lean forward to reach down for the salmon that were beside and between my legs and, as I did so, I shipped water over the top of the waders which quickly began to fill. I went on for as long as I could with the waders filling to the extent that I looked rather like the Michelin Man and the quite cold water off the hills was beginning to affect me. I had to give in. The spectators had to drag me from the pool since I was carrying so much water I simply could not move. They soon cured that by several of them holding me upside down and letting all the water run out of the waders.

A hot bath, a couple of malt whiskies and I was none the worse.

Two more brief fishing stories. On one never to be forgotten day, I was fishing the Cassley in high summer conditions, that is not much water, blazing sunshine and a clear blue sky. I fished most of the sections of the river that were reasonably accessible from the road without even seeing a fish, still less touching or catching one. I decided to walk to a part of the river that was furthest away from the road and I suppose I must have walked for a mile or two up the right bank of the Cassley when I came upon a quite small pool at a bend in the river and lo and behold, a fish showed. I went upstream of the bend and then fished down very carefully – bang – a decent fish on and in a few minutes on the bank. I waded back into the river, put out another cast pretty well over the same piece of water and bang! a second fish. This happened yet again and, instead of a totally blank day which is what one might have expected in those conditions, I had three handsome salmon lying on the bank. I was very well pleased, but then my problems began. I was on the far side of the deer fence which runs down that part of Glencassley and consequently I had to climb over an eight foot fence whilst carrying three good fish, a two handed rod and the rest of my fishing kit. I suppose it was inevitable that I would fall off the top of the fence, fortunately without any serious injury, rather than using my brains and shoving the fish and all my tackle through the fence before trying to climb it.

On another occasion a little further up the Cassley I hooked a fish at the bottom of the junction pool. My problem was that the bank from which I was fishing was about three feet higher than the surface of the water where I had now got the fish under control. I remembered what all the good books say and I led the salmon like a dog on the end of a lead some fifty yards upstream to where I knew there was a rocky piece of bank sloping gently down into the water. Just the place to bring the salmon ashore. I really had him only a matter of feet away and about to begin to slide up the rock and into my grasp. I bent down to grab him by the tail and in one extraordinary moment my feet slipped, I fell headfirst into the river, the hook came out of the salmon's mouth and inserted itself very firmly beneath my finger nail and with me thus firmly attached to my rod and line, the salmon lay gasping in the crook of my right arm. Desperately I tried to grab him by the tail, desperately he tried to wriggle away. He succeeded, I failed. The end of a long day's fishing found me sitting at the side of the pool, pretty wet and with a salmon fly firmly imbedded in my finger. I cut my line and then contemplated trying to remove the now extremely painful barbed hook. Clearly the wine of Scotland was the first essential. I gave myself a stiff dram and poured a little whisky over the throbbing finger in the hope that this might anaesthetise it to some extent. When I tried to remove the hook I quickly learned that, whilst malt whisky is a splendid restorative, it is a very poor local anaesthetic. I returned sadly to my car, put away all my tackle one-handed, then set off to drive down the glen to seek medical aid in Bonar Bridge. Halfway down the glen, who should I see but my friend and fellow fisher Tom Waite. 'How have you gone on?' he asked as we stopped with our cars side by side, I said nothing but simply showed him my bleeding and well-hooked finger.

'I can get that out for you,' he said kindly and reached underneath his dashboard and produced a pair of rusty pliers, I hastily thanked him for the suggestion, but then continued on my way and later had the hook removed with the benefit of a local anaesthetic. Score line – Salmon 1 Greenwood 0.

Just two more shooting stories from Glencalvie. There are not many grouse in the actual Highlands, since there are so many predators regarding them as fair game. It is further south in, for example, Perthshire that grouse moors tended by gamekeepers are to be found with large stocks of the birds. Consequently there is no question of having grouse driven towards you in the Highlands. There simply are not enough of them and also the areas to be covered are far too large. The technique is to shoot them over dogs, particularly Pointers and Setters. One of the joys of Glencalvie was going out with John Gordon and his two excellent dogs, one of which – Beech was a beautiful and graceful Red Setter. The other – Sweep was a burly German short-haired Pointer. We would go out, ideally as a team of four guns accompanying John who was also accompanied by Robert, and a pair of Labradors to pick up any birds that we shot.

Usually when we were on one of the vast heather-clad lower slopes, Beech would be first to go. He would tear off to the right for perhaps two or three hundred yards, then zig-zag back to the left for a similar distance whilst we walked slowly behind him. Came the moment when he caught a scent of grouse and immediately – as that breed of dog's name implies – he would 'set' standing quite still and with his tail out and you could be quite confident that a line from his tail to his head was pointing at grouse in the heather somewhere in front of him. Then the technique was for John to walk forwards slowly, gently brushing the heather in front of him with the end of his thumb-stick. Two guns would be to his right and two guns to his left, the intention being that if the grouse broke to the left, those two guns would try and shoot them, if they broke to the right it was for the right-hand guns to try and if they went straight away from us, probably all four would have a bang.

You could, almost without exception trust the dog. As the line walked very slowly and silently forward with John brushing the heather, there would be a heart-stopping flurry of wings and the covey of grouse, that's to say a family of grouse, would spring from the heather and fly quickly away. You had to be both quick and accurate to bring one of them down before they had disappeared out of shot.

When Beech was tired it was Sweep's turn. A Pointer covers about a quarter – if that – of the ground over which a Setter dashes. Sweep would plod fairly slowly and methodically forward, veering from left to right until he caught a scent. Then he would obligingly point to where the grouse were. One can say point, since, apart from his body being aligned straight at the source of the scent, he would lift one paw as if to say, 'That's where they are'.

All this activity would usually be taking place in lovely weather with glorious purple heather stretching all around us and with the mountains and high tops forming a background to the scene beneath a blue sky. We used to walk for miles and counted ourselves very lucky if we shot more than five or six brace, but the shooting was not necessarily the most important part. The splendid scenery and the sight of the dogs working so well was, together with the fresh air and healthy exercise, enough to make anyone forget their cares and enjoy a blissful day.

I must not give the impression that Highland holidays, even in August, are all blue skies and sunshine. Far from it. Sometimes the weather could be really foul, but that didn't stop the deerstalking, where wind and wet are just part of the sport. We welcomed the rain on the river since it soon stirred up the fish and, if enough fell, they began to move upstream and fight their way up the Glencalvie falls. There was one downside to damp days. A damp but warm atmosphere is just the condition that the infamous Highland midges prefer. Never underestimate the misery that Highland midges can inflict on you!

Sometimes they were so bad that the only way you could continue fishing was with tightly fastened clothes, a pair of gloves and, over your head netting, rather like a bee-keeper's headdress. A wide variety of creams, sprays etc. usually had very little effect against the tiny horrors, which could do you real damage. There are many Highland sportsmen who have come off the river with swollen hands and lumps and bumps all over their faces. Even the deer hated the midges and at times when the midges were about in plenty, you could be sure that the deer had gone up to the highest ground where the breezes kept the little devils away.

Just occasionally you got more than breezes on the high tops. One day at Glencalvie we went out to try for a few ptarmigan, which are very much like grouse but with white and pale grey plumage. It is almost unbelievable how well the birds are camouflaged when they are amongst the rock, stones and scree on the tops. When trying for ptarmigan you do not use Setters or Pointers but you will need dogs to retrieve any that you are able to shoot. We would walk over the high tops about ten yards apart and sometimes the birds would remain perfectly still until you were no more than a pace or two from them. Then up they would get and away they would go. They would not fly upwards or straight and level but rather tear away down the side of the hill so that you had the most unusual situation of trying to shoot at something descending rapidly below the level of your feet and probably curling around the contour of the hill at the same time. We never shot more than a handful of them, nor did we wish to. For my part, I was content to have one or two on each excursion, not least so as to be able to have them looking at me from a glass case.

On one never-to-be-forgotten day, we were moving slowly across the very top of the high hill at the head of the glen behind Glencalvie Lodge. It was a breezy day when we started and by the time we had climbed to the top it was quite windy. The wind quickly developed into a fierce gale and we quickly realised that we were in a pretty dangerous situation. The gale was so strong that one man's cap was blown off and, rather than dropping to the ground a few feet in front of him, it simply disappeared, travelling horizontally out over the edge of the hill. We began to struggle down from the top but the wind was now so strong that it literally blew us off our feet. One way or another we scrambled down the hill to where we had left cars on the road below. I struggled to open the door of son-in-law Stewart's car. As I opened it the wind caught the door and simply tore it from its hinges, such was its force. When we had assembled I was extremely worried to see that one of our party – my son David – was missing. He had been marching at the far side of our line and my fear was that he had been blown over an edge and was lying injured, or worse, somewhere up there. Fortunately he had had the good sense not to try and struggle across the top of the mountain to re-join us, but had sheltered out of the worst of the wind until the storm had passed.

After our regular visits to Glencalvie, we frequently stayed at the Oykel Bridge Hotel to fish the lower Oykel of which splendid river we were part-owners for a number of years. The lower Oykel begins at the falls just behind the hotel and, for the first half mile of its length, runs between jagged rocks interspersed with small pools which are difficult to fish, but can be rewarding. There are in fact two Oykel bridges. The centuries-old one is no longer used for traffic which is now carried by the comparatively new second bridge. It is an attractive spot on the road from Bonar Bridge to Ullapool and coach tours frequently stop there for passengers to take photographs. I remember fishing just below the new bridge one day when I hooked a particularly lively salmon. He was dashing about between the rocks trying to rush downstream whilst I was trying to get him back up towards me. Partway through the excitement I looked over my shoulder to find that I had got some forty odd spectators, most of whom had their cameras out watching the struggle with great interest. I was beginning to look forward to playing the fish out and then lifting him up for the benefit of the coach-load of amateur photographers when he made a final downstream rush. He jumped several feet out of the water, slapped against a slab of rock, out came the hook and he was away at which point my audience who were clearly not on my side burst into loud applause!

There was one evening at the Oykel Bridge Hotel which sticks in my memory. It was my granddaughter Emily's birthday – I can't remember which – but she was only quite a little girl at the time. We were just finishing dinner in the hotel when, to our surprise, the Bonar Bridge Pipe Band in full Highland dress appeared on the main road outside the hotel windows and began to play stirring music on their bagpipes. It transpired that son-in-law Stewart had bribed them to make this special journey and appearance so that little Emily would have a surprise for her birthday.

It was a good idea, save for one thing. When my family – and all the rest of the guests in the hotel – had gone outside to hear all the pipers, we soon found that the dreaded Highland midges were also apparently music lovers. All we faint-hearted Sassenachs hastily beat a retreat into the hotel and watched from behind glass. The stoical and hardy Highlanders played on with each piper surrounded by his or her personal cloud of midges. They're bad enough when you're wearing trousers. What it must be like when you are wearing a kilt – and what are Scotsmen meant to where under their kilts? – hardly bears thinking about!

And now one final Scottish story, otherwise this chapter will become a book-full of Scottish reminiscences. On one of the many occasions, whilst staying at the Oykel Bridge Hotel, fishing conditions were poor during the day and I decided to go out after dinner in the gloaming, as the Scots call that evening time when the sun is long gone, but there is still a fair amount of light. I drove down to beat two and then walked down to a very good pool where the river had just rushed around a corner and then slowed down, so as to provide a perfect place for salmon to pause on their upstream journey. It was quiet and still and I was about a mile away from anybody. As I approached the pool I realised that all its surface was covered with a yellowish powder. I had read and heard much about how professional gangs of poachers used cymag to poison salmon pools before gathering up, in large nets, the fish that had floated to the surface. Apparently, sometimes hundreds of fish could be taken with one such foul deed. I had no idea what the surface of a pool which had been so treated looked like, but there was certainly something very odd indeed about that pool on that evening. Every stone at the edge had its rim of the powder.

It dawned on me that, if this pool that I was staring at had been recently poisoned, then those who had done so might very well be watching me from the trees on the other bank. I hastily returned to my car, drove back to the hotel and asked the manager if he knew what a cymagged pool looked like. Like me, he had no idea, so I telephoned George Ross who was the Fisheries' Manager or Head Ghillie and told him what I had seen. Apparently George was no wiser than me, so he called out the Police and several of his colleagues to both stop any traffic on the road and then accompany him down to the pool.

Their hopes of catching the poaching gang were dashed and I ended up acutely embarrassed when it turned out that the cause of the alarm was not the use of poison, but rather a dusting of pollen from one solitary laburnum tree which stood by the bend of the river and which an earlier breeze had disturbed enough to spread the pollen just over that particular pool and nowhere else.

In the event, no one criticised me harshly and apparently the Police and all the others who turned out to help them took the view that it had been a worthwhile exercise since poaching, and the fear of it, are ever present concerns in the Highlands, the worst examples of poaching being the carefully planned raids by organised gangs who would drive up a valley such as Glencassley at night when deer had come down to feed on the grass near the river. A van-load – literally – of deer could be shot and driven away for a very profitable sale of poached venison. I learned evidence of that when a number of severed stags heads were discovered, having been thrown over a bridge on the Ullapool road.

However, ugly thoughts of cruel and, of course, highly illegal taking of game, must not mar any thoughts about the Scottish Highlands which this chapter has produced. We are fortunate indeed in Britain to still have this substantial, virtually unspoiled area of our crowded island to enjoy.

CHAPTER 14

Deals We Did and Deals We Didn't

Let's start with some interesting deals which were very seriously considered, but which did not come to fruition.

The fact that we contemplated all of these very seriously will, I trust, convince you that we were very expansion-minded. I saw it as my role to be the spokesman for the family in most of the negotiations that took place in both unsuccessful and successful deals. My father, although an expert salesman in one-on-one situations, never enjoyed public speaking or speaking to a group of individuals and he was happy for me to be the 'mouthpiece'. My brother, Denis, usually played the very necessary role of restraining influence and, if there were potential dangers or snags in a possible deal, it was usually Denis who would see them first.

The first major deal we did not do was when we did not become part of Great Universal Stores. In the fifties, Isaac Wolfson's G.U.S. was buying up private and small public companies in all directions. G.U.S. already had a significant menswear division, including such now almost forgotten multiples as Hope Brothers, Hector Powe Tailors and Masters of Cardiff. Greenwood's were obviously on their hit list and we were duly approached with the temptation that, if we were to sell out to them, Denis and I would be offered joint leadership of the whole G.U.S. menswear division. Even with that temptation we had no difficulty in refusing promptly.

Mentioning Hope Brothers reminds me that we had already attempted to take over that company before G.U.S. acquired it. With the advice of Myers & Co. – London stockbrokers – we had produced an elaborate plan for a bid for Hope Brothers' shares but the snag was that the quite complex transaction would have meant that we would have had to become a public company and that was a hurdle we decided not to jump.

Another deal which did not come off, but was very seriously discussed, in the early fifties, was our proposal to Burtons – who were at that time simply a massive (some 600 shops) mens tailoring firm, that we should add a Greenwood's 'shop-within-a-shop' unit to, say, 200 of their larger branches. At that time Burtons were trading poorly and clearly needed a significant change in their operations. Finally, they turned us down and instead purchased their fast-growing rivals – Jackson the Tailor – primarily, I think, in order to secure the Jacksons' management who over the next few years certainly pulled Burtons round.

Our successful acquisition of the Bunney's departmental stores in Liverpool and Llandudno sent me searching for similar opportunities and one where we unfortunately failed was Hanningtons' Brighton departmental store. We also tried, and failed, to acquire a chain of sweet shops mostly around Glasgow with the object of converting the larger ones into Greenwood's units and holding the remainder as property investments for our now quite active property subsidiary company, Shop & Store Developments Ltd.

Through Shop & Store we were full of ambition. We worked hard on a town centre redevelopment scheme for Widnes. We attempted to buy the Bradford Wool Exchange Company so as to obtain control of that very valuable building. We came quite close to a successful scheme for the development of Bradford's Kirkgate Market which was later carried out by Arndale. And, of all things, we put quite a bit of work into a potential purchase of the Blackpool Tower Company. There were sound economic reasons for this last idea. The Blackpool Tower Company owned not only the famous tower but also the adjoining block which occupied a key position and, in the 1960s looked to be ripe for redevelopment. It was in fact later pulled down and replaced with a modern retail block.

There were numerous smaller misses and it sometimes seemed that, for every ten properties we thought about, eight of them would come to nothing; one would result in some serious efforts but no success, and the tenth would ring the bell and we would have a deal.

We were not short of funds for these deals. Apart from the family's wish to cash in on at least part of the retail and property empire which we were building, there was a further reason for floating Shop & Store as a public company in November 1959. As a public company it was very much easier to borrow large sums from the London-based institutions and we soon had a modest long-term mortgage deal with the Legal & General which was then followed with a much larger deal with the Friends Provident Insurance Society. It sounds incredible now, but, at that point in time, it was possible to arrange for a long-term mortgage facility for twenty, twenty-five or even forty years at a fixed rate of interest – fixed for the whole term – of around 5%. We made such long-term arrangements for sums, which in today's money, would be well over £50m. In addition to the availability of these long-term mortgage funds we were, of course, generating good profits and retaining almost all of these within the business for further expansion.

Whilst, of course, we did numerous straight-forward property deals we tended to be most interested in acquiring existing businesses. As mentioned earlier we were ready to buy any business which had accumulated tax losses which we could use to our advantage. Such purchases ranged from an ironmongery company – Entwistle & Nutter Ltd. in Darwen, Lancashire, where I found myself trying to take stock of nails, screws, nuts and bolts in a myriad of different sizes, to easier transactions, such as Stephens Cloth Company in Liverpool which required very little effort to turn it into a retail menswear operation.

All the deals were interesting. Some were genuinely exciting – such as my purchase of a derelict block in the High Street of Rhyl, North Wales. It occupied an excellent position and was clearly long overdue for redevelopment as four shops. I journeyed to Rhyl to negotiate with the charming lady who was the owner of this property. I was prepared to go up to about £80,000 which would, of course, be over a million in today's money. The lady and I met in Forte's cafe not far from the property and had a thoroughly good haggle. I, apparently grudgingly, went up to £75K. She was adamant that she would take no less than £80K and so, of course, I knew that if the worst came to the worst, I was going to buy the property. Obviously, if I could persuade her to accept a lower price, so much the better. I therefore dug my heels in and stuck at £75K. She dug hers in and stuck at £80K and it appeared we had reached an impasse.

Then to my shock and horror she cheerfully said, 'I'll tell you what, let's toss up for the difference!' Remember the £5,000 then involved would be over £70,000 today.

The prospect of gambling for that kind of figure on the spin of a coin no doubt set all my ancestors spinning in their graves, but, as far as I could see, it was heads I would win and tails I didn't lose, since the worst case was that I would end up paying what was actually my ultimate bottom line figure. I produced half a crown (those were the days of real money!) and suggested I spun the coin, caught it and put it down on the table – hand over it – whilst she called.

'That will be fine,' she said. 'Oh, isn't this exciting?' I must admit, it was.

Up went the half crown, I caught it, slapped it on the table, put my hand over it and she called, 'Heads!' I took my hand away and it was tails. She was as good as her word and we bought the property at £75,000, demolished it and built a block of four fine shops.

In 1962 our constant look-out for departmental store businesses that might be acquired was rewarded when we heard that Lowes of Wigan could be bought. Lowes' store, on the market square in front of Wigan Parish Church, was a typical medium-sized, family-owned, department store. It had begun as a modest draper's shop in 1887, and over the years had acquired adjoining properties so as to have a substantial frontage to the market place. The store traded from basement, ground, first and second floor levels with various departments – the most important of which was, as is usually the case with department stores, ladieswear which occupied the whole of the first floor. There were particularly good departments for glass and china and also for soft furnishings, together with other less significant sections. When we had agreed terms to buy all the shares in the company, it was our intention to do as we had done with Bunney's of Liverpool, namely to clear all existing stocks, and run the store with just menswear and ladieswear until plans for its demolition and rebuilding as a block of shops could be completed.

However, I recall Father and I standing on the pavement outside Lowes and Father saying, 'Do you think we could run this place as a store?' I was happy to agree to try and do so and thus, for the next twenty-odd years, Lowes of Wigan was an active trading element in what was now a group of businesses.

A little later we acquired another small store in the adjoining Lancashire town of Leigh and ran Danbys of Leigh more or less as a branch of Lowes of Wigan for quite a number of years before finally splitting it into shop units.

We did an interesting property deal in the early sixties when we bought the Leeds Safe Deposit Company which owned only one property – but it was a good one – in a prime position in Albion Street, Leeds. Our intention was to refurbish the building and then let or sell it. In the event we were able to sell it profitably and it was later pulled down and is part of the site which included the old *Yorkshire Post* building and which was entirely rebuilt as a major office block. However, Father and I were after more than just a profit on a property deal.

As the name implies, the Leeds Safe Deposit Company had, in the basement of its premises, hundreds of strong boxes which were let to anyone who wanted bank vault level security for their papers, jewellery, cash, or whatever. The terms of those lettings meant that we, in our new capacity as directors of the safe deposit company had to give all the box holders due notice that they must clear their boxes by a certain date and thereafter the vaults would be ready for redevelopment.

As we anticipated, many of the box holders had died or disappeared or for some reason simply ignored the notices that we had served. The upshot was that, after the expiry of the due date, Father and I went into the basement vaults together with workmen armed with crowbars and sledge hammers. Along each wall were the rows of strong boxes, mostly with the doors hanging open and the contents cleared. But there was a quite significant number still closed and locked. It seemed to us very likely that we should come across some long forgotten jewels or possibly bundles of cash, the proceeds of some illegal or improper dealings.

One by one the boxes were burst open and slowly our spirits sank. Rather than 'the bonus' we were hoping for, all we seemed to find were old documents of no current value, one or two love letters which might have been valuable, but only for blackmail, and some odd souvenirs.

There was absolutely nothing of real current value. Which only goes to show that the good people of Leeds – particularly the businessmen – do not forget where they have deposited their well-gotten or ill-gotten gains.

We made our first move outside the north of England as far back as 1960. We heard that a small chain – five shops – trading as Griffiths, could be bought. I went to inspect the shops in Cardiff (two), Newport, Port Talbot and Barry. They were in reasonable positions, well-stocked and with competent staff, so I was happy to persuade my father and brother that we should buy them. I had in mind the fact that, if we had five units out on a limb, i.e. a long way from the rest of our branches, it would be necessary to open more shops in that new area and also gradually fill in the areas of the country in between. We started down that road when I found more branches in South Wales and soon we had a viable group of thirteen units in South Wales. Two or three of those additional shops came as part of a poor deal which at the time had looked to be a very clever move.

A London-based retail chain, trading under the name Maxwell, had shops in three parts of the country. They had a handful of units in South Wales, a further modest-sized group in Yorkshire, and the rest of their branches in the Greater London area. How that had come about I have no idea, but it seemed to me that to acquire their South Wales and Yorkshire shops would be a shrewd way of expanding our chain and particularly so in the South Wales area. After the usual haggling, I agreed terms with them. Fortunately, not a lot of money was involved, since all the units were leasehold and there was therefore no large sum required for the property element.

The deal proved to be a poor one for several reasons. Firstly Maxwell's class of trade was aimed at the youth market. Secondly, like many lower class retailers, Maxwell took club cheques, a lucrative system, for the provider, whereby the hard-up made regular modest payments until they were entitled to a cheque which could be spent only at such retailers as would accept them. Our class of trade was always a notch or two above the club cheque level. The third and final problem with the Maxwell deal was that the staff were mostly a poor bunch. With one or two exceptions, they were either poor salesmen and unskilled outfitters or − worse still − they were not strictly honest. Suffice it to say that stocktaking results at the ex-Maxwell branches threw up some ugly deficiencies.

There was one Maxwell unit which taught me a lesson. They had a branch in the small South Wales town of Bargoed. When I was dashing about South Wales inspecting their branches prior to finalising the deal, Bargoed was just too far up the valleys for me to visit conveniently. I therefore just assumed it was like their other Welsh shops and did not go to see it. It was the only shop of the dozens − make that hundreds − that I have bought which I did not first see myself. What a mistake! When I finally got to Bargoed, a month or two after the deal was done, I soon realised why the figures from that branch were appallingly low. The shop was in a rotten position, the last one in a street that led up to the Welsh hills beyond. On the day I first saw it such was the foot flow, i.e. weight of pedestrian traffic, that, sleeping soundly in the shop doorway was a sheep off the hills! We ended up selling most the Maxwell units and at the end of the day, I suppose we about broke even on the whole deal.

Some good did come out of my excursions into South Wales. I came to know the area well and therefore when, in 1963, we got the chance to take over Hodges & Sons, a fine old-established South Wales business, I was ready to go after it hard.

Hodges had thirty-nine branches, most of which were freeholds in good positions. The branch list included representation in most South Wales towns but also some excellent branches in such south-western English towns as Torquay, Gloucester, Taunton, Bristol and Hereford. Their business was primarily clothing, with outfitting given less attention. Their clothing business was – at that time – based on an excellent bespoke tailoring service from their own factory at Fforestfach, Swansea. The factory premises also included the company's head office and warehouse.

It was blindingly obvious that Hodges was just what we wanted. With one deal, our modest presence in South Wales could be changed into the area's leading menswear retailer and, we would have a presence in the south-west, edging up towards the Midlands.

Whilst we were negotiating to purchase the Hodges company, we took a decision which had very significant long-term repercussions. At that time – before the motorway network was completed – it seemed logical to let the head office and warehouse operation of Hodges continue to supply and administer both the Hodges chain and the South Wales Greenwood's shops, which were quickly renamed as Hodges. Subsequent expansion in the south-west was also to be under the Hodges' name.

This might have been logical in terms of geography and the length of delivery journeys and also in the fact that Hodges' name carried great goodwill in the towns where they traded. However, with hindsight, I now realise that a wiser move would have been to integrate the south-west and South Wales operations entirely into the Greenwood business which would, in due course, have meant massive savings in head office expenses. Effectively, from 1963 onwards, our retail business had two head offices and warehouses. One could have done the job.

Hodges was an archetypal family business. Many of their shops had been open for more than half a century. Their branch managers were well-known figures in their local communities and virtually all of them had been with the firm since starting as junior assistants.

In true Welsh fashion, managers were never known by their Christian names and thus Dick Jones, manager of Aberystwyth branch, was 'Jones Aberystwyth'. We had 'Evans Swansea', 'James Newport', 'Evans Black-wood', and so on.

The staff at the branches were nearly all male, with just the occasional female assistant, some of whom had been recruited during the war years and were still there twenty years later. Of the 250 staff at the factory and head office in Swansea, the majority were, of course, female machinists but there, as at the branches, long service was the order of day and there were sewing machinists in the factory whose mothers had worked for Hodges before them.

Before a deal was done, it was my task to visit every branch and this time I most certainly saw every one of them. I studied the position of each from the outside, hurriedly sketching a street plan showing the location of major multiples in relation to the Hodges branch, and sketching the style and shape of the shop front and interior and adding two estimates. I tried to estimate what would be a rental value for each unit and also what I thought that shop's annual sales might total. I was pretty accurate as regards my estimate of the rental value of the branches when other expert eyes and closer experience confirmed just how much the properties were worth. I was, however, miles out in my guesstimate of the turnover of the branches. Every one of them was doing significantly more than I would have expected. This was, of course, a consequence of their being long-established, well-managed shops and also due to the fact that they were all doing a significant bespoke tailoring business, which was something we had only dabbled in at a few Greenwood's branches.

Altogether, Hodges was a splendid purchase for us. I had the pleasure and privilege of finally agreeing a price with Mr Willy Hodges in his home on the Gower Peninsula near Swansea, but it was still necessary that there be a formal meeting to finalise all the details.

The Hodges family and the other Hodges directors were very anxious that there should be no premature disclosure of their decision to sell out. Therefore it was agreed that the final meeting – hopefully – would be held secretly in the hotel adjoining Paddington Station in London. A meeting room was rented for the day and we lined up on two sides of a long table. In the centre of each team of directors, lawyers and accountants were the respective chairmen with my father facing Mr Willie Hodges. After an hour or two, all details had been satisfactorily resolved. I rang reception and asked them to send up a tray of tea and biscuits and a waiter duly appeared. After depositing the tea things he stood for a moment hesitantly with the bill for same in his hand. No one seemed to be in a hurry to take it from him, so he put it in the middle of the table between the two older gentlemen who he rightly assumed to be the principal players.

Father said, 'Well, Mr Hodges, we've agreed to pay you a jolly good price so I think it's for you to buy us a cup of tea.' With that, he pushed the bill across to Mr Willie.

'Oh, no. You've driven a very hard bargain, Mr Greenwood,' said Mr Willie with his Welsh accent. 'I think this bill is for you,' and he pushed it across to Father.

I knew my father well enough to realise that he was thinking this was a bit of Welsh meanness, so he pushed the bill back across the table pointing out, 'We've come the furthest for this meeting so I think the tea should be on you.'

Mr Willie was clearly thinking what a hard lot these Yorkshiremen were and it was beginning to be a point of honour with him not to pay this bill. Back across the table it came.

'I'm surprised, Mr Greenwood, you instigated these negotiations. I'm sure this bill is your responsibility'.

The situation was in fact becoming ugly. Both the elderly principals were showing signs of a red flush. Our accountant, Harry Clough, who was sitting next to me whispered urgently in my ear, 'Brian, give me the bloody bill. I'll settle it! If these two go on any longer the whole deal will be off!'

I think he was right. The two chairmen were both capable of having a major fall-out over this trivial cost, which was nothing when compared to the multi-million pound (in today's terms) deal that had just been agreed.

The sale of the business came as a great shock to all of the Hodges staff. I was able to reassure the factory staff and the trade unions who represented them that we had no intention of closing the bespoke tailoring operation but, on the contrary, intended to include the service in as many as possible of the Greenwood's branches in the north. As regards the retail staff, we explained to them that we had no intention of closing any branches – quite the reverse, it was our intention that the Greenwood's shops in South Wales would immediately become part of the Hodges operation and new shops would be opened throughout the south-west.

We kept our promise as regards branch expansion, so much so that by 1970 Hodges branch list had lengthened to sixty-four units and a lot of work had been done in refitting many of the original thirty-nine.

We took over another quite significant menswear retailer in 1970 – William Blackburn & Co. Ltd. – who operated twenty shops from their Leeds headquarters. The twenty branches were very well spread since, apparently, the first Mr Blackburn worked on the principle of having all his branches in different types of trading area. Thus, there were one or two shops in mining areas, others in resort towns, others in textiles towns and so on.

This wide spread of shops suited us very well because we simply added the southern Blackburns units to the Hodges chain. Such branches as Bath, Brighton, Bristol, Cheltenham and Gloucester were obviously good places for Hodges to be. In the north there was no problem for Greenwood's in assimilating shops in Bradford, Castleford, Doncaster, Leeds and Stockton, etc.

I suppose it would be boring just to add a list of the various property acquisitions which Shop & Store made in the sixties and seventies, but I think two deserve a mention. The first is Airedale House in Albion Street, Leeds. It was one of the first of the wave of office developments which have swept the city in the last forty years. Airedale House was, and still is, a sound office block development with Barclays Bank and some shops on the ground floor. It was, for many years, one of the most valuable of Shop & Store's assets.

The other deal that we did do was not particularly profitable but it was interesting. Having failed to buy Blackpool Tower, we succeeded in buying the Morecambe Tower. Yes, there actually was one but it was never completed. The base of the tower was built and around it the old-time developers provided a ballroom, a cinema, shops and cafes. But the tower itself never rose above two or three storeys high and I suppose few people realised that the four massive 'feet' of a tower were hidden inside the facilities just described. We bought the partly vacant and already semi-derelict buildings in order to demolish them and build a bowling alley which in later years became a bingo hall.

I'm afraid the building we put up at Morecambe did nothing to enhance the beauty of that seaside resort and I have to confess that a lot of the smaller shop developments that we built in the sixties were typical of their era – comparatively ugly brick-built boxes. Property developers had it too easy in those days – perhaps they still do?

CHAPTER 15

The Joys of Shopkeeping

R UNNING A CHAIN OF SHOPS is bound to be an interesting experience. I certainly found it so. Unlike some hi-tech businesses, you are bound to need a large number of staff and that means a lot of time spent on personnel matters. For many years I tried to interview all the branch managers personally before they were appointed and, even when I had to leave some managerial appointments to the discretion of area managers or the sales directors of Greenwood's and Hodges, I made a point of meeting each new manager as early as possible in his career.

We tried hard to maintain contact with the managers and other staff and for that reason published the group's house magazine, *Contact*, usually every two months. Each issue was full of photographs and information and, whilst the regular 'Directors' Letter' tried to set out group policy, *Contact* was very much more than a branch circular.

It had been the custom at Greenwood's for many years to hold an annual staff dinner and dance. These began way back before the war and continued into the sixties. At Hodges the custom had been to have an annual dinner for the managers. However, from 1966 onwards each of the two main companies held an annual convention with the day being devoted to discussion, lectures, displays and fashion parades of forthcoming merchandise – all of which was then followed by a black tie reception and dinner in the evening.

Greenwood's had long followed the practice of presenting a gold watch to any member of staff who had completed twenty-one years of service. When we acquired Hodges and sought to introduce the same custom we found that virtually every manager immediately qualified. So for a year or two the qualifying period was made slightly longer so as to keep the total number of recipients down to a level where the occasion could be regarded as notable.

The managers' dinners for Hodges, always held in or near Swansea, were particularly enjoyable. At the first such event where my family was involved, the Hodges' directors, from whom we had just bought the business, were guests of honour. I recall that, after the formal dinner, toasts and speeches, Mr Hodges said to us, 'At this stage Mr Greenwood, the directors usually retire since the managers can become a little boisterous.'

We most certainly were not going to retire. If there were to be a party, we wanted to be part of it. The whisky flowed and, as you might expect when a large number of Welshmen get together, the singing was loud, prolonged and of pretty good quality. Two incidents stick in my mind.

I was standing watching the boisterous proceedings when one Hodges manager weaved his way unsteadily across the floor and stood in front of me, swaying gently. He opened his mouth and began to speak and then passed out like a light! He fell with a thud at my feet and, quickly, two of his colleagues rushed to him. With a hand under each arm, they dragged him away. I can still recall the twin lines in the carpet which his trailing legs and shoes left behind. His colleagues were, I suspect, shocked that one of their number might have disgraced himself in front of the new directors.

As they disappeared, one of them called over his shoulder, 'Do not worry, Mr Greenwood, only stumbled he has'.

A little later another Hodges manager staggered up and, for a moment, I thought he was going to thump me. In fact, he patted me on the shoulder and said, 'Mr Greenwood, when I heard you had bought our business, I hated your bloody guts. Now I wish you had bought it twenty years ago.'

That inebriated comment showed once and for all that our efforts to be on good terms with the Hodges' personnel had proved successful.

Later that evening – and at all subsequent Hodges' conventions – the informal Hodges Male Voice Choir, led by branch manager Jones Aberystwyth, was in very good voice and they added the Yorkshireman's anthem, 'On Ilkley Moor bar t'at' to their repertoire.

For my part, I found myself inducted into the choir. After a few drinks, I seemed to have acquired an instant mastery of Welsh and found myself singing 'Sospan Bach' and 'Calon Lan' with the best of them.

A characteristic of the Welsh is that, when they have plenty to drink, they don't sing dirty rugby songs. Instead, they sing hymns. One of the high spots of the evening was always, for example, hearing Jones Aberystwyth leading the choir in 'Jesu, Lover of My Soul' to – of course – the tune 'Aberystwyth'. With perspiration rolling down his face, his jacket off and bow-tie awry, Jones would urge us to give it more 'hoel' and we would do our best.

Incidentally, that particular Hodges manager was a salesman of similar quality to my old teacher in my shop assistant days, Ronnie Buckley. I could never understand why the Hodges Aberystwyth branch had a particularly good bespoke tailoring trade. More orders for suits-to-measure came through from Aberystwyth than from other shops in much larger communities, and clearly there had to be a reason for this. I learned that Jones' technique for boosting his bespoke trade was unusual.

You might have seen him standing in the shop doorway and, when farmer, Mr Evans, walked by, Jones would have called out, 'Mr Evans, your suit has come!'

'What suit is that? I don't remember ordering one,' the farmer might reply.

'Ah, yes,' said Jones. 'But we have just had this season's patterns delivered and, when I saw this lovely lovat-green with a faint overcheck, I said to myself at once, *Perfect for Mr Evans!* So I took the liberty of ordering a suit for you in that cloth.' He apparently got away with that technique regularly and the result was the excellent bespoke trade at his branch. Some of the best-dressed farmers and others in west Wales were to be found in and around Aberystwyth.

I could certainly depend on brother Denis to ensure that relationships with our suppliers were always very good. He had deservedly earned a high reputation with them all.

I think we also had a good reputation in the property world. I took the view that, if we gave our word on any transaction that would be totally binding and, whilst formal contracts and other documentation might follow in due course, there was no way we would ever renege on a deal. Our policy was to negotiate as hard and as skilfully as possible but then, once we had committed ourselves, there would be no change.

There was, however, one exception to this that I recall. After lengthy discussions throughout the day I had reached agreement with the retiring owner of a menswear business in Bristol. I had agreed a price for everything – stock, fittings, fixtures and property and had shaken the vendor's hand. He and his wife were living in the flat above the shop and, before I set off on the long drive back to Yorkshire, he kindly invited me to have a cup of tea. He and his wife were clearly looking forward very much to their retirement and this had been one reason, I suppose, why he had been really anxious to agree a deal with me.

We were half way through our tea when I said to him, 'I've been thinking about the price we've just agreed'.

A look of horror came over both their faces, but it quickly lifted when I went on to say, 'I don't think we're paying you enough'. I had decided that perhaps I had pressed too hard for the keenest possible price, so I told the vendor that, whilst the price would remain the same, we would pay all his expenses – solicitors' fees, estate agents' charges, advertising costs and any other costs in which he might be involved so that the price he received would be net in his hands. He and his wife were, of course, delighted.

Apart from personnel and merchandise matters, running a retail chain obviously involves working on the layout of the branches and window displays and advertising. It was a pleasant experience to be involved frequently and deeply in all these.

As regards shop fitting and shop layout the basic rule was standardisation. All multiple firms try to decide what is the best layout for a typical branch and then to replicate this at all their units. We did the same at both Hodges and Greenwood's and it soon became the case that the only difference between a Hodges branch in, say, Torquay, and a Greenwood's branch in say, Newcastle was the name on the facia. Much of the merchandise was the same and it was labelled with an 'HG' logo as our own brand. There were, however, some significant differences between Hodges in the south and Greenwood's in the north. Whilst the bespoke tailoring trade was, in fact, a slowly dying business, thanks to the constantly improving quality of ready-to-wear garments, a significant part of Hodges' sales still came from the bespoke business. Also, if anything, Hodges always had a slightly higher class of trade than Greenwood's. After all, the northern shops in the early years even had a significant business in working clothes – overalls, etc. That was now all history, but Greenwood's customers still included many whose first consideration was price.

Hodges window displays in the old days had been mixed, with a few shirts, ties, items of knitwear, hats and caps etc., among displays of suits, jackets, trousers and, of course, lengths of cloth to emphasise the availability of the bespoke service. Once under our control, displays became rather more specialised with one window full of clothing and the other full of outfitting.

When it came to advertising, again there was a difference between the two companies. In the north we did virtually no general advertising, though the opening of a new branch, or the reopening following a refit, would mean some use of the local press and also leaflet advertising.

Hodges, however, had a specially favourable situation. The Welsh TV area conveniently covered very many Hodges units and we therefore decided that some television advertising would be justifiable. We ran TV adverts for a year or two, but frankly I don't think they did us a great deal of good and hardly justified their cost but we had a few laughs in producing TV adverts. One advert featured a James Bond-like character with his clearly labelled Hodges clothes neatly packed in a special suitcase. That resulted in customers in several branches asking if they could have a gun with their suit.

I sent in a TV script myself which, naturally, I thought was very good but which the TV authorities rejected on grounds of taste. My script showed a well-dressed man driving an open sports car over a hump-backed bridge and, hearing a scream from the river below, he jumps from the car and looks over the bridge to see an attractive young lady apparently drowning. He rips off his Hodges jacket (label clearly shown), as she goes down for the first time. He pulls open his Hodges shirt (label noticeable!) as she goes down for the second time. He is about to dive in, still wearing shirt and trousers when a 'voice-over' reminds him Hodges clothes are really too good to spoil. He sadly picks up his jacket as she finally disappears.

I still think it would have been effective – however bad the taste!

Throughout the seventies, our trading policy was to try to edge the Greenwood's class of trade upwards with an increasing emphasis on clothing so that the per unit sales figure would increase. At Hodges the aim was to build a first class outfitting trade on the firm foundation of its clothing and tailoring business.

We were reasonably successful in these endeavours as the figures for, say, 1978 show. In that year, Group turnover was some £14 million, which would be the equivalent of £60–70 million today and pre-tax profits of £1.25 million then would be some £6 million in present terms.

We were showing these respectable trading profits after spending a lot of money on the refurbishing and re-equipping of the branches. During the 1970s, a standard shop front for both Greenwood's and Hodges – and also for the former Blackburns units as and when they were integrated into the northern and southern chains – was composed of blue pearl granite. A capital letter G or H in an illuminated square panel was fixed to the left side of the facia and the name Greenwoods or Hodges in a separate illuminated box sign to the right. This was a costly style of shop fitting, but we thought the price worth paying in our efforts to improve the class of trade, particularly of the Greenwood's branches.

Inside the shops we introduced what we called 'County Rooms'. This was simply the clothing and tailoring area of the shop. There would be a table and chairs, and a good quality carpet, as well as the usual hanging fixtures, and the walls would be decorated with shields – coats of arms – for all the counties in which we were represented.

As well as improving our premises, we tried hard to make improvements in staff affairs. We introduced a grade of assistant staff known as DSMs which stood for 'Deputy Shop Managers'. For an assistant – male or female – to achieve DSM status they had to pass an examination which tested their familiarity with our bookkeeping procedures, ensured they had the right basic knowledge for stock keeping and general branch upkeep and, finally, that they could manage some fairly basic display work. Those who passed received a pay rise, and it was clearly understood that it would be from the ranks of the DSMs that we would look first when seeking managers for the new branches which were steadily appearing, or to replace those managers we lost through retirement or other causes.

We also established the category of 'Senior Manager' who were the long serving men and, later a few ladies. Staff outings for these Senior Managers, such as trips from the north to Hodges tailoring factory in Swansea, became a regular feature.

Generally we had few staffing problems thanks, I suppose, to our policy of internal promotion wherever possible and also our policies regarding remuneration which were always very much on the basis of payment by results. This was achieved both by regular weekly commissions on the shop sales and also bonuses paid against the achievement of target figures. These arrangements together with the stocktaking bonus and spiff schemes which I mentioned earlier did mean that able and hard-working staff could achieve earnings which compared favourably with other menswear retailers.

My shopkeeping activities were not limited to the sale of menswear, since with the two small departmental stores, in Wigan and Leigh, I had to take an intelligent interest in all departments which they included. The most important of these was, of course, ladieswear but Lowes of Wigan also had a particularly good glass and china department. The store also boasted a large ladies' hairdressing operation and a restaurant, both of which I organised by letting the appropriate floor space within the store to a successful ladies' hairdresser and a local restaurateur.

As for ladieswear, I found that many of the principles of display, stock keeping and salesmanship were much the same as for menswear. I tried to have a smattering of the necessary knowledge of all aspects of the trade and thus sat in on a staff training session where we were lectured on the skill of bra fitting! Apparently then – and probably still – 60% or 70% of British women wear the wrong size, so accurate measurement, both round and below, is of critical importance.

It was one shopkeeping skill which I never had to perform and I must say I always approached the lingerie and corsetry departments with discretion, unlike the Wigan husband who, when accompanying his wife into the department, was seen by her to be leering lasciviously in the direction of the fitting rooms. Whereupon his wife, a Lancashire housewife – clearly of the kind with whom one did not trifle – slapped his face so hard that his false teeth shot out and flew some distance across the lingerie department!

Parallel to the expansion of Greenwood's in the north and Hodges in the south, Shop & Store Developments Ltd. had, of course, continued to grow. Back in 1965, changes to corporate taxation arrangements made it advantageous for our family to control all the shares in the company and we therefore made a public offer to buy back those shares that were in the hands of the general public. I think all the outside shareholders were reasonably satisfied with their investment since we paid rather more than the then market price for the shares which was quite a bit higher than the original flotation price.

I had been appointed Chairman of the company by that time, my father having decided he absolutely hated conducting the company's annual general meetings. After almost a lifetime as his own boss, he did not take kindly to shareholders' questions or, worse still, implied criticisms from the floor.

Reg Newiss's office was still providing most of the development opportunities on which we worked and although most of my time was spent 'shopkeeping' in the next ten years, amongst other deals and developments, we built a modest supermarket in Bradford, a pair of shops in Preston, a fine new office block with six shops below in Bury, a block of five shops in Beverley, a small supermarket and half a dozen shops in Baildon near Bradford, and another supermarket with adjoining shops in Kendal.

From 1968 Shop & Store was involved in the management and development of the Whittington Estate with its 1,200 acres of farms and forestry. In 1970 I bought The Shambles in Settle. This was a most interesting old property with six cottages perched on the top of six small shops and forming the focal point in the market place of this charming little Dales town.

I bought The Shambles primarily because it looked an awful mess. I used to drive past it frequently on my way to and from Whittington and the old building was painful to see since it was festooned with advertising signs, all six cottages were painted different colours as were the signs on the shops below. The cottage chimneys each had ugly TV aerials and altogether it cried out for better management. I learned that the property was unusual in other respects in as much as it was not a freehold but rather was held on the residue of a lease for no less than two thousand years.

I well recall reporting to my father after I had purchased it for a ludicrously small price.

'Oh, that's good,' he said when I told him of the modest figure involved. 'It is a freehold, of course?'

I replied, 'No, but it's a two thousand year lease.'

'Yes,' said Father, looking worried. 'But how much of the lease has gone?'

Keeping my face straight, I advised him that since some two hundred and fifty years of the lease had passed, we now had the anxious situation whereby our newly acquired leasehold interest had only one thousand seven hundred and fifty years still left!'

Three Shop & Store schemes in the early seventies were a supermarket with a multi-storey car park above it in Carlisle, Airedale House in Albion Street, Leeds – a seriously valuable office block with a large Barclays Bank and several shop units on the ground floor, and the Low Hall Restaurant in Horsforth near Leeds. I found myself as Chairman of Low Hall Restaurant Ltd. as a result of rather unusual circumstances.

My daughter, Patricia, after leaving school, had worked briefly for Shop & Store inspecting its various properties. She then decided to move to London which caused her mother and I some anxiety as she was still a teenager. To lessen that anxiety I found her an absolutely excellent flat almost opposite Harrods' front door.

After a spell as a society photographer's receptionist, she found herself an extremely interesting job in the wholesale diamond trade. When we went to see her at work I was very impressed at being admitted through a heavy steel door complete with a 'speak-easy' type spy hole and then to find my nineteen-year-old daughter sitting at a desk sorting out on a sheet of white paper what was probably a small fortune in diamonds.

During this phase of her young life we took Patricia with us on a trip to South Africa and in the course of the lengthy voyage, both there and back, she and one of the ship's catering officers struck up a mutual attraction. Since the affair continued after the voyage, I found myself contemplating the possibility that my daughter might end up marrying a fairly impecunious young man whose skills all lay in the catering or restaurant trade.

Quite coincidentally at that time a well-known West Yorkshire restaurateur – Kenneth Monkman – rang me to say he had found the site for what could be a splendid restaurant and would my company buy it, rebuild it and then lease it to him. Apart from the fact that this was quite a sensible proposition in economic terms I saw at once a way of ensuring that Tricia's boyfriend could have a worthwhile career in Yorkshire.

We formed a company – Low Hall Restaurant Ltd. – of which Kenneth Monkman had 49.5%, Tricia's young man was able to raise enough to take a similar 49.5% and I held 1% acting as Chairman and obviously having the deciding vote. Shop & Store did indeed acquire the old manor house, known as Low Hall, together with the derelict former manor house at the rear thereof. Very extensive rebuilding and renovation works resulted in a first class restaurant in the front part of the property, excellent kitchens and other facilities in the middle and two floors at the rear – either or both of which could be used for functions. With ample car parking in what had been the grounds to the old hall, Low Hall was for a number of years a very successful restaurant and functions venue benefiting from its semi-rural location almost equidistant from Leeds and Bradford.

I quite enjoyed setting up this operation and being involved right down to such details as selecting the cutlery but my efforts all came to nothing! Tricia fell out with her boy friend having met someone who was very much more attractive to her. Ken Monkman then bought out his youthful partner and I passed my 1% holding to him. Thereafter Low Hall was the Monkman family business for some years.

The man Tricia had met – now her husband of over thirty years' standing and the father of my two eldest granddaughters, Sophie and Emily – was Stewart Urry. At the time he and Tricia met and later married Stewart was, at a young age for such a position, a partner in

London-based accountants Binder Hamlyn & Co. Apart from his accountancy qualifications, Stewart was also a barrister. He specialised in tax law and particularly matters affecting family businesses and family estates – family fortunes, if you like. As a keen sportsman to boot, he was most clearly the sort of son-in-law that an over-involved Yorkshire businessman would very happily welcome into the family.

Thus it was that Stewart and Tricia's wedding in October 1974 was a high point in Enid's life and mine.

Whittington was a superb venue for a wedding. A marquee on the croquet lawn supplemented the large reception rooms in the Hall itself. The weather was a golden October day and Whittington village's church was only a pleasing stroll away along what was known as 'the lady's walk'. It is gratifying for the father of a bride to be able to reflect many years later that of all the weddings I have ever attended I think my daughter's was the best.

Stewart and Tricia's first home was in the Holland Park area of London and later they moved to a splendid country house not far from Guildford in Surrey.

By the mid-seventies, our son, David, had left Woodhouse Grove School where, despite the handicap of being the son of the Chairman of Governors, he had done well, ending as Deputy Head Boy. His ambition was for a spell in the Army and he had set his mind on joining the Coldstream Guards. Probably because he had heard my mother often speaking about that regiment in which her brother had served. David duly gave up the opportunity of going to university and attempted the officer selection course at Pirbright, which he passed. However, he later failed the Regular Commission Board and then chose to join the family business.

Until Father's death in 1971 we had been very much a family business. The Directors of Greenwood's were initially simply Father and Mother. Then at a later stage my brother and I were made Directors and Father's younger brother, Harold, joined the board. As previously mentioned Sales Manager George Eley had 'risen from the ranks' to be Sales Director and in the late sixties Barry Tyldsley had risen from his position as Property Manager to a directorship of Shop & Store.

The managing directorship of the Hodges subsidiary in South Wales and the south west had been in the hands of E.P. (Phil) Clayton ever since we acquired the company. Since the tailoring factory in Swansea was such an important part of the Hodges' business we had realised at the outset that we must find someone to join the local directors who would remain with us after we bought the company and effectively run Hodges on our behalf.

Phil Clayton was the logical man for the job since he, too, was a former pupil of Woodhouse Grove and a personal friend of both my brother and me having for a number of years, been a stalwart in our lacrosse team. More importantly for the post at Hodges, he had many years' experience in clothing manufacture.

After Father's death and with what was by now a substantial group of companies, some reorganisation at the top was necessary. We, therefore, set up a Group Board which initially consisted of Phil Clayton, George Eley, my brother and me. Later Barry Tyldsley (Managing Director of Shop & Store) and Stephen Rawson, Denis's son-in-law, the Group Accountant joined us.

CHAPTER 16

Through Sadness and Sickness to Ducal Splendour

TOWARDS THE END OF 1967 my father came into my office to ask, 'Are you doing anything really important today?' Whilst there was always plenty to do I had nothing particularly pressing so I was able to answer, 'No.'

'Right,' said he. 'I want you to come with me. I'm going to show you my house.'

Naturally this puzzled me since I knew his main house, Briaden intimately, having spent most of my youth therein. I was also quite familiar with the handsome bungalow on the cliffs between Morecambe and Heysham which was a favourite retreat for both Mother and Father.

When I asked for clarification he explained, 'No, I don't mean those. I've seen a house that I'm going to buy and I want you to have a look at it.'

With my curiosity aroused, we set off in my car for the small village of Whittington which is just beyond Kirkby Lonsdale on what you might call the back road to Morecambe. We drove up the road behind Whittington Hall and stopped the car. There before me was the house which Father apparently coveted. By any standards Whittington Hall is a large and imposing country mansion but the side view from which you could see the staff cottages and other outbuildings at the rear made it look enormous.

'What do you think of that?' said Father. 'If that's ever on the market, I'm going to buy it.'

My opinion was short and plain. 'You must be barmy!'

Apparently Father had been using the back road to Morecambe and, when driving past the south lodge of Whittington Hall he had decided to be cheeky enough to sneak up the front drive and have a good look at it. Snarling dogs from the Home Farm half way up the front drive had forced him to beat a hasty retreat but he had seen enough to have decided that this was something he really wanted.

I was happy to go along with this fantasy that perhaps some day the place would be for sale and, we could then think seriously about buying it, but I certainly did not anticipate such a development in the near future. In fact, within a few months of Father showing me his ideal home, the entire Whittington Estate was on the market! There had been a death in the family of the owners and the impact of estate duty (as inheritance tax was then known) was such that the family had to sell. The vendors were in fact the second family to have lived at Whittington Hall which had been built in the early 1830s by Thomas Greene, MP, whose family had lived there until 1925 when death duties had resulted in a sale to the Haworth family who were prosperous and prominent figures in the West Yorkshire textile industry.

The Haworths had put the sale in the hands of John H. Raby & Son, Bradford estate agents, which was perhaps rather a surprising choice since one would normally have expected one of the leading London agencies such as Savills to deal with such a property. However, Rabys were to sell it and an auction date of 1 May 1968 had been fixed.

For the first time in his life Father was ready to do something really rash. At this stage of his life he liked me to do most of the negotiating in any significant property transaction and his suggestion to me was simple.

'Go see the agents. Find out how much they'll take to sell it before the auction and do a deal with them.'

I spoke with the agents and learned that there was no possibility of a pre-auction sale. Their instructions were clear. The property would be sold by auction at the Royal Hotel, Kirkby Lonsdale, on 1 May at 3 p.m.

We had time to look around the whole estate which, apart from the Hall and grounds, the two lodges and three staff cottages, included four farms, woodlands, a handsome detached house in the village and also a block of three flats. The whole estate covered almost twelve hundred acres. The estate and particularly the Hall itself were not in very good condition and it was clear that, apart from the purchase price, a lot of money would have to be spent on the property.

Father's plan was simple. He would buy the whole lot and then break up the estate and, in his own words, 'Be left with the Hall for nothing.'

Fortunately by this time I had learned a little about land values and agricultural property generally thanks to my own farm at Hutton Hill and I therefore suggested an alternative plan. My proposal was that if we could buy the whole estate Shop & Store could end up owning all the farms, woodlands and let property etc. and leave Father simply with the ownership of the Hall, staff cottages and lodges. He was entirely happy with that, given only the clear understanding that managing the estate would be down to me.

When you read in a moment or two how little we had to pay for this fine property, do please remember two things. First, inflation had not really taken off and in subsequent years, particularly quite recently, there has been a massive increase in the demand for country estates. If Whittington were to be sold today it would fetch the thick end of £10 million, maybe even more. Secondly, it should be remembered that we were very fortunate in that there was no really keen competition bidding against us and we bought at the lowest possible price as you will now learn.

The sale of a country estate in a local hotel was bound to attract a lot of attention and the dining room of the Royal Hotel was packed on the day of the auction. Father and I had decided we would happily pay up to £160,000 and would probably have gone further if we'd had to (doesn't that sound a trifling sum in today's money!).

Having answered a few pre-auction questions the auctioneer suggested that bidding might start at, say, £200,000. No such bid was forthcoming so he invited his audience to, 'Start where you like'. Then the bids rattled in. Seventy thousand. Eighty thousand . . . ninety thousand. One hundred thousand . . . up to one hundred and thirty thousand before my father had even had the opportunity to put up his hand. 'One hundred and forty thousand,' someone called. And then from across the room, 'One hundred and fifty thousand'.

'Now we're beginning to get somewhere,' the auctioneer said. 'Who'll give me a hundred and sixty?' Silence.

At this meaningful pause in the bidding, I nudged Father and said, 'Try him with a hundred and fifty-five.' Father called this out.

'All right,' said the auctioneer. 'I'll take five thousands. Now, who'll say one hundred and sixty?' There was complete silence. Desperately the auctioneer tried to coax more bids. None came and he was forced into a lengthy discussion with the vendor's solicitors.

At its end of the discussion, the auctioneer announced that the property was, 'In the market'. This very important phrase means that the bidding had reached a level at which the auctioneer was empowered to sell the estate as a whole without recourse to splitting it into separate lots and it was also a formal confirmation that there was no question of any withdrawal from sale. It would have been normal for a renewed burst of bidding to follow such an announcement and it was clear that the auctioneer expected this. Despite his repeated efforts he was to be disappointed and he invited bids at only £1,000 intervals. No one answered his plea for a bid of one hundred and fifty-six thousand.

So with obvious reluctance, it was, 'Going once . . . going twice . . . and sold,' as the hammer descended.

And so, for a consideration of only £155,000 Whittington Hall and its estate had changed hands. By a happy coincidence our one and only bid had clearly been at the reserve price level, i.e. the lowest level acceptable to the vendors for the estate as a whole. Father was delighted to sign the formal contract and pay the 10% deposit.

A *Yorkshire Post* reporter had been sent to cover the proceedings and he asked Father, 'Would you mind telling me why you've bought the property, Mr Greenwood?'

Father's reply was typical of his ready wit. 'I've always fancied a country cottage.'

It was Father's intention to make Whittington Hall his permanent home but Mother was having none of that. Under no circumstances was she prepared to leave Briaden. Nor was she willing to give up the bungalow in Morecambe and therefore Father's joke ended up with a ring of truth. Whittington Hall was destined to be no more than a weekend or occasional retreat.

A great deal of work had to be done and before this could begin – completion of the sale was set for the end of August 1968 – Father was taken seriously ill. He, Denis and I were travelling to Belfast on the overnight ferry from Heysham to meet our principal clothing suppliers. When we saw him the following morning, although he was up and dressed, he looked ill but bravely told us he had had a bad bout of indigestion during the night. We did not believe him and summoned a doctor who immediately pronounced that he had suffered a coronary thrombosis. He spent several weeks in a Belfast hospital and then went to his Morecambe bungalow to convalesce.

Father's illness changed our plans for Whittington Hall. We now decided the whole estate would be owned, managed and maintained by Shop & Store Ltd. who would, therefore, meet the heavy costs of renovation with the intention that in the future Father, Denis and I would all make occasional use of the Hall. With a struggle, most of the repairs and necessary works were completed in time for Father's sixty-eighth birthday on 12 January 1969.

Father made a good recovery from his coronary but obviously his days of deep involvement in the business were over. In fact, he was happy spending much of his time overseeing the final works and the refurbishing of Whittington Hall. My mother had no intention of living there permanently but she, too, spent quite a bit of time there organising things, including recruiting domestic staff, so that by August 1969 the Hall was a splendid venue for a family party to celebrate the twenty-first birthday of Denise Rawson, Father's eldest grandchild.

We were sorry to lose Grandfather Willie Greenwood who died in 1970 aged ninety-two, after more than forty years of retirement. You may recall that Grandfather, too, had suffered a coronary. In his case it was probably deserved as the story told back on page 11 indicates.

Willie had not only a very long but also a very happy retirement. He and Grandma were reconciled and they lived comfortably until her death with Grandfather devoting his time to his garden, following Yorkshire cricket, and making full use of the full-size billiards table in his large house at Daisy Hill, and then moving to a smaller bungalow a mile or two away. It was probably the only bungalow in Bradford with a full-size billiards room incorporated. Grandfather was a sad sight as a widower but at least he had a good housekeeper, May, to look after him.

I had an amusing incident a year or so after Grandmother had gone when I walked into the bar of the Stansfield Arms to meet some of my lacrosse-playing pals. Tom Whitfield and Tom Horsfall were at the bar looking depressed. I asked them what were their problems. Tom Horsfall said sadly, 'My daughter is pregnant.' This was obviously poor news as she was a single girl.

Tom Whitfield said, 'That's nothing. Cynthia's pregnant.' Cynthia, Tom's wife, had just informed him that they were to have a much-belated addition to their family. They already had a boy and a girl, both teenagers, and now there was a surprise package on the way.

I said, 'I can top that. My grandfather has just got married.'

Willie had, in fact, married his housekeeper without his family knowing anything about it until the deed was done. The older generation – my father and his two brothers – were shocked that their aged father – he was in his mid-eighties – had taken such a step. My generation of the family members thought the old man had done the sensible thing. May took even better care of him as his wife than she had as his housekeeper. She was a sensible woman in her sixties and the result of their belated matrimony was that Grandfather had a comfortable extreme old age.

Sadly it was not long after Grandfather's death that we learned that Father was suffering from an inoperable cancer which he fought with characteristic courage. He had plenty to occupy his mind during the last months of his life. He remained keenly interested in the progress of the business to which he had contributed so much. His three homes, Briaden, Whittington Hall, and the bungalow at Morecambe, continued to give him pleasure. He had taken up a further interest in the form of Daisy Hill Methodist Chapel. The Greenwood family had been associated with this chapel since it was first built in the middle of the previous century. Moses Greenwood had contributed towards it and had laid a foundation stone. Willie Greenwood had been a regular attender and so had my father during his boyhood. When Father learned that the chapel was to be closed and the building pulled down his reaction was characteristic. He bought the fine old building, then modernised and renovated the interior and did the same with the nearby Sunday school. That was used first as a youth club, complete with discotheque, dance floor, loud speakers, and special lighting etc., but later it became a meeting place for the elderly of the district.

As for the chapel itself, this re-opened in May 1970 to provide a weekly 'Songs of Praise' service similar to the well-known television programme. Guest speakers, musicians, choirs and brass bands were all persuaded to appear there for a simple service consisting mainly of popular hymns together with a short Bible reading and prayers. 'Songs of Praise' at Daisy Hill Chapel remained a part of the life of that part of Bradford for the next two decades.

Around the turn of the year Father's health deteriorated rapidly. Mother, who had been an operating theatre nurse during the war, and was most certainly a very competent woman, refused to have him go into hospital for his last days. Instead she cared for him at Briaden where he died on 9 January 1971, three days short of his seventieth birthday.

We published a special edition of the house magazine which we produced bi-monthly for the staff in the main companies making up the Greenwood Group at that time – Greenwoods (Menswear) Ltd., Hodges Menswear Ltd., James Lowe (Wigan) Ltd., Shop & Store Developments Ltd., and Wm. Blackburn & Company Ltd. (the latter being a recent acquisition). That edition of the company magazine, *Contact*, as Father had named it when it began life as a duplicated staff circular in pre-war days, charted Father's life briefly from his birth in the rooms over the family shop at Westgate, Bradford, to the end of his days and included a list of the branches and properties.

At the time of Father's death, there were 181 Greenwood's branches. The Hodges chain in South Wales and the south-west had been expanded to fifty-eight shops and the recently acquired Blackburn business added a further twenty. So Father had seen the family business grow from one modest shop in Bradford to 259 well-equipped units as far apart as Newcastle and Torquay. In addition were the departmental store operations – Lowes of Wigan and Danbys of Leigh. Alongside these retail operations was the Hodges clothing factory in Swansea and, more importantly, the ever-lengthening Shop & Store Developments Ltd. property portfolio. In early 1971 Shop & Store had some 350 tenants, mostly retailers, but including numerous office lettings and, of course, the agricultural holdings at Whittington.

It is surely undeniable that the 'smart boy' who had begun as a shop assistant in 1917, earning 12s 6d. (62½p) per week had come a long, long way.

Father's death meant many changes. I had been acting as Chairman of Shop & Store ever since he decided that the chairmanship of a p.l.c. was not his forte and I had, of course, retained that chairmanship when we took the company back into our private hands in 1964. When we acquired Hodges, we agreed that Denis would be Chairman of that company but Father retained chairmanship of the parent company until his death. Afterwards, my brother and I had no difficulty in deciding that we should be Joint Chairmen and Co-Managing Directors of Greenwood's. For a number of years this arrangement worked quite well – not least because Denis remained primarily interested in the merchandising side of the business whilst my interest was in sales and property.

For two years after Father's death I was particularly busy. Adding new branches to both Greenwood's in the north and Hodges in the south meant an awful lot of driving. As had been the case for many years, I was clocking up around 40,000 miles a year, mostly on business, but with frequent visits to Whittington where a lot was happening.

I was there most weekends. We negotiated vacant possession of one of the farms and ran High House Farm 'in hand'. Indeed I established a small company – Greenwood Farms Ltd. – for that operation. We were employing a full-time forester who was steadily improving the woods and with the aid of the veteran gamekeeper, Fred Boughen, who we had inherited with the estate, I had begun to develop a first-class pheasant shoot. In the winter months regular shooting parties and a house full of guests were beginning to be a feature of life at Whittington and my invitations to different shooting friends inevitably led to an increasing number of invitations for me to shoot with them.

As if all this activity were not enough I was heavily involved with the chairmanship of the Board of Governors of Woodhouse Grove School. Furthermore, since July 1969, I had been serving as a magistrate on the Otley Bench which was a significant diary commitment. I enjoyed my work as a JP and think I made a useful contribution.

In the early seventies the Otley Bench had quite a reputation for firmness. I remember one occasion when the Chairman asked me to change my rota dates and sit with him at a special court held with the intention of dealing firmly with Otley's weekly problem – drunk and disorderly behaviour on Market Day. These, of course, were the days when licensing hours were strictly upheld but there was a special dispensation for Market Day in Otley and the pubs were open all day long. The result was that some pretty rough elements from Leeds, Bradford, or wherever, were attracted to the town and 'D & D', as the offence was usually known, was a serious problem.

The police decided on that particular Market Day that every drunk behaving in a disorderly manner would be arrested and our special court was waiting for them. All the defendants who were hauled up before us either pleaded guilty or there was adequate evidence to convict them and the Chairman and I spent the day handing out the maximum fine which the law would permit. We grew increasingly frustrated with the fact that the worst offenders could not be hit a little harder. However, our chance came.

One man had been arrested for – to put it politely – spending a penny on a grave in the Parish Churchyard. The Clerk of the Court happily advised us that in those circumstances some ancient ecclesiastical law, or ruling, came into effect and we were free to impose a heavy fine. We did so with alacrity. I should think the offender thought for a long time afterwards that that was the most expensive penny he had ever spent!

I recall another case from those interesting days sitting as a magistrate.

A most respectable-looking man was before us charged with indecently exposing himself to a little girl. He denied the accusation vehemently and it boiled down to the fact that it was going to be his word against what the child told us. The problem was that she would not say anything. The elderly Chairman, a grandfather I should think, tackled the situation admirably. First he cleared the court of all save those who had to be there. Then he invited the little girl to come and sit up on the Bench between him and me. Then, speaking softly, he asked the little girl if she had seen the man before and she nodded her head. 'Was it in the woods on the Chevin?' he asked referring to a wooded area just outside the town. She nodded again.

'Did he show you something which surprised you?' Again she nodded. Now came the crunch question. 'What was it?' asked the Chairman. There was no reply.

I pointed to the pad on which I had been making notes. The Chairman understood. 'If you don't want to say it, will you write it down for us?' The child nodded.

We gave her a pad and a pencil and the chairman said, 'Just write down what it was he showed you.'

The little girl wrote, 'His peanuts.'

At that we immediately found him guilty and could ask if there were any previous convictions – he had a string of them for similar offences.

That case had me wondering then, and I still wonder, if denying the court any knowledge of previous convictions until after a verdict is truly the best way of achieving justice.

In the early seventies there was a major planning debate as to whether the Leeds/Bradford Airport should be extended. Some of us took the view that the airport, situated at Yeadon on the outskirts of Leeds, was just not an appropriate site for what would sooner or later become a major airport. A group known as LACAN (Leeds and Bradford Association for the Control of Aircraft Noise) was the main objector to the airport extension plans. I attended one of their meetings and before it was over I found myself Chairman of the association and leading a campaign which pressed for a major airport to be built near the motorway network on low grade land known as Thorne Waste. We also argued vehemently that if Manchester Airport was to become a major international operation then extensive development of Leeds/Bradford was more an exercise in civic pride than a sensible use of public funds.

The LACAN struggle inevitably added a lot more dates to my already crowded diary.

The planning battle over the runway extension at Yeadon – as the Leeds/Bradford Airport was locally known – was hard fought. It culminated in a public enquiry held in Guiseley Town Hall. I was mildly amused to learn that the Airport Authorities' expert witnesses etc. had anticipated that the hearing would be all over in a day. In fact it took several days of hard argument before the enquiry was concluded.

There was, of course, much local interest in the matter and I even found myself appearing in front of the television cameras arguing the case against extending Yeadon. It was not a very happy moment since the TV crew decided to film me standing on the tarmac outside the then fairly modest terminal buildings and all the people in the background were airport staff who were far from pleased to hear me advocating a replacement airport at a different location.

In the event the decision went against us and the airport runway was duly extended. I am quite unrepentant in my view that this was a mistake and I believe it is the case that for years Leeds/Bradford topped the list of airports listed for the most aircraft diversions due to bad weather. The site on Yeadon Moor is often fog bound. The airport still lacks convenient motorway access and to my mind proves the point that airport development in Britain has always been a haphazard matter. There should have been a carefully considered national plan half a century ago which would probably have ensured that all major airports were both close to the coast (to avoid aircraft noise and danger of accidents over densely populated areas) and also tied in to the motorway network. However, that's all history now.

The pressure of all my various activities finally caught up with me. On Saturday 24 March 1973 I was refereeing a school lacrosse match at Woodhouse Grove when I felt distinctly unwell. I drove home and lay on the settee feeling even worse. I got upstairs and into bed and then suffered all the classic symptoms of a coronary thrombosis – pain right across the chest, pain in the forearms, sweaty forehead, etc. Enid summoned the doctor who took one look and immediately summoned the ambulance and I found myself en route to Bradford Royal Infirmary where there was a whole large ward devoted to coronary cases.

I recall lying in my hospital bed the following day and watching with grim fascination the monitor screen standing on the table over my bed.

There were the peaks and troughs generated by my heart beats and I could not help thinking that, if that line began to flatten out, it would be the last thing I would ever see.

One of the doctors spoke to me and I remember the conversation clearly. 'You smoke cigarettes, don't you?'

'Yes, doctor,' I replied.

'You realise that's one of the principal reasons why you've suffered a heart attack?'

'Yes, doctor.'

'Are you going to give up smoking?'

'Yes, doctor.'

And I have never touched a cigarette since that day.

That heart ward was laid out in the old fashioned manner – a line of beds down each side and a wide central aisle. Halfway down the ward was a cross-aisle. The beds on each side at the top of the ward were for those who had just been wheeled in or were in poor condition. Indeed, some of the occupants of the beds near me when I was in that section died there, which certainly concentrated the mind. However if, after a few days, it seemed you were on the road to recovery, you were moved down the ward below the cross-aisle and you could reasonably hope that was the start of the road to recovery.

I passed some of my time in that recovery section by conducting a quiz around the entire ward to find out how many of my fellow patients were cigarette smokers. The result was 100% – everyone in that ward, and they were men of all ages, sizes and backgrounds, had suffered a coronary. The one thing we all had in common was that we were cigarette smokers. That was enough to convince me totally and for ever that cigarette smoking is a major contributory factor in heart disease.

Another factor in my case possibly lay in the fact that for the previous three Februarys I had taken a long, very enjoyable and quite restful break in South Africa, travelling each way on the splendid Union Castle liners. But in 1973 I decided I was too busy to accompany my mother, who had been in the habit of spending February in South Africa for quite a number of years, voyaging on the *Pendennis Castle*. Instead I had had a particularly busy and stressful time which may have been the trigger to my attack.

The misery I was feeling as a forty-five-year-old who thought his active life was over was made much worse when my mother on her return from South Africa came to see me in hospital.

She walked up the ward towards my bed looking tanned and healthy, sat down on the chair at my bedside and said, 'Oh, Brian, I do feel tired.' She slid off the chair and collapsed on the floor.

The nurses took her into a side ward and she died shortly thereafter. My recovery had not progressed far enough for me to be able to go to her funeral – a grim business.

I got home and began convalescence. I sought advice from several different specialists and doctors and because my recovery seemed smooth and uneventful, and in the absence of all the modern technology now used in coronary care, I thought that I had suffered only a mild heart attack. In fact, I was told quite recently by the cardiologist with whom I have regular check ups that if, back in 1973, ultra-sound scans had been available and he or anyone else had had the opportunity then to look closely at my heart, they would have rated my chances of survival as thirty in a thousand – i.e. only a 3% chance. I don't think I would have enjoyed being told that, although it might have prevented me taking the too-relaxed view that I took of my state of health. So much so that I started shooting again and a strenuous day shooting with friends in Swaledale in the autumn of that year provoked a second but thankfully milder heart attack.

I dropped some of my commitments, including retiring from the Otley Bench and coaching and playing lacrosse. I tried to cut down on business commitments and made a special point of taking a rest in the middle of every day.

It was not a happy time. Anyone who has ever suffered a coronary – or who is close to someone who has – will know that the slightest pain in your chest brings a moment of fear that another attack, possibly fatal, is on its way. Any general feeling of illness starts the mind imagining the worst. I learned one or two valuable tips which helped me and might be helpful to you, or people you know, who have coronary anxieties. For example, if you have a pain in your chest, and you can put your hand on it, it is almost certainly *not* the first sign of a heart attack. Only if the pain is over a wider area, or indeed across the whole chest, should you start seeking medical help.

Another tip was to look in the mirror and see if the lobes of your ears remain pink. Apparently if your circulation is failing that is one of the first visible signs. If you do feel you are on the verge of a coronary, have a large stiff whisky, not brandy which is a stimulant – but whisky, which apparently helps to dilate the arteries. Whether or not it does dilate the arteries, a stiff whisky – or two or three – will indubitably relax you and make you feel better!

After a few months I was back at work but was taking great care to do nothing strenuous. I continued to have a rest in the middle of each day and avoided stressful situations. I suppose I was behaving like an old man and I was certainly far from happy. Then came a turning point.

I was told there was a particularly good cardiologist practising in Liverpool and I arranged an appointment with him at his consulting rooms not far from St George's Cathedral. He examined me carefully and thoroughly and then delivered his 'verdict', which amazed me.

He said, 'You're too fat. You need more exercise and stop feeling sorry for yourself.'

He explained in more detail that I needed to lose a few pounds in weight which would be no particular problem since I really was not fat, just a little overweight. As regards exercise, he recommended that I began a graded exercise programme. He told me to buy a Penguin book which explained what was apparently the Canadian Air Force air crew exercise programme. He went on to tell me to amend my drinking habits so that henceforward I would only drink whisky and wine, preferably red wine – I have never found taking that advice to be a hardship!

I bought the Penguin book, *Physical Fitness*, which sets out the 5BX Exercise Programme. You start at the lowest level and have a week or two thereon before moving up a grade, continuing to progress up the grades until you reach the amount of exercise appropriate for a person of your age. At first you need to do the exercises every day but in due course, when you have reached the level for your age, one serious exercise session per week will enable you to maintain that level of fitness.

I followed the programme fully and within twelve months had just about reached my level. Certainly by the time I hit age fifty, I could comfortably manage the exercises for that age which – if this is not too boring for you – consisted of:

- Exercise 1 – stretch up and touch the ground between your feet twenty times
- Exercise 2 – lie flat on the floor and sit up fifteen times
- Exercise 3 – lying on stomach lift head and shoulders and also legs and feet twenty-one times

- Exercise 4 – do fourteen full press ups
- Exercise 5 – running on the spot, 425 paces, i.e. count one each time left foot hits the floor. Also, after each seventy-five such runs, do ten astride or 'star' jumps

All the above are to be completed in eleven minutes. Unfortunately, the 5BX programme stops at age sixty so, for the last twenty years, I have gradually reduced the exercises shown above and settle now for fifteen of exercise 1, twelve of exercise 2, fifteen of exercise 3, twelve of exercise 4, and 350 of exercise 5.

I do sincerely believe that graduated exercise programme changed my life. The cardiologist also recommended me to go back to playing tennis, which I still do, and taking whatever other exercise – within reason – I might fancy. For example, from my mid-sixties onwards I have played a lot of enjoyable albeit low quality golf. I continued my fishing and shooting pastimes although I did give up deerstalking once I had had the pleasure of a day's stalking in the company of both my son and grandson in my seventy-seventh year.

I have gone on a bit about recovering from a coronary condition since I hope there will be quite a number of people who will read these words and find them an encouragement or a comfort if they have ever suffered a heart problem or are frightened of one.

My recovery, thanks to all the above exercises, which I also back up with a daily arm-swing and stretching routine, has certainly been well worth the effort.

I did even have a final fling at lacrosse when someone organised a veterans' match for former members of the Old Grovians' team to play one of our regular opponents from the old days – the Heaton Mersey Club from Lancashire – in 1979.

Fate was kind to me that day. I had taken a small bottle of whisky to revive myself in case I pushed myself a bit too far, together with the Glyceryl Trinitrate spray which I have always carried for the last thirty-five years. I didn't need either. I look at a photograph of that match, hanging on the wall of my study, and captioned, 'One of the Last', which has caught me just about to shoot one of the five goals I scored on that day. Grovians' Veterans beat Heaton Mersey 11–9 and the Lancashire club did me the honour after the match of making me a life member. They suggested I should start playing regularly again but for once I had more sense. That was a remarkable day. I felt I was as fit as anyone of my age (fifty-one) at that point but there was no point in pushing my luck and thereafter I have been more than content with all the other sports mentioned above. Of course, I still take care of myself and I remember the excellent advice that the Liverpool specialist gave me.

Regular check-ups become a part of your life once you have suffered a life-threatening illness or attack.

For some twenty plus years the regular attention of our family doctor, Dr David Fieldhouse, and the particular skills of cardiac specialist, Dr Paul Silverton, have served me very well.

I did have one other particularly interesting medical experience in 1997 when Dr Silverton decided that I should have two doses of the angioplasty treatment which, as you may know, is a sort of arterial 'flue-cleaning'. Through an incision in your groin a long flexible wire travels up into the arteries around your heart and widens out the narrowed sections with – I think – a tiny balloon. I had four arteries apparently needing such attention and went to the Sheffield Hospital for the first session which was a bit of a non-event. There was discomfort and anxiety, as I lay there, wideawake, watching on a TV monitor the wires travelling up into the arteries around my heart. But it was soon over. The plan was that I was to go back a week or so later and they did forewarn me that the next session would be more difficult – it most certainly was!

The Sheffield Hospital had a unit devoted to angioplasty and once again I found myself lying on the operating table therein. Confidence was not greatly enhanced when you saw that all along one wall of that operating theatre were dozens of the wires in varying lengths from which, in due course, one would be selected to reach your heart. Indeed, in the dim light there was something of the atmosphere of a torture chamber!

They set to work as they had done previously with the Sheffield professor in charge. I had known it was going to be difficult since the plan was to insert stents into arteries at the site of my 1973 damage. A stent is, incidentally, a small wire mesh tube which when put in the right position will hold the artery walls permanently wider. They had put one stent in position but were having real difficulties with the second. Try as they might they could not manoeuvre the long wire from my groin to my heart into the right position.

Time passed. I think they had been working on me for the best part of an hour when things went very wrong.

They had put a drip into my arm, presumably to keep my blood pressure up, and I knew I was in real trouble when I heard the person who was monitoring my blood pressure tell the professor that it was falling steeply.

'Squeeze the bag, nurse!' came the instruction – so I supposed the drip became a squirt.

I was now feeling all the pain of a heart attack and indeed I was suffering one. Later the professor told me there was much scar tissue in the area where they were trying to fit that stent and some of this tissue had been dislodged and had blocked an artery, thus producing a coronary thrombosis.

In the next few seconds I learned exactly what it feels like to die. I knew we were into a desperately dangerous situation when I heard someone say, 'We'll need electricity,' and someone ran off to fetch one of those electrical contraptions which can – sometimes – awaken the dead by giving an inert heart an electric shock.

What does it feel like to be very close to death? I felt as if the room was shrinking around me and I had a feeling of being in a vortex or a downward spiral. I spoke to them with what could have been my last words. Happily we were able to laugh about them afterwards.

'I'm sorry, but I think I'm going,' I said. At least I was being courteous to what seemed to me to be the end!

Thankfully I suddenly began to feel a little better. I heard them say my blood pressure was rising and I knew I was going to survive.

They wheeled me into the intensive care unit and a little later the professor came to speak with me. He explained that I had started with four arteries all of which had needed angioplasty. They had treated three of them, which were now much improved, but their attempts on the fourth had totally failed. It was his view – and time proved him right – that the improvements in the three would more than compensate for failure with the fourth.

Nevertheless, I had suffered a third coronary which did not exactly please me since I had read somewhere that the third is usually fatal. Obviously I had to go through the convalescence and recovery period just as had been the case twenty-four years previously with my first attack.

After just a couple of nights in the Sheffield intensive care unit it was decided to move me to the Yorkshire Clinic at Bingley which should have been no problem. As it was, some fool – I never troubled to make detailed enquiries – arranged for my transfer from Sheffield to Bingley to be, not horizontal in an ambulance, but sitting in the back of a glorified Transit van as it bumped and rattled its way, making one stop en route over the thirty or forty mile journey. I survived the journey but when my own doctor and the staff at the clinic learned how I had been conveyed only forty-eight hours after a heart attack they were furious and there were some questions asked.

In any event I managed the convalescence and recovery pretty well and as the professor had predicted I definitely felt better with three fully functioning arteries than I had been before the treatment. Since then, touch wood, there has been no recurrence.

To complete these medical passages so that we can get back into something like a proper chronology with the rest of the story I will simply mention that in the last decade two shoulder operations following falls have been my only serious medical events.

I must not give the impression that in recent years I have been a stumbling old man. The first of the falls was the result of tripping over a stone trough whilst heaving on a garden hose-pipe. The other, a couple of years later, was a slip on a wet tennis court when I was trying too hard to reach a drop shot.

I headed this chapter 'Through Sorrow and Sadness to Ducal Splendour'. You may well wonder where the ducal splendour came in.

It did not all come with a rush and, before I was enjoying a lifestyle which probably compared favourably with that of some dukes, lots of other things had to happen. See the next chapter for example. However, I did reach a plateau which included having three homes of which Whittington Hall and its 1,500 acre estate was perhaps the most significant, and not far from there we leased no fewer than three grouse moors in the beautiful Trough of Bowland.

The other two homes were a splendid house in northern Scotland, close to the River Oykel – of which we owned a share – on the edge of our 17,500 acre Invercassley Estate.

My third home was The Mews, an aptly named flat adjoining my then business headquarters, Burley House, Burley-in-Wharfedale, a most handsome listed Georgian building.

I ran seven cars which were a Rolls, a Jaguar XJS, a Range Rover, a hot BMW for Enid, an elderly Land Rover which we still have and regard as part of the family, together with two small cars, one for the housekeeper at Whittington and another for the housekeeper/caretaker in Scotland.

I had about a dozen personal staff consisting of a Scottish lady, a daily help at The Mews flat and then, at Whittington, a housekeeper, a cook, two daily cleaners (wives of estate workers), two gardeners, two gamekeepers and a forester/handyman, and finally a company chauffeur to look after the above mentioned cars and very occasionally drive us.

We travelled first class on our foreign travels, used Concorde for a number of US trips and lived, altogether I think, sufficiently 'high on the hog' to justify the 'ducal splendour' tag. I have to say it was all very nice while it lasted but as you will discover if you have the patience to read to the end of this book it did, as they say, like 'all good things come to an end'!

CHAPTER 17

Lune Valley Life

THE PART OF MY LIFE spent at Whittington deserves, I think, a full chapter since it was full of activity and interest. Ownership of a country mansion and its attendant estate involves both particular pleasures and sometimes onerous obligations!

The pleasures include wonderful facilities for parties, especially those involving shooting, fishing and other country sports, as well as the satisfaction to be gained from planting woods, laying roads, creating a lake, changing a river and all the other improvements I was able to make to the Whittington Estate. I shall describe some of those activities shortly.

On the other hand, there were indeed some onerous obligations, we frequently had to arrange visits for various groups who were interested in the Hall's architecture or the conduct of the Estate. It was understood that we would support all the local charities and were an obvious venue for coffee mornings etc.

I took a very serious interest in Whittington, so much so that when the Ministry of Agriculture approached me in 1977 to see if the Estate could be the subject of an intensive survey, by a variety of experts in everything from forestry to wildlife. I happily agreed and thus some twenty experts in such fields as nature conservation, landscape, country sports, ornithology etc., etc. spent months producing a detailed report under the heading – 'Conservation and Rural Estate Management'.

A local historian – Major B.M. Copeland was invited to write the historical notes for this report. At the same time I was trying to keep an estate diary covering all the changes on which we were working. I decided to turn over that task to Major Copeland and suggested that he write some introductory notes covering the history of the property. His first rough notes were sufficiently impressive for me to decide that, rather than simply produce a few paragraphs as the introduction to an estate diary he should instead be commissioned to write a book which I would publish privately. Thus in 1981 '*Whittington, the story of a country estate*' was published by our company Shop and Store Developments Ltd. who were the freeholders of the estate. The book was printed by W.S. Maney & Son Ltd. of Leeds whose principal was a fellow old boy of Woodhouse Grove School and which firm had a well deserved reputation for extremely high quality print work. Suffice it to say that a fair number of copies were sold through book shops in the north-west and it was – and is – regarded as a useful piece of social history.

As the years passed I had been able to extend the estate size by some 300 acres through the purchase of adjoining pieces of pasture land and also to improve its sporting potential by a series of purchases of stretches of the river Lune. In the early days at Whittington our only access to that fine river was on to a 400 yards stretch of the north bank which we leased from the North family's adjoining Newton estate. I first acquired the freehold of that stretch and then with the series of purchases ended up with nearly a mile of double bank salmon and sea trout fishing with some fifteen named pools in the stretch.

Readers who know a bit about fishing will be interested to read that most of the water which I purchased was flat and uninteresting. To create salmon lies I constructed a series of V shaped groynes which had the effect of accelerating the flow in the centre of the river and thus quite quickly channelling out a deeper stretch which provided suitable places for salmon to pause on their journey upstream.

One word of warning, if any reader ever contemplates doing something similar on another river, beware of back-eddies! The accelerated water flow produces these and the result can be massive river bank erosion for quite a long distance downstream from the groyne. We had that problem on the Lune and it cost a lot to replace and reinforce the banks.

During my time at Whittington the best of the salmon fishing had passed. The Lune did very well in the 1960s but by the 1970s and 1980s there was no run of spring fish but there was certainly a worthwhile late run in the early autumn and we were able to take around thirty salmon in a season at that time. The figure could have been higher if the river had been more intensively fished. Usually the only rod on the water was your author at a weekend, sometimes accompanied by a friend.

Sea trout fishing on the Lune was good, with over 150 being taken in a season when I let the weekday fishing to a syndicate, one of whom took a sea trout of over 14 lbs. from our stretch.

The salmon and sea trout ran up the small feeder streams to spawn. One of these streams ran through the middle of the park in front of the Hall and up a stone weir which adjoined one of the woodland paths around the Hall. It was a very pleasing sight to see salmon and sea trout struggling up this obstacle.

Studying this little stream – known as Newton Beck set me thinking about the possibility of creating a lake in the fifty or so acres of parkland to the south of the Hall. Creating a lake of some three acres was a very interesting project. Digging it out and removing the surplus soil is simple enough but the clever touches come in remembering to preserve a piece of the area so as to produce an island refuge for wild fowl in the middle of the lake. Also, a thoughtful lake designer will take care that the lake has varying depths as well as shallows around the edges. The end result of such care will be a lake with which fish are very happy and which wild fowl will use. We were successful in both respects and after a year to two it was a joy to see a pair of wild swans nesting and rearing their young on the island and, to have an excellent fishery only a short walk from the Hall's front door.

There was one particularly interesting feature about the lake. The land where it was sited sloped gently down in the direction of the Lune. Consequently at both ends of the lake, that is, where Newton Beck flowed in and also where it flowed out there needed to be a step several feet high. Such a step would have made it impossible for salmon and sea trout to get up it and therefore with the aid of a Victorian encyclopaedia, which was the only place I could find any advice on the construction of salmon ladders, I designed and built three stone-masonry lined 'pots' at each end of the lake. The Victorian encyclopaedia had indicated the necessary depth for each such pot to enable the fish to jump from it up a foot or two into the next one and from the third into the lake itself. Similarly their route beyond the lake was via a stone-lined pot ladder.

Happily it worked like a charm and fish were able – as they had no doubt done for centuries – to swim up Newton Beck to find spawning grounds but in doing so to swim through or rest within my lake.

The park lake was not the only still-water fishery on the Whittington Estate. On the high ground known as Docker Moor was an old quarry from which most of the stone for the house had come. Over the years this had filled with water and had become a very deep pool occupied by a handful of hungry brown trout. This was obviously an ideal location to be stocked with rainbow trout and every year I would buy 200 lbs. weight of fish and restock the quarry. The trick in stocking a fishing pool is not to purchase, say, 200 fish all of 1 lb. weight but to have your supplier provide fish of all sizes including some 'biggies' of 3 or 4 lbs. This ensured that when you hooked a fish it might be anything from a recently stocked small fish weighing less than 1 lb. up to a 'biggy' which had thrived and was pushing 10 lbs. in weight. This personal and very private fishery afforded me much joy and many were the evenings when I would chug in the old Land Rover up the concrete roads which I had laid all over the estate, to Docker Moor for a quiet evening's fishing, usually with a floating fly or if that failed, something fished just below the surface and moved in such a way as to attract the rainbows cruising in the deep water.

The quarry gave me the chance to teach all my grandchildren how to fish. Incidentally, let me observe there are few gifts a grandfather can give grandchildren better than an interest in fishing and other sports.

A visit to the quarry was part of the tour of the estate that I would give to any visiting friends. I particularly remember one such occasion when my guests were Christopher Hibbert, the author and historian, together with his wife and a solicitor friend of mine Godfrey Whitelock and his wife.

As we drove up to the quarry I explained to the four visitors that my fish in the quarry were very unusual in as much as I had taught them all to appreciate music. As you will imagine the suggestion was treated with scepticism and derision. Godfrey Whitelock was a fly fisherman and I had told him to bring a rod with him. When we reached the quarry, it was flat calm and on a bright sunny day not a fish was showing. I selected a fishing fly from his fly box told him to put it on and then stand on a large rock at the side of the pool. I then lined up the other three beside him, instructed Godfrey to aerialise his line (that simply means wave it about backwards and forwards in the air) and then told the three to start to sing.

Somewhat embarrassed and probably thinking their host was crazy they told me they didn't know what to sing. I assured them that the fish would react to music and that anything sung loud enough would do the trick. Therefore, they must all sing 'God Save the Queen' as loudly at they could. Hesitantly at first but louder with my urging the trio began to sing lustily.

'Now!' I shouted to Godfrey and he let his fly drop on to the surface of the water. Immediately up came a good-sized rainbow trout which grabbed the fly and then tore off across the quarry. A minute or two later I was able to net it out, knock it on the head and then note their reactions. There was shock, amazement and disbelief in that order. Chris Hibbert summed up the visitors' feelings when he said, 'I don't know anything about fishing but I don't believe that's anything to do with music. Is it something to do with sonic vibrations?'

I continued the tour of the estate and let them meditate on the mystery for some little time before finally revealing the truth. The fact was that at that particular point I frequently fed the rainbow trout in the quarry with floating fish pellets and they had come to appreciate that a figure standing on the rock probably meant that lunch was on the way. The fly I selected was the same colour and as close as I could get in general appearance to a fish-feed pellet. Thus I'd hoped that the instant the fly hit the surface a greedy fish would want to be first in for lunch and I was lucky enough that the ploy worked first time.

Incidentally you may think the story proves that rainbow trout are easy to catch. Not so! Elsewhere in the quarry you might have fished all afternoon with 'nary a knock'.

With the lake, the quarry, two other ponds and a mile of the River Lune there was never any shortage of fishing and in due course, after I had carried out a number of improvements, the Whittington Estate provided excellent shooting for my family, my Yorkshire friends and my Lune Valley neighbours. When we first bought the estate Fred Boughen, the elderly gamekeeper, was rearing only 250 pheasants in the old-fashioned manner, that is using broody hens to hatch and mother the pheasant eggs and resultant chicks. Virtually all the shooting was confined to the Big Wood – some seventy acres of mature woodland in the middle of the estate – together with some duck flighting on a modest pond and some of the rougher ground.

Twenty years later the Big Wood had been extended, several small plantations had been placed at strategic locations, the duck pond had been materially enlarged – with explosives! Another pond had been created by damming a small stream. We had an extremely efficient and modern pheasant rearing operation producing some 6,500 birds for release all over the estate and thus providing no less than eighteen different drives of which I would select six for a typical day's pheasant shooting.

For the first half of my time at Whittington all the shoots were strictly private, I would usually invite six friends to join my son and me to make up a party of eight guns. Frequently wives would accompany them and the shooting on the Saturday would be preceded by dinner at the Hall on the Friday evening.

For most of the twenty-five years when I ran the shoot my key man was gamekeeper Sid Watts who had joined me at first as general handyman, but later developed into an excellent and much respected keeper. Watts always organised an excellent team of beaters, usually numbering about sixteen and which included all kinds of people ranging from a senior police officer to lads from the village, together with the Estate staff. These comprised an assistant keeper, forester/handyman, two gardeners and the young man Ken Armer who I had originally engaged to run the 'in-hand' farm nearest to the Hall and who later took a tenancy thereof. We would usually have three or four drives in the morning with the last of them close to the Hall so that we could go straight in to the gun room which contained a bar and a table which could seat as many as eighteen, for an excellent shooters' lunch. Then we would go out for two or at the most three drives in the afternoon.

Later in the seasons as the days grew shorter we would, as shooting men say − 'shoot through' − that is to say we would not stop for lunch but would instead take a break for coffee, sloe gin and soup or snacks in the old shooting bothy which stood up on Docker Moor close to the quarry. The bothy was a typical piece of Victoriana − simply a small stone building with two doors and a dividing wall thus permitting the gentlemen to be kept separate from the beaters. I had the dividing wall removed and extended the bothy so as to provide a w.c. and wash-hand basin. The keeper's wife would go up there in the morning and light two log fires which made it a warm and welcoming place on a cold or wet shooting day.

Until the 1984/85 season everyone who shot at Whittington was there as my guest and as the shoot developed this became increasingly expensive. I therefore decided that we would let one or two days each season and thus generate a little more income to add to the receipts from the sale of game. I used to sell the pheasants we had shot at first to a restaurant in Yorkshire and later to a game dealer.

Even with two or three let days, running the shoot was a very expensive hobby costing in total over £50,000 per annum by the end of the 1980s. By that time we were shooting over 3,000 pheasants from eight family shoots, together with two or three let days and the keeper's day making twelve full days per season. My son David and his wife Judith usually acted as host and hostess on the let days, pretty well all of which went smoothly and happily and to the visitors' satisfaction. As a consequence of inviting so many guests to our family days I found myself regularly receiving reciprocal invitations to shoot all over the place.

Regrettably, I didn't get anything like as much grouse shooting as I wished. I think every shooting man would agree that shooting driven grouse is indeed la crème de la crème. So much so that nowadays teams of guns cheerfully pay around £160 or more, per brace for grouse shooting.

Most of my grouse shooting was with a syndicate on the Langbar and Denton Moors near Ilkley and at Fleensop high up Coverdale, one of the smaller Yorkshire Dales. However, shortly before the end of my time in the Lune Valley, son David succeeded in negotiating leases of no fewer than three grouse moors which were only a fairly short drive away from Whittington, in the beautiful Trough of Bowland.

Part of the pleasure of being invited as a shooting guest to a variety of difference places, lies in the fact that you meet all sorts of interesting people. I recall, for example, shooting at Barbon with what seemed to be a significant part of the House of Lords. Lord Charlie Shuttleworth was the host but fellow guests included the Duke of Westminster, the Earl of Stafford and Lord Zouche. I spent most of the day on the next peg to Stafford who was an absolutely superb shot and on his form that day the best pheasant shot I have ever seen – and over the years I have seen some very good ones. In company like that the pleasure and interest in meeting people from outside your normal circle can be marred by the inevitable anxiety that you will at least shoot reasonably competently.

I shall never forget the first time I was a guest at Barbon, when on the very first drive we lined out well below a hill top wood from which the birds were to be driven. Before the drive had really begun a single cock pheasant rose from the back of the wood and climbed higher and higher into a clear blue sky. To my horror I realised it was flying absolutely straight towards me and in a second or two would be passing high over my head. I mounted my gun, swung through it remembering the old adage – 'bum – belly – beak' i.e. start at the back of the bird and keep swinging through it and because of its really serious height kept on swinging well in front of it before squeezing the trigger. Down he came with a resounding thump some sixty yards behind me and on the strength of that one – probably lucky – shot I immediately had a reputation amongst my fellow guests as a very good shot.

The opposite can be true also. On one occasion I was shooting at Stockeld Park and was at number one, that is the right-hand end of the line of guns, when they tried a new drive from a belt of trees adjoining the park in front of the Hall. The drive did not go as planned and the majority of birds headed off across the park in my direction, rather than to the centre of the line. Some forty yards to my right stood a fine park tree and the pheasants appeared to make that their aiming point and flew in a steady stream over the top of it, which of course meant that I had pheasant after pheasant passing me at extreme range on my right-hand side. The result was that for ten or fifteen minutes the rest of the team of guns stood and watched me going bang, bang miss – bang, bang, miss until I was almost ankle deep in cartridge cases. One or two birds came a little closer but as far as the observers – especially those a long way away could see the number one gun had fired some fifty or sixty shots for some two or three birds and he must therefore be a very poor performer indeed.

Shooting is not all about skill and certainly not all about statistics. There is room for plenty of laughter given only that the golden rule – safety is paramount – is always remembered. Here are a few lighter moments – I remember when the late Noel Stockdale, former Chairman of Asda, who was a member of the Langbar grouse shoot was granted a knighthood. When next he turned up to shoot with us on the moor and began to walk across the heather towards the butt which had been allocated to him, he was impressed to find that a lengthy red carpet led him to it!

Then there was the occasion when my family bought for my sixtieth birthday a walking stick gun which was in fact a .410 shot gun inside a most handsome snakeskin cover, together with a suitably inscribed gold band. The rest of the team clearly thought I had 'flipped my lid' when I walked on to the moor twiddling this walking stick, much as Charlie Chaplin used to twiddle his stick in the ancient movies and informed them that the grouse on this moor were so easy, I proposed to simply knock them down with my stick as they flew past!

Once I was in my butt I surreptitiously slipped a cartridge into the walking stick and was then lucky enough to have a small covey of grouse come straight at me. Up went the stick – bang! and down came a bird.

Early in my shooting career I had a night duck flighting with my old friend Dick Atkinson. The elderly gamekeeper who we had 'inherited' with the Estate came out with us to assist with the pick up. It was a good evening flight and the wild duck kept coming and Dick and I kept banging away at them with only modest success. Boughen was not shooting although he had his gun with him in order to dispatch any

54. *Whittington. The view from the Shelter Belt. Outfield farm is on the right, the Hall is lost in the trees to the far left. The distant hill is Ingleborough.*

55. The Drawing Room. Whittington Hall

56. The Swimming Pool

57. Burley House, Burley-in-Wharfedale, West Yorkshire

58. My office at Burley House

59. The Mews, Burley House

60. 'Tricia and Stewart's 1973 wedding

61. David and Judith's wedding in 1981

62. *Woodhouse Grove School from the South. The Sports Hall on the right*

63. Woodhouse Grove south front

64. The W.G.S. 'Greenwood Building' formerly the Business Management School. This building, opened by the Rt. Hon. Michael Heseltine MP in November 1988, together with the squash courts behind it, was a major part of the improvements carried out during David Miller's Headship

65. The entrance to the 'Davy Music and Performing Arts Centre'. Opened 2009

66. The Fforestfach, Swansea Headquarters of Dunn & Co

67. Part of Dunn's 75,000 sq. ft warehouse and offices

68. Regent Street, London branch

69. Regent Street, London. Lower level sales floor

70. Bristol, The Horsefair branch

71. Birmingham, New Street

wounded birds if necessary, at the end of the flight. He was of the generation when it was certainly not a keeper's place to shoot with his employer. I called across the pond to him – 'join in Mr Boughen, feel free to shoot whenever you wish'. The flight was coming to an end but a pair of mallard appeared high over the pond 'bang'! went Boughen's gun and down fell both birds stone dead. That was in fact the only shot he fired since evening flight then came to an end. As we picked up I said to him, 'That was a good shot Mr Boughen. You don't often get two high duck with one shot.'

'Arrh,' said the old villain, 'you must remember Mr Greenwood when I were a lad money was very tight and my old father taught me, always get two or even three with one shot, you just have to wait 'till one's above the other then shoot them both.'

In my naivety I was enormously impressed. Here was an old man who had been trained as a boy to achieve regularly, what happened only very rarely to ordinary shooting men and when it did it was simply a fluke. For a year or more I deluded myself that my old gamekeeper was an extraordinary marksman and as I told visitors to the shoot about him, he happily basked in the warm glow of their admiration. That was until the day when we were a gun short and I insisted that he join in one of our pheasant shoots and take a peg beside me. He was no super-shot just an ordinarily competent performer but also a very convincing liar!

The social life in the Lune Valley was delightfully old-fashioned. Whilst sometimes an invitation to dinner would be verbal, it was usually written, dress was almost always black tie and courteous letters of thanks invariably reached host and hostess shortly afterwards.

Our immediate neighbours on the west side were the Norths of Newton Estate and on our eastern side George and Judy Gray occupied a fine old property known as Sellet Hall. On the other side of Kirkby Lonsdale was Charlie Shuttleworth's seat Leck Hall. Further downstream in the valley was Horace Spencer at Storrs Hall which was a somewhat smaller version of Whittington, having been designed by the same architect, George Webster of Kendall. Across the valley in Thurland Castle lived Judy Von Rugemeer and her husband Karl. With the Fairhursts of Arkholme, the Boddys a little further on and several others, we had quite a circle of friends and acquaintances with similar tastes and responsibilities. Sadly our nearest neighbour Richard North of Newton died at a comparatively early age, but a few years later his widow Sue remarried and she and her husband Tim Kimber were our good friends. Incidentally it makes country living very much more enjoyable if you are on good terms with your neighbours and I am happy to record that in my time relations between the Whittington Estate and the Newton Estate were always excellent. Sue Kimber and I were the two Church Wardens for Whittington's fine old church which was only a brief stroll along the 'ladies' walk' from Whittington Hall.

Horace Spencer at Storrs Hall was a man I greatly admired and would like to emulate. The first time I visited him and we were having a drink together he asked me, 'Tell me, where do you buy your whisky'? This seemed to me a peculiar question, since the honest answer would have been the local wine and spirit merchants or sometimes one of Threshers' wine shops or sometimes from a supermarket. However, Horace assumed that like him I bought whisky by the barrel straight from the distillery and that stashed away in my cellars there were various barrels to which one could descend jug in hand at regular intervals. I am afraid I never did get round to laying down malt whisky by the barrel.

I did, however, have the pleasant experience of giving the local wine and spirit merchant the best day in his business life. Kirkby Lonsdale, only two miles away from Whittington, was and is a fine little town and amongst its numerous interesting shops was the long established wine and spirit merchant – Plato Harrison. The then incumbent was not Plato Harrison himself who I assume had founded the business but rather a descendant named George. Nevertheless, everyone in the district referred to him as Plato. Not long after we had moved into Whittington I went in to see him and began the discussion by saying – 'Mr Harrison I have come to make your day.'

'How is that Mr Greenwood?' he replied.

'I am here to buy a cellar,' was my answer.

I explained to him that I anticipated doing a lot of entertaining at Whittington and it was logical for me to establish a full cellar with an appropriate range of wines as well as a stock of spirits and liqueurs. We had a most interesting series of conversations and some tasting sessions whilst we compiled a list covering all kinds of fine wines. In due course Plato delivered all the many cases to the Hall. Rather than keep them in the rather damp and gloomy cellars below the house, I had decided that the game larder, a north-facing tiled room adjoining the gun room would be the ideal place to keep wine and had it lined with wine racks. After

Plato had delivered my 'cellar' he also delivered his bill which let's just say, was quite a significant sum and felt more like a property purchase than a bill for consumables. In any event it proved to be very good value. For the next twenty years visitors to Whittington drank well and in fact only recently did I – sadly – finish the last 1982 claret that was a part of that transaction.

The people across the valley at Thurland Castle were an interesting couple and I shall certainly not forget our first visit there. Together with neighbours George and Judy Gray we had been invited to Thurland which is an enormous place, now split up into several apartments. On opening the castle door you were faced with a large portrait of Kaiser Wilhelm. Clearly Karl Von Rugemeer (although I think from Minnesota) was proud of his German ancestry but some of the very old people in the valley e.g. Horace Spencer felt the same about a picture of 'Kaiser Bill' as in recent days we might have thought if someone had Adolf Hitler's portrait hanging by their front door.

Once inside Thurland evidence of Karl and Judy's rather unusual relationship was immediately clear. Judy was – so I was informed – a seriously wealthy heiress, with one side of her family's money coming from the Hoover business and the other from ownership of the *New York Times* and possibly other newspaper interests. Apparently Judy had always coveted an English castle and her first husband had not disappointed her by buying Thurland then in a poor state of repair. Judy brought over Karl Von Rugemeer who was apparently a highly respected interior designer. Before very long she had divorced her first husband and married Karl.

Karl had had a free run at Thurland and some of the changes he had brought about were quite remarkable. For example, the sitting room was decorated in only two colours – black and white for everything in it. The dining room which was a very big room, was illuminated for dinner, only by an enormous chandelier. When I say chandelier I mean chandelier in as much as it had dozens and I mean dozens of flickering candles. In the gloom at the far end of the room on a large dresser two or three rows of gold plates reflected the candlelight.

The ballroom was even more surprising with its ornate fittings and furniture and one wondered where on earth Karl had obtained such items, to which the answer was he had purchased them from MGM Studios and most of the items came from the set of *Ben Hur*. All of which is to say that the social life in the Lune Valley included some interesting people and places.

Not far away from Thurland on the other side of the valley was Gresgarth Hall the home of Mark and Arabella Lennox-Boyd. Mark was our local MP and also served as Margaret Thatcher's PPS. I was an enthusiastic Conservative supporter, then and now including for example one general election where rather than simply signing a large cheque for the party's funds, I rang up Central Office and asked them for a list of the most marginal constituencies in the land. Armed with that list I contacted a dozen of those local associations, all of whom required a computer (which was in those days a seriously costly item) for their membership records etc. To the surprise and pleasure of all those constituency chairmen I had my business pay for one in each constituency.

We frequently helped the Tory party with functions at Whittington to help the local association's fund raising and at Mark's suggestion arranged several dinner parties during the period that the annual Conservative conference was being held, not so far away, in Blackpool. Consequently we had the interesting company on different occasions of Douglas Hurd, the then Foreign Secretary and his wife, Norman Lamont, the then Financial Secretary and also Chris Patten and his wife.

The most interesting bit of political hosting came very shortly after Margaret Thatcher had been deposed. Mark Lennox-Boyd rang me to ask if I would host a function for her. She was going to stay for a day or two with him and he thought that a reception full of her committed supporters might cheer her up at that obviously very low point in her political life. I readily agreed albeit unaware at that point of the security implications of a visit from the IRA's number one target.

The local police chief rang me to say that his men needed to make a thorough inspection of the Hall, access routes and the grounds. That was no particular problem but then twenty-four hours before Mrs Thatcher's visit a police bus rolled up and disgorged a team of professional searchers. Their leader explained to me that they would not be carrying out their most thorough search – which involved taking up floor boards, removing panelling etc. but nevertheless he and his men needed to carry out a 'level two' search. Enid and I were about to go into Kirkby Lonsdale for a pub lunch, so I told them to get on with it but first I hid a large key in the inside pocket of one of the many garments hanging in the Hall's cloakroom. I told the chief searcher that I would know how thorough his men had been since there was a hidden key that they might or might not find.

When we returned from Kirkby Lonsdale the head searcher not only waggled under my nose, the key I had hidden but also produced two others which we had lost! All of which is to say that his team and the sniffer dogs that accompanied them had thoroughly searched the forty or so rooms that Whittington Hall contained.

The policeman told me that their sniffer dogs had been very active in front of a locked cupboard in my study and he wondered why this should be so. I was as puzzled as he until I opened the cupboard and there at the back of the shelf was a small sealed box containing some .22 blank cartridges which I used for gun-dog training. It was incredible to me that their dog had so fine a nose for explosives that it had scented these through a half inch thick door and a cardboard box.

Suffice it to say, the police were extraordinarily thorough. After searching the house they left one or two constables on guard duty around the house until the function was over. One of them got the shock of his life. The gardener at Whittington regularly used to set the old fashioned Victorian alarm guns. These were not fire-arms but rather a simple spring-loaded plunger with a split pin through it, into which you could put a twelve bore blank cartridge. Nylon could then be threaded amongst trees and bushes for a considerable distance and if anyone walked into the virtually invisible nylon line, it pulled out the split pin and bang went the alarm gun. Their purpose, of course, was to deter people from poaching pheasants.

Apparently, that particular policeman was on his radio to the central control in Lancaster and had just reported in to say – 'I'm just checking the gardens at the back of Whittington Hall' when 'bang!' and he went off the air having fallen over with surprise at what he naturally first thought was a shot at him. I gather that when he picked himself up and spoke again to the central control to tell them that – 'I seem to have detonated some sort of alarm'; he was only just in time to stop them dispatching an armed force!

The evening reception for Mrs Thatcher proved to be a great success. The large drawing-room was full of local Conservative supporters, all looking forward to meeting the former Prime Minister. Mrs T. swept in and then 'worked the room' with all the skill of a thoroughly able politician. She spoke to everyone and although the conversations were inevitably brief I think everyone there had the feeling that they had enjoyed a serious conversation with her. We drank her health in champagne and the time came for her to speak to us all. We moved into the hall from which rose a fine oak staircase and I suggested to her that she might care to speak from a few steps up the stairs, which she duly did. As always she spoke well but on this occasion with an inevitable tinge of sadness. I particularly remember her pausing to look around the room before remarking – 'This is a very fine house, it reminds me of Chequers – I wish I were there!'

My reward for hosting this event came the following evening when Enid and I went across the valley to the Lennox-Boyds' home for a small dinner party. I recall that apart from Mrs T. the other guests included newspaper magnate Conrad Black and his wife. I enjoyed lengthy conversations with the great lady, both before and during dinner. I was seated beside her at the dinner table and oddly enough we found ourselves in a deep and serious conversation about – of all places – Kazakhstan. I was not surprised at her depth of knowledge of the peripheral parts of the Soviet Empire then in its breaking-up stage but I suspect she was mildly surprised to find a north country business-man with a keen interest in such matters.

Other social gatherings in the Lune Valley included a most enjoyable evening at Horace Spencer's home Storrs Hall. Although in his nineties he still cut an elegant figure in a velvet smoking jacket, cigarette in a Noel Coward-style holder and a seriously brown looking whisky and soda in the other hand. I thought then and still do, that if I could be like that in my nineties it would do very well indeed! Actually Horace did not last long after that happy evening but the manner of his going is worth telling. He was apparently fishing for salmon in Scotland with some younger companions. During the morning his companions thought that Horace did not look very well so they persuaded him to return to the hotel and summoned the local doctor. He examined Horace and told him that clearly he had just suffered a heart attack, to which Horace replied – 'Does that mean I can't fish this afternoon?' The doctor's advice was that he should have several days of rest and convalescence etc. etc. Horace's response was that he would compromise with him and take the afternoon off and then resume fishing in the morning. I believe that is just what he did but in fact he died a few days later – not a bad way to go!

Another important part of Lune Valley life was the use of the land adjoining the river for point-to-point races. Part of the course was over our land and we regularly sponsored one of the races. Besides providing the usual modest cash prizes we put up a handsome silver salver engraved with an illustration of Whittington Hall and appropriate phrases. Hopefully that trophy continues to be presented to the winner of one of the Whittington point-to-point races.

As many readers will know a feature of point-to-point meetings, apart from the quite serious gambling which goes on via both the tote and numerous bookies, is the car back or car boot partying. At Whittington the high ground overlooking the racecourse was always filled with cars, particularly 4 × 4s and just about every vehicle would be well stocked with food and drink. Since all this was happening immediately outside our front gates, I didn't have to hold back from the hospitality offered by numerous friends and acquaintances from their car-borne supplies. So much so that on one occasion with senses mildly dulled I stopped to look at the display of Jaguar cars which formed part of the commercial presence and marquees beside the course. A gleaming pale blue XJS two seater coupé with its massive V12 engine was irresistible and I bought it on the spot.

It was not really a suitable car for a man in his sixties but in fact I very much enjoyed driving it – probably trying to recapture lost youth I suppose – so much so that when I had clocked up a fair mileage on it I bought an identical replacement and thus for quite a number of years a lot of my motoring both business and pleasure was in that very fast machine.

I did have one poor experience with the car when driving up to the far north of Scotland for fishing, I was going up the A9 beyond Aviemore at a fair speed. It was our custom then to break our journey with a roadside picnic during which I would enjoy a whisky and water with my sandwiches and then let Enid drive for forty or fifty miles before I completed the journey. On that particular day we were rolling along nicely, the sun was shining, the traffic was light and I was enjoying driving. 'Let's not bother to stop,' I said, 'just feed me my sandwiches as we're going,' which Enid duly did. She also fed me my whisky and water. I had seen signs along the road advising 'unmarked police cars operate in this area' but frankly didn't really believe them. Only when I glanced in my mirror and saw the radiator grille of a blue Vauxhall behind me suddenly begin to flash with blue lights did I realise that the signs most certainly told the truth. My problem was that I was driving with a whisky glass in my left hand and Enid was just enjoying a glass of sherry. I hastily thrust the glass at Enid. One or the other of the drinks was immediately spilled as the unmarked police car overtook me and flashed the stop sign in his rear window. We put down both windows of the car as one of Scotland's finest approached and enquired, 'What sort of a speed do you think you were doing?'

I told him that we were doing about the same speed as all the other cars, since on that particular stretch of the A9 virtually every vehicle that passed was exceeding the speed limit. It was a sixty mph stretch immediately after a dual carriageway section where seventy mph was permissible and where − let's face it − just about everyone on the long journey towards Inverness would have been travelling at more than that.

'Why did you pick on me?' I enquired sadly.

'Just consider yourself unlucky,' was the reply. 'Now just come and sit in our car'. When I had done so he was able to show me on his miniature radar screen that I had been doing around eighty (as of course had everyone else) and I simply agreed that it was 'a fair cop'. Only when he produced the breathalyser did I become alarmed. I had never been breathalysed before (nor have I since, touch wood!) but it seemed to me that at that moment time was of the essence so I played for it. I had the officer explain just how the breathalyser worked and he confirmed that when the green light came on that told him that there was a genuine reading. If there was alcohol in my breath then the yellow light would be illuminated. When I asked what would happen if the red light came on, his answer was swift − he was getting rather impatient by this time − 'We tak you to Inverness and put you in the cells'. With fear and trepidation I blew into the contraption, on came the green light, on came the yellow light then to my great relief and to the officer's very obvious extreme disappointment the red light did not so he sadly observed, 'Well we'll just have to book you for the speeding then'.

Shooting days in the pheasant season were the high spots in my Lune Valley life. Looking into the Estate game books, which I kept with care and accuracy, helps me to describe a typical day's shooting there.

On one day in the early 1990s, I see that there were six of us shooting. My five guests were Norman Tebbit who, towards the end of his more active political life, had become a keen and very competent shot, together with four well known north-country sportsmen, Martin Vallance, Tom Barnes, Duncan Marsden and Ted Palm. The six of us on that day shot 267 pheasants, a brace of partridge and the odd woodcock for a total bag of 270 head. We fired between us 636 cartridges, thus producing a kill to cartridge ratio of 2.35 which is a quite acceptable outcome in the

Whittington conditions. Most of the shooting was from woodland rides and you had to be quick as well as accurate to nail the birds.

I see that on that day we had 149 in the bag when we adjourned to the Victorian bothy on the high ground for coffee and sloe gin whilst the beaters took a break. The ladies would usually join us in the bothy and be spectators for the later drives. Sometimes – as on that particular occasion – they would be actively involved as dog-handlers and the game book tells me that on that particular day Joan Marsden and Pip Valance were very good pickers-up.

One of the best drives at Whittington sometimes followed the coffee break. I would deliberately slow things down and give the keeper time to accumulate a large number of pheasants in the plantation which we named 'the shelter belt' and alongside which we always planted an area of game crop. On those occasions the guns would drive down from the bothy and take up their pegs on ground around 150 feet lower down the hillside. The result was that pheasants flushed from the shelter belt would pour over the line of guns at just about the maximum shootable height. Sometimes the keeper was able to contrive such a weight of birds in the shelter belt drive, that as they fanned out one looked up at perhaps 200 pheasants flying over the entire line of guns with as many as eight men shooting simultaneously. The quality of the drive is easily illustrated when I turn the page in the estate game book and see that when we had eight estate agents shooting as my son-in-law Stewart's guests, they fired 197 cartridges between them on that one drive, for only thirty-four birds picked i.e. a kills to cartridge ratio of almost six bangs per bird.

I suppose that of all the good times I enjoyed at Whittington, if I could have only one again it would be as one of the guns on the shelter belt drive when it went really well with every successful shot feeling something of a triumph and the dead birds falling way behind us, into and even over the big wood. Then of course I would want to end the day, as we always did, with a merry shooting lunch in the gun room back at the hall.

Whilst we lived at Whittington, I carried out a number of minor improvements to the Hall, including designing a stained-glass window beside the rear staircase, which replicated the view from the Hall towards that well-known north-country hill – Ingleborough.

Shortly before the onset of major business problems I did, however, carry out one major improvement. I designed and had built a superb indoor swimming pool, together with changing rooms and a lounge area at the pool side. A feature of the pool was that on two sides the water therein ran right up to the walls which were tiled with hand-painted tiles depicting banks of reeds, wild fowl and a view across the park, again featuring Ingleborough in the distance. The effect was really most impressive and I suppose that one of the things that I do miss about leaving the Hall was the pleasure of swimming in that particularly attractive pool.

Incidentally, my Victorian predecessor had designated the site I chose for a swimming pool to be his private chapel. His plans for that were for a most handsome design but, of course, I was glad that he had never executed them since the days for private chapels in country mansions are surely long gone.

I must not close this chapter on Lune Valley life without mentioning what came to be known amongst my friends as 'Brian's Edwardian Weeks' or as I called them 'Whittington Weeks'. I decided that once a year we would have a house party lasting about a week, when we really would live in the grand manner, much as would have been the case in Victorian and Edwardian days. I would invite six or eight guests to stay with us for a week in October when there were salmon to be caught in the Lune, an early day at pheasants was practicable and grouse shooting in the Trough of Bowland was also available. I would supplement the Whittington staff by engaging an additional cook of Cordon Bleu capability and we would therefore eat extremely well.

Each day would begin with a traditional English breakfast with the dining-room sideboard laden with bacon, eggs, grilled kidneys, sausages etc. etc. After which the men in the party would go out, either shooting or fishing. Besides the pheasants and grouse we would always have one day of competitive clay pigeon shooting.

The ladies in the party would usually take two or three days to drive out into the Lake District or visit local museums etc. etc. In the evenings we would, of course, all dress for dinner which was a lengthy and enjoyable affair before the men disappeared into the billiards room and the ladies into the drawing-room. Altogether we did in fact live like the Edwardians in a country house party.

To lighten the burden of hosting such days, I established the principle of having a 'lady and gentleman of the day', for which role my guests took turns. The lady of the day oversaw morning coffee and afternoon tea as well as luncheon and dinner. The man of the day's particular duties were to ensure that a generous supply of wines and other drinks were available at the appropriate times. For their day on duty the wine cellar was open for their choice not mine. These Whittington weeks were thoroughly enjoyable or at least the house guests and my neighbours who sometimes supplemented the house party all seemed to think so. There is certainly something to be said for an occasional throw-back to old-fashioned ways.

When catastrophic business problems meant that I had to sell the Whittington Estate and leave the Lune Valley as you will shortly read, it was with a mixture of feelings. We had most certainly very much enjoyed the many years spent there but we could see that as we grew older the problems and responsibilities of a country estate would begin to outweigh the advantages. Let's just conclude this chapter by saying our Lune Valley life was very good while it lasted.

CHAPTER 18

How Fare the Family Fortunes?

BEFORE THINKING OF FACTS and figures regarding the business, perhaps I should at this point explain just who are the family involved in this story.

Apart from Enid and myself as I have already mentioned, for most of my business life I worked in close partnership with my brother Denis. His wife Marjorie like Enid was never directly involved in business affairs other than, I suppose, as a beneficiary of our efforts.

I have already mentioned my daughter Tricia's marriage to Stewart Urry, which in due time produced my first granddaughter Sophie, who was born in July 1978 followed by her sister Emily four years later.

My son David was also very fortunate in his partner. He married Judith in September 1981 and she very quickly became a close and much loved part of my family.

The family list was not completed until the late 1980s when David and Judith had their first child, my third granddaughter Elizabeth, who was born in November 1986 and then the final name on my family register appeared in August 1988 when David and Judith had their second child, my grandson Edward.

In the late 1970s, the family fortunes were faring so well that I came up with a grand plan to add even more pleasure to our then quite happy existence. I decided that our property company – Shop & Store Developments Ltd. should purchase some overseas properties in locations which would be a pleasure to visit. Top of my mental list was the United States and after some quite serious thought I concluded – I think rightly – that Florida was the place to aim for. Obviously property interests in Florida would mean regular opportunities for visits to its sunny shores at the company's expense. Preliminary visits/holidays convinced me that there were three particularly suitable locations in Florida.

My interest was – inevitably I suppose – in retail property about which in terms of British locations I could reasonably claim to be knowledgeable. However, I soon learned enough about the American retail scene to realise just how fluid it was. In the first case, the concept of long leases did not apply. In those days in Britain twenty-one year leases originally without even seven yearly rent reviews were the norm. In the US a ten-year lease would have been thought of as quite a long one, with five, three or even one year terms frequently being arranged. Furthermore, the problem with US locations compared to those in the UK was the ever-continuing sprawl of shopping locations. You could build a small shopping centre just outside a US town and before your tenants had comfortably settled in, someone would have started building a bigger and better centre half a mile further down the road.

What I wanted to find were established locations that would remain good trading areas for as far as one could see into the future. I identified three such. The first was Worth Avenue in Palm Beach, one of – perhaps the most – exclusive retail locations in the land. Over some years I looked at several properties there but never found a good deal.

The second location which I identified was St Armand's Circle at the end of Long-Boat Key on the Gulf of Mexico coast of Florida. In due time I was able to buy the freehold of a very well known restaurant, known as 'Charlie's Crab'. This was a substantial property and we held it for many years.

The third Floridian retail location which seemed to me to be certain to remain a good area was Park Avenue, Winter Park. This was a separate small city but effectively an upper-class suburb of the city of Orlando, which when I first saw it was a modest-sized place but which has over the years been one of the fastest growing centres in the USA with its phenomenal growth due largely to the Disney Corporation's Disney World and Epcot Centre and other tourist attractions which followed them.

I had made several annual exploratory visits to Florida before buying properties. It was in 1981 that we made three interesting purchases in Park Avenue, Winter Park. First we purchased a small retail development comprising a restaurant and several small shops and offices. Then we acquired the adjoining block which comprised three small, rather run-down apartment buildings immediately adjoining the retail property. The acquisition of some rear land meant that these two acquisitions could later be redeveloped into an attractive small unit development known as 'Brandywine Square'. Our third purchase was to acquire the freehold of the Jacobsons departmental store which was the largest retail business in the street. These Winter Park properties were followed by the acquisition of the Charlie's Crab Restaurant on St Armand's Circle near Sarasota already mentioned and together all these properties meant that we had a valuable stake in the fast growing Florida economy.

Helping me with these acquisitions was a local estate agent or as he would describe himself – 'realtor' – named Blair Rugh. When I had agreed my first purchase in Winter Park I asked him if he knew of a good lawyer who could act for us and he suggested we should go and see Gene Godbold. I was impressed when I walked into Gene's office for the first time and noted that on the wall behind his desk besides all the framed law degrees etc. was a handsomely mounted and framed slogan reading – 'Sue the Bastards'. Clearly Mr Godbold was a man of action which he duly proved when I asked him how quickly the documentation for my proposed purchase could be provided. The same question to an English solicitor would almost certainly have provoked a reply such as, 'Well probably in a couple of weeks' or 'If you press us by the end of next week'.

Gene's reply was different, he looked at his watch – it was early afternoon and then replied – 'About mid-day.'

'Mid-day when?' I asked.

'Tomorrow,' was his answer.

'How on earth will you manage that?' I queried. He shrugged his shoulders and replied, 'So several of us will work all night.' I was mightily impressed and ever since Gene's firm has looked after our Floridian interests with both speed and efficiency.

These American acquisitions by Shop and Store Developments Ltd. followed a decade of steady progress by our property company. At the start of the 1970s, Shop and Store had a rent roll of just over £330,000 per annum (the equivalent perhaps of about £3.5m today). By the end of the decade the rent roll was nearly £900,000 per annum and with this steady growth in income as a consequence of new acquisitions, developments and of course rent reviews, the company's profits were the equivalent of about £1 million a year in today's money.

Despite the obvious potential of our property business, I still thought of myself as a retailer. The retail businesses had their ups and downs during the period that Shop and Store was steadily growing. The parent company – Greenwoods (Menswear) Ltd. continued to extend its branch list and by the end of the decade was operating as far apart as Dumfries and Berwick-on-Tweed in the north, throughout all the northern counties and moving down into the Midlands through Staffordshire.

Some of the more recent branches had been part of our takeover of the William Blackburn business at the start of the decade. Another particularly valuable addition to the chain came with our purchase of the Newcastle-based Anthony Donald business. This company operated twenty shops throughout the north-east and its purchase in December 1974 strengthened still further Greenwood's representation up to and indeed just over the border.

By the end of the 1970s, sales from the Greenwood's branches had reached a level of around £50m in current values. Profits had reached the modern equivalent of about £2.5m in 1978. However, the latter part of the decade particularly 1980 were significantly more difficult years.

As might be expected a similar pattern to the trading results of Greenwood's up north was being followed by our Hodges business in South Wales and the south-west. Hodges like Greenwood's was steadily expanding and they too had had the benefit of the addition of some former Blackburns' shops to the business that was being operated from a separate office and warehouse adjoining the Hodges bespoke tailoring factory.

During the 1970s the Hodges branch list grew from fifty-eight to seventy-six. To these additions in numbers should be added the fact that during the decade many of the branches were completely refitted. Thanks perhaps to the influence of Hodges' long-established tailoring and clothing business, in both north and south we placed an ever-increasing emphasis on the clothing, as opposed to the outfitting side of our menswear businesses. In the good year of 1978 the Hodges business produced profits for which the modern day equivalent would be around £1.5m.

However, the dark cloud on the horizon lay over the bespoke tailoring business. In days long gone the bespoke trade was the main part of Hodges business but even thirty years ago fewer and fewer men were willing to wait for a suit made to their personal measurements. The long-term prospects for Hodges factory were therefore bleak. It had, of course, benefited from the tailoring business generated by all the Greenwood's branches in the north which became part of its captive market but both north and south and indeed nationally and internationally bespoke tailoring for a middle class market was slowly dying. By 1980 the Swansea factory was operating at a substantial loss.

In reviewing the whole of our family business we must not ignore the small but interesting department store operation Lowes of Wigan and its modest off-shoot Danbys of Leigh.

Ever since we acquired the Wigan store in 1962 Jimmy Lowe, great-grandson of the store's founder, had operated the business on our behalf. It was a constant struggle to do better than break even but over the whole period of our ownership of the business the operation was modestly in the black. Thus considering all of the above facts and figures together the fair answer to the question which heads this chapter – 'How Fare the Family Fortunes'? would be – pretty well thank you.

As a family we were operating nearly 300 men's shops which in a decent year could produce profits in the order of £4m in today's money and to which could be added a further million from Shop and Store Developments Ltd.'s activities. Also the value of Shop and Store's investment properties and the many freehold Greenwood's and Hodges shops was increasing yearly.

I have never thought that figures alone define the standing of a business, although of course sensible profitability is essential. I believe that other factors such as the relationship with your staff and with your suppliers is important. So too is the public's view of you.

We can fairly say that our staff relations were excellent. We genuinely tried hard – and I think succeeded – to maintain a family atmosphere throughout the whole business. Our principle of always promoting internally whenever possible certainly helped as did, I think such arrangements as our 'Gold Watch Club' for long serving members of staff, the regular production of the group's house magazine *Contact*, the annual conventions both north and south and the regular branch visits by senior executives and family members.

As I have already mentioned our reputation with suppliers was always first class, thanks mainly I suppose, to my brother's completely fair, straight-forward but also amiable approach.

My son David had joined the business during the period just described, after his unsuccessful attempt at a military career. I was anxious that he should learn every aspect of our affairs and that of course included spending some time in a shop. He very quickly grasped all the essentials of branch management and I remember in his very early days sending him to 'relieve' at Otley branch – 'relieve' in the multiple retail trade means act as temporary manager.

You can be sure that I made a point of visiting Otley branch whilst he was in charge to see where I could pick faults. The trouble was I couldn't find any! The shop was immaculate with everything from displays to book-keeping in impeccable order. I wracked my brains to think of some peg on which I could hang a need for improvement and finally hit on one. 'Have you remembered to wash the coat hangers?' I asked him.

'No,' said he looking rather puzzled.

'Ah,' said I, 'for perfect care of hanging stock you should occasionally wipe down all the coat hangers with a damp cloth so as to remove every bit of dust.' They may do that in high fashion ladies' stores but to be honest I think it would be just about unheard of for the hangers carrying men's coats and jackets.

Having illustrated that the family's financial affairs were in pretty good shape in those days, it might be interesting, before we turn to the trials and tribulations of my latter years in business, if I tell you a little more of how some of the proceeds from all the hard work that went into building a substantial business were spent.

I spent quite a lot of money then – and pretty frequently since – on lengthy trips to South Africa. That country was on my list as a possible place to make serious property investments and I learned that when and if the time comes that you can afford both the time and cost of a visit to South Africa, it is indeed a very good place to spend February.

Travelling by sea to South Africa in the 1960s and 1970s was just about the best travel experience one could have. Indeed short of having your own private jet or a very large yacht, I can think of nothing to compare with it and for me foreign travel has been downhill ever since those happy days spent on the Union Castle Liners.

Union Castle had operated a weekly liner service to and from South Africa for generations. Besides passengers and cargo the ships carried the mail and were indeed known to most South Africans simply as 'the mail ships'. For Enid and me a voyage would go like this – we would drive down to the Polygon Hotel in Southampton in the Rolls with my company chauffeur following behind in a van which contained our cabin trunks. No struggling to pack as much as possible into one or two suitcases but instead the pleasure for Enid of putting outfit after outfit into her trunk and for me, the now lost forever joy of opening my massive trunk which when standing open could accommodate ten or a dozen coat hangers on one side with five drawers for smaller items on the other.

A leisurely drive to the docks on the following morning, minimal problems boarding the vessel and you are in your cabin or state room. Which incidentally if you wanted a good one, you had booked a year previously and which was then to be your very comfortable billet for the next thirteen nights.

The weather was usually pretty poor, since our usual departure dates would have been a Friday in early or mid-February. The first night at sea almost invariably proved embarrassing for someone. First class passengers knew that on these liners you dressed for dinner and as far as the ladies went, each evening was an opportunity to wear some glamorous new creation. However, it was a long-standing shipboard convention that one did not dress formally on the first night after leaving a port. Consequently all the experienced passengers would be in lounge suits but there would be one or two poor fellows descending into the elegant dining room in their dinner jackets, only to suffer the embarrassment of indicating thereby that they were not seasoned voyagers.

Once the ship was through the Bay of Biscay the voyage became pure bliss. After three days the mail ships always called at Las Palmas to take on fuel oil which was presumably less expensive there. The brief stop permitted a few hours ashore if you wished it and then in the early evening away you steamed. Then for nine delightful days one never saw land unless when passing Dakar on the bulge of Africa you could discern something faint on the eastern horizon. You usually saw no land, but what you did see were the flying fish zipping along beside the bows of the ship, sometimes pods of dolphins and occasionally whales.

You quickly settled in to shipboard life which consisted of all the traditional deck games during the day and buffet luncheons beside the swimming pool often washed down with excellent South African wines. My lunch time favourite was Lanzerac Rosé. When you returned to your state room in the early evening you would find your evening clothes laid out ready for you by your bedroom steward who became a cross between a valet and a ladies' maid. One minor problem was that a fair percentage of the stewards tilted towards the ladies' maid side or – to use, reluctantly, in its modern sense that otherwise happy little word, they were gay.

As a result of friendship with some of the ship's officers, on one occasion I attended the crew concert which included several very convincing female impersonators. I fully appreciated that transvestism is – or so it then seemed – quite common on ocean liners, when Enid indignantly observed whilst looking through her clothes in our state room – 'Someone has pinched my strapless bra!'

The first-class passengers on those Union Castle liners were most certainly an interesting lot. The majority were elderly, so much so that, on one of our earlier trips on the *Edinburgh Castle* one of the pursers told me that the three youngest passengers in first class were my daughter Patricia, then came Enid and then came me. I suppose it was fairly obvious that most of the first-class cabin occupiers were older, since to make the voyage you had to be prepared to spend a lot of money and also be able to give up quite a lot of time. In any event most of our fellow passengers were interesting people and such evening entertainments as quizzes were of a high intellectual standard. Evenings often began with cocktail parties going on all over the place, some were in state rooms others in some of the smaller public spaces, some were in the officers' cabins and all were good fun.

Dinner was always a meal of the highest quality and after dinner there were various kinds of entertainment and usually at some stage, dancing to the ship's small band. I recall one evening which was organised as a casino night and I was standing near a crowded roulette table, making a few modest bets. Standing alongside me was fellow passenger Jack Cohen, the founder of the Tesco empire. One of my bets near the centre of the table came up and before I could reach out for my winnings, Jack Cohen had reached out for the pile of chips, I literally slapped his wrist and having had several friendly conversations with him on deck previously I felt quite free to say – 'Get your thieving hands off Jack you know damn well that's not yours!'

To which he took not the slightest exception but grinned broadly and replied – 'You'd be surprised how often I get away with it!'

If you wanted a particularly elegant evening on board ship the thing to do was give a cocktail party for a modest number, say twelve then make use of the ship's private dining room which as a seasoned traveller you had booked before leaving Southampton. These rooms were always beautifully furnished and appointed and the catering staff could provide just about any kind of menu that you chose. It was indeed a first-class way to travel.

These Union Castle liners had been designed for three purposes. There was a limited amount of first-class accommodation, usually for about 200 people but in addition there was much space devoted to tourist-class passengers who in earlier days on the outward voyage had frequently been people emigrating to South Africa and other southern parts of the African continent. The stream of emigrants of earlier days had dwindled to a trickle by the time I was making the voyage an annual event, as a result, of political concerns in the apartheid era. The third purpose of the ships was to carry cargo, including of course, mail.

You did not need to be a genius to realise that loading cargo through hatches could not compare economically with containers. I recall leaning on the ship's rail and watching one of the new – as they were at that time – container ships ploughing north laden with dozens of the steel containers that are today such a common sight at every port around the world. My ship's officer friend sadly observed, 'That's what's going to put us out of business within the next year or two'. He was right. One by one the Union Castle liners disappeared. For a year or two the South African government operated some of the ships in order to maintain the weekly service together with the now depleted Union Castle fleet.

Finally, we saw the sad photographs of the – in my view – best of the Union Castle liners, the *Pendennis Castle* driven on to an Asian beach and then being totally demolished down to the last rivet. Just the stern of the ship existed when the photograph was taken, producing a weird picture, since the stern was absolutely intact and untouched but the bows and the centre part of the ship had totally disappeared.

The last ship to go was the biggest, the *Windsor Castle* and whilst we enjoyed very much its final 'blue' voyage (blue voyages were those at the most sought-after time of year, namely February), all the regular passengers felt pretty sad when it carried them back to Southampton for the last time.

I have a small memento of my last voyage on the *Windsor Castle* in the form of the prize for winning the deck tennis tournament. Deck tennis played with a rope ring on a court which is marked out like a miniature tennis court and over a six-feet high net is in fact a very good game requiring agility and dexterity as well as know-how. A few years after my voyaging days were over I actually wrote a set of rules for the game to be played under the title – 'Ring Tennis' and formed a small company to see if the game could be commercially exploited. I got fairly close to selling the project to a major American sporting company on the back of a sales promotion video produced at Burley House, my then corporate head-quarters which starred, if that is the right word, my friend Dick Atkinson's young son and some of his teenage friends. The voice-over commentary I did myself.

Unfortunately other commercial pressures at the time when everything was going badly wrong caused me to let the Ring Tennis Ltd. project drop but I do believe it could be resurrected if someone young enough and enthusiastic enough were to get behind it.

Something else came out of that final voyage from South Africa. That was the formation of what we chose to call the 'Castle Club'. Eight of us who had enjoyed each other's company so much on the voyages decided that we would meet regularly, at least once a year and spend a few nights in some good quality hotel. We set the club up properly with six of its members having an official title – President, Vice President, Secretary, Treasurer etc. and just two of us being the 'Indians' to the other six 'Chiefs'. The club continues to this day and we occasionally meet when the club ties and ladies' scarves must be worn. These are blue with a small reproduction of the *Windsor Castle* thereon. The club has visited some twenty of the best country house hotels and restaurants and I have on occasion had some innocent amusement from telling the manager or head waiter that he was being favoured with a visit from the international travel body – the 'famous Castle Club'. Perhaps he would like to so inform the chef against the possibility that we might make an award. Actually we never got round to having award plaques which we thought of as being composed of anchors, with three anchors being at least as good a recommendation as three Michelin stars. It was interesting to see the puzzlement on a manager's or a head waiter's face.

Obviously they were afraid to show their ignorance of what might just be a significant international group by questioning just what was the Castle Club. Instead they usually put their best foot forward and we stayed and dined always with the best attention. The years have claimed two of our membership and perhaps we shall no longer manage official get-togethers but like so much of my life it was a lot of fun whilst it lasted.

One of the high spots of those South African voyages was the morning thirteen days after leaving Southampton when the ship approached Cape Town. Arrival was usually timed for about 6 o'clock in the morning but nevertheless many passengers got up particularly early to see the beautiful sight of Table Mountain, perhaps with its 'table cloth' of snow-white cloud, dwarfing the city of Cape Town at its foot.

To finish the story of these voyages I should mention that they did not terminate in Cape Town. You could if you wished leave the ship there and re-join it for the homeward journey ten days later. That would permit you to travel inland perhaps up to the game reserves in the north or perhaps for a few days in the beautiful Cape itself with visits to say

Stellenbosch and Franschhoek. Many passengers simply got off the ship and moved straight in to the Union Castle owned Mount Nelson Hotel, in those days definitely one of the world's finest.

The alternative was to stay on board the ship and enjoy what was known as the coastal voyage, with the ship steaming first to Port Elizabeth for morning arrival and evening departure and on the following day a similar call at East London. Then on the day after that arriving at Durban where it would stay for two nights and most of a third day before returning to Cape Town with repeat calls at East London and Port Elizabeth.

Two days later the ships would set sail for home, leaving Cape Town usually in the mid-afternoon and thereafter re-tracing the outbound voyage. Usually on the voyages at some point the southbound liner passed its northbound sister-ship with much blowing of hooters and waving of hands by the passengers. The sight of a fast-steaming ocean liner in an otherwise – as far as the eye could see – empty ocean was a fine one.

After all the above about getting to and from South Africa I must say something about the time spent out there which included a number of interesting events.

On different visits we did all the obvious things e.g. travelled on the Blue Train from Cape Town through Johannesburg to Pretoria, drove the 'Garden Route' between Port Elizabeth and Cape Town, stayed in the Drackensburg Mountains and of course visited several of the game reserves in the north, including of course the Kruger National Park but best of all was the stay at Londozoli, famous for its leopards. Most of the earlier trips to the reserves and the remaining wilderness areas were purely for sightseeing but later I did try my hand at hunting with a rifle.

One sightseeing trip could all too easily have been our last. Enid and I were travelling with our then teenage daughter Patricia and her cousin, my brother's youngest daughter Melissa. Whilst visiting a game reserve near the St Lucia estuary (north-east corner of the country) our driver/guide took us to meet a game warden with whom he was friendly, at his post on the banks of the great river. The warden took the six of us – we four, plus the driver and himself, in a small jet speed boat, only about twelve feet in length. We whizzed off up the river and saw all kinds of wildlife. I remember particularly the squadrons of white pelicans flying alongside and also the goliath heron which was certainly the biggest bird I have ever seen in my life. With its long legs, its head could reach up to – it must have been twice a man's height.

The stupid warden began to show off with two particularly alarming tricks. When he saw a party of hippos in the middle of the river, he would drive straight at them assuming (thank heavens correctly), that at the last minute the hippos would sink and we could whizz over their backs. One such trick would have been quite sufficient but the trouble was he repeated it whenever the opportunity arose.

Even worse, was his trick when he saw crocodiles (of which there were very many) sunning themselves on the muddy bank side. He would roar up to them and then at the last minute spin the wheel so that the crocodiles got a spray of river water to awaken them from their slumbers. They of course immediately charged down the bank and into the river but we were well on our way.

He tried running close to the bank once too often and managed to ground us in the shallows. Clearly someone had to get out and push the boat off, it certainly wasn't going to be me! With obvious anxiety our guide and the warden jumped over the side into the muddy waters which could well have concealed a crocodile and pushed us off before resuming our trip up stream.

We were several miles away from the landing stage, where incidentally the warden told us 'one of my boys was taken by a crocodile last month' – when we drove through a sharp bend in the river which had created a large almost still pool. It was full of crocodiles. They lay on both banks of the river and all around the pool and naturally we were glad to zip through it and continue upstream.

It was on the return journey that disaster – or nearly – struck. Just as we reached the crocodile pool the guide shouted to the warden – 'You're losing oil'. We looked below the dashboard of the little speed boat to see a fractured pipe squirting engine oil all over the floor. The warden immediately cut the engine since of course there was a danger of the engine seizing up leaving us without power. Consequently we drifted slowly to the centre of the pool full of crocodiles, several of which entered the water to join those already there and we had the hideous sight of many pairs of eyes just above the surface looking at our small boat from all directions.

The fool of a warden had not brought a pair of oars or a paddle, nor was he armed. We sat in silence for a minute or two all trying to think if there was any way out. Some of the crocodiles were longer than the boat we were in and obviously any one of them could have tipped us over. I weighed up our chances of all trying to swim for the nearest shore and frankly decided they were nil. There was no way the six of us were going to swim through dozens – and that is the literal truth – of crocodiles for fifty or sixty yards and step out safely at the other side. The flow of the river was sluggish in all parts but at this wide corner it was so slow as to do no more than let the little boat very slowly rotate.

I have never been so scared in my life as at that moment. A revolting death for all of us seemed to me to be just a matter of time when one of them would either swim under the boat and capsise it or lash it with its tail.

With the engine turned off, spurting oil had of course ceased but the dripping pipe showed clearly what was the cause of our problem. It was simply a slim copper tube leading to the oil pressure gauge on the dashboard which had broken.

Our daughter Patricia who had said absolutely nothing for several minutes suddenly shouted out, 'Can't you bash up the pipe with something?'

'Hell-fire yes,' said the warden and with an old spanner he brayed the broken pipe into a right angled bend and then hammered it more or less flat.

Thank heavens the engine re-started and we were away. None of us had anything to say until we drove away from the landing stage in the VW combi which is the vehicle of choice for many game park visitors. I think all six who were in that boat will remember the incident with the clarity with which it is burned on my memory.

On other trips I did try my hand at hunting and the heads which presently adorn my billiards room prove that I had some success. Two instances, are worth a mention.

One was the time that I determined to try to take a kudu, which is the approximately cow-sized African antelope with the long spirally twisted horns which can be four feet or more in length. Long-time South African friends in Port Elizabeth told me that if I was prepared to get up very early and make a long drive, there was a large area where plains game including kudu roamed freely. So with a borrowed rifle I made the long drive, met the Afrikaaner who owned a large area and who for an appropriate fee would let you try for a kudu or indeed other types of buck.

After a couple of test shots with the borrowed rifle, he drove me in his pick-up to a pretty remote spot in the barren area. There were very few decent trees but a lot of scrubby thorn bushes covering the stony ground as far as the eye could see. My instructions were simply to hide behind a thorn bush and then he and his boys would try and move the game towards me. This was not what I had expected. I was anticipating that we would stalk the kudu much as one stalked deer. Whilst I have shot thousands of driven birds, driven kudu was certainly something different. He impressed on me – unnecessarily – that I should only try and shoot a mature bull and only if I was pretty sure I could kill it cleanly.

I settled down behind a thorn bush as he drove away to join up with his team of beaters. Then I waited and waited until I heard in the distance the rattling of stones on tin. The method my host and his boys used for driving animals before them was to walk, each about a hundred or two yards apart, each carrying a biscuit tin full of pebbles. Some ten people shaking biscuit tins full of stones certainly provided enough noise to disturb the animals and a variety of game including kudu came in sight of me but none passed within a reasonable range.

He tried another similar drive from a different direction but this too was without success so he decided on a different tactic.

He sent the beaters off into the distance whilst he drove me to the main railway line which passed his property a mile or two away from where I had last been stationed. There were twin railway tracks with a dirt road beside each, then came a thick thorn bush fence and then a two metre high wire fence. To my surprise he took us through a gated opening onto the railway lines and then stationed me against the wire fence on the northern side.

Through a gap in the thorn bushes and looking across the railway tracks and both dirt roads to my left I had a fair field of fire, so despite my amazement at what was obviously his plan to have his beaters try and drive animals straight down the main railway tracks towards me, I settled down and waited patiently.

In the distance I could hear the rattle of stones on tin and then I noticed that the wire fence on which I was leaning was moving rhythmically. I shifted my gaze away from the railway tracks and dirt roads to the narrow passageway between the hedge and the fence. Coming towards me at full gallop was a kudu bull bouncing into the fence with every step thus producing the movement.

My host shouted, 'Shoot him in the chest man, quick,' and then took to his heels, I swung up the rifle as the animal charged straight at me and by the time I had the telescopic sight on to him he was so close that all I could see in the 'scope were the hairs on his chest. There was time for just one shot – boom! went the rifle.

Thank heavens I hit him right in the chest and he dropped dead not more than five paces from me. I have no doubt if I had missed him or only wounded him it would have been kudu one, hunter nil and I would have been at least hospitalised and more probably dead. Thus it was with much relief that I left the place having made arrangements for a local taxidermist to set up the head which after some months reached my home.

My second hunting story began when South African friends David and Mary Marshall found someone I always thought of as the 'great white hunter' who would guide me on a serious hunting expedition – Johann D. Schyff by name. We drove in two cars, one towing a trailer full of kit to an area not far from the Kruger National Park. We reached the camp in daylight and Johann fished out of the trailer a collapsible table, some small sandbags and a folding chair, together with a metal target frame, some paper targets and a Yugoslav-made .270 win. rifle which had a variable power telescope from $3 \times$ to $9 \times$. I watched with interest as he set up the target, table with sand bags on which to rest the rifle and the chair in which to sit comfortably whilst testing it. I was amazed when he put up the target at a distance of only forty yards and naturally thought, if we are going to get so close to the game I shall have no trouble at all in shooting straight. My Scottish stalking had usually been with shots taken between say 100 and 180 yards.

I had no problem in putting several shots through the bullseye at the limited range Johann had set up and we therefore promptly adjourned to a splendid barbecue (a *braivleis* in South Africa), the roaring log fire and several bottles of good South African wine. I was greatly enjoying the evening until Johann asked me to fetch more logs from the log pile adjoining one of the rondavels (thatched mud huts) which were to be our quarters.

Clutching two large logs, I took them back and tossed them on the fire, only to see a large scorpion emerge from the log which I had just been holding close to my chest. Consequently despite the bonhomie produced by the good red wine we remembered to look carefully for scorpions and other 'nasties' before climbing into the camp beds.

The next morning we set off as a party of six. Mary Marshall with Enid were the spectators in the raised back seat of the open truck. Johann was the driver, David was the front seat passenger and a Zulu tracker/skinner named Joachim and I were standing in the truck section in the rear.

We bumped along the rough forest tracks and occasional open areas early in the morning. Joachim who had magnificent eyesight suddenly called – quietly – for Johann to stop the vehicle and look where the Zulu was pointing. There only about 100 yards away was a handsome nyala. I got out quietly, expecting that Johann and I would try and stalk up to him, perhaps to the sort of close range that the previous evening's target practice had suggested. Not so, 'Shoot him from here,' was the order so I knelt down in the back of the truck and shot him. Happily it was a perfect bulls eye and he went over and never moved. We loaded him into the back of the truck.

A little later we saw an impala ram on his own in a small clearing. Johann and I left the truck together and this time we did try to stalk to within a reasonable range and were probably just inside a hundred yards when I was told to take him. This had to be a standing shot with just a small sapling providing some support for my left hand. Nevertheless, I hit him with what I was sure was a good heart shot but as often happens the beast galloped off into the brush. Johann was quite confident that he was dead and so was I, since from my Scottish deerstalking experience I knew full well an animal even with a shattered heart can run for a surprising distance before keeling over and then lying motionless. Spectators and all were called from the truck and we began a search for the impala in increasingly widening circles. Only when Johann casually mentioned, 'Keep your eyes open for snakes,' did the spectators decide immediately to abandon the search! The Zulu, he and I looked for another minute or two, then Johann shrugged his shoulders and simply said, 'We'll leave him for the leopards'.

This was quite different from deerstalking, where you would have carried on searching regardless of time to find a beast which had been shot in that way. However, as Johann had explained it made no sense to spend a lot of time looking for a wounded or even a dead animal when the area was full of carnivores which would be glad of the kill. We re-boarded the truck and continued searching, our objective being if possible to shoot a trophy impala ram i.e. one with a really good head.

We came to a big open area, part of which was just a dusty plain and the nearer area was covered with knee-high or maybe in places waist-high grass. Joachim suddenly called to Johann to stop and pointed towards the middle of the large grassy area. We all looked where he was pointing but I used my small binoculars and still could see nothing. Johann said, 'Go

with Joachim, I'm sure there is a buck in there, be ready.' Off the Zulu
and I went, I still seeing nothing and he confident that we would see an
animal lying in the long grass. We came to a large anthill some eight feet
tall. The Zulu and I climbed on top of it and standing on top he pointed
again. Still I could not see what he was looking at. I therefore gestured to
him to keep pointing and then laid the rifle on top of the woolly knitted
hat that he and many other Zulus liked to wear. I then pointed the rifle
along the line of his outstretched arm, looked through the telescopic sight
and lo and behold there were two slim horns just sticking up above the
long grass.

Johann the great white hunter had followed us. 'There is something
there,' I told him, 'I can see two horns.'

'Shoot it then,' said he.

'But I can only see the horns,' I replied.

'Well just shoot below them.' You do as you're told! So I aimed a round
about a foot below the horns. They never moved.

'Give him another one,' came the order. I fired a second round, again
the horns did not move.

'You must have killed him,' said Johann as we scrambled down from
the anthill and began walking through the grass. We got to within thirty
or forty yards and suddenly a reed buck, for that was what it was, jumped
to his feet and tore away madly first bursting out of the long grass and
then racing in an arc across the dusty plain from our right to our left. To
my surprise Johann flung up his rifle and fired a shot at the rapidly
disappearing buck. I was surprised since in deerstalking it was unheard of
to try and shoot a galloping beast other than if it were definitely wounded.
However, I thought to myself, well if he can have a shot so can I. I swung
my rifle on to the buck as it galloped full tilt throwing up clouds of dust,
I can still see the picture in the telescopic sight. I swung through it just as
you swing through a crossing grouse with a shot gun. As the cross hairs of
the sight passed the front of the buck, I squeezed the trigger. The result
was spectacular, he went down head first and then cartwheeled half a
dozen times before lying still and stone dead a long way away.

The Zulu ran to him and came back chattering madly. 'What's he
saying?' I asked Johann.

Johann translated. 'He's says it is a magic shot, he has hunted all his life
and never has he seen such a shot.' We looked at the dead buck and there
was the bullet hole just at the base of his neck and he had died instantly,

but both his horns lacked their last three or four inches. 'Look at that,' said I pointing at the horns.

'You must have shot them off from the anthill,' said Johann. I certainly did not believe that and told him – 'I may know nothing about hunting in Africa but I know damn well an animal is not going to sit there while someone shoots both his horn tips off'. The Zulu had the answer. He had gone back thirty or forty yards to the point where the animal had first hit the ground. He bent down and pulled out the two horn tips. They had been driven into the ground and as he started to cartwheel both tips had been snapped off neatly.

Araldite in due course re-secured them and his head looks down as we play snooker in my billiard room and reminds me of what was unquestionably the best – probably that really means the luckiest – shot I have ever fired myself or ever seen fired.

I was the hero of the hour when we returned to the camp, Joachim had his entire family – several young Zulus aged about four upwards lined up and I was presented to them as some kind of mighty hunter!

Another happy evening by the camp fire, a few more bottles of South African Merlot had us in good form for the following day. We set off determined to find a really good impala. Joachim, the Zulu and I left the truck at least half a dozen times to stalk the impala in clumps of bush but without getting a shot. One attempt included a belly-crawl over a kopje (small hill). As I crawled through the dead leaves following Joachim, it seemed to me that this would be a very good place to live if one were a snake. Consequently when the Zulu turned round and waved what I thought was a snake in my face and cheerfully announced – 'Boomslang' I nearly had a heart attack that being the name of a particularly poisonous reptile. In fact what the Zulu had picked up was the skin of one which had recently sloughed it off. This at first reassured me and then the thought dawned that if its old skin was there probably it was not far away and thus I was very relieved when Joachim called off that particular stalk. I later attempted an almost impossible shot at an impala ram standing on the sky-line but with the beast only partially visible this time I had a clean miss.

Later in the day, this time at a distance I would estimate as over 200 yards – so far that I certainly allowed almost a foot for the drop of the bullet – I tried for another impala ram. Johann thought I had missed it but when my Zulu friend ran on to it, he found that not only was my ram stone dead but so was a younger impala which had been standing immediately behind it.

A little later we tried for another group of impalas, going a fair way from the truck before deciding that we did not like the look of a large male ostrich, who by his behaviour, so Johann informed me could best be described as a randy male! We 'spooked' the impala so returned promptly to the truck with the ostrich chasing us.

About half a mile further on we saw on the skyline a pair of impalas at a very long range, probably 300 yards or even more. They were effectively standing looking at us. I sighted on the left-hand one in an attempt at a shot straight into his chest. I deliberately aimed over the top of his head to allow for the bullet drop. I had a good rest on the bonnet of the truck and made the shot. Down he went but as we drove up to him it was clear he was still alive and needed the *coup de grâce*. Johann went to do so. Just as with deer the thing to do is to put a bullet into the base of the neck, but he missed. It was then that we realised that the male ostrich had followed us for the last half mile and was now charging towards Johann to attack him. The ostrich towered over him trying to slash him with its foot. Ostriches have two toes and the long one with its claw at the end could rip a man open with one blow. Johann fired a shot, not at the ostrich, simply thinking the bang would frighten it away. It did nothing of the sort and the claw struck down on him. Johann went down on his back, the giant bird stamped on his chest, ran on for a yard or two and paused for a moment. We later learned that having his rifle up in the air had saved Johann's life since the claw struck his left hand and the rifle barrel which he was holding out in front of himself.

It was as if a cleaver had hit his hand with one finger now become two. I swung my rifle on to the ostrich and was just about to shoot when Joachim used the only two words of English that he knew – his vocabulary was limited to 'shoot' or 'no shoot'.

'No shoot,' he screamed. He explained afterwards that any shot I had fired into the body of the ostrich was highly unlikely to kill it but was certain to have enraged it and it would have attacked Johann again and perhaps killed him as he lay helpless on the ground.

David Marshall acted quickly. He jumped into the driver's seat of the truck and drove it straight at the bird which of course ran a few yards away. The Zulu slashed the dying buck's throat with his knife and threw it into the back of the truck and we helped Johann aboard.

His injury meant an overnight visit to the hospital in Hluhluwe. When he came back the following day heavily bandaged it was obvious the rest of our hunting trip was to be abandoned.

It had been interesting and exciting while it lasted. I particularly enjoyed the nights in camp when if you shone a flashlight into the bushes and trees a lot of eyes looked back at you. Mostly hyenas but maybe the odd leopard.

I regret not having another serious attempt but for one reason or another the opportunity never presented itself before I reached the age when that kind of excursion would not have been very sensible.

As regards finding business properties in South Africa again there is cause for regret. With a shipboard friend who subsequently became a very close friend – Ralph Sutcliffe, I looked at numerous commercial properties out there, but never closed a deal. With the perfect vision of hindsight I am now quite sure that one block in particular – in Wynberg, near Cape Town – would have been an extremely good investment. However, as I said at the start of this perhaps overlong chapter family fortunes were generally in very good shape throughout the 1970s and 1980s. Not so a little later as you will shortly read.

CHAPTER 19

The Great Divide

B EFORE I TURN TO THE division of the entire family business which took place early in 1982, I think there are a number of other matters which I need to cover if this book is to be anything like comprehensive. Let's mention first my educational involvement.

I continued to be very busy with the affairs of Woodhouse Grove School in my ongoing capacity as Chairman of Governors. Dr Cyril Pritchard, who at the start of his career had taught me, as a very small boy, retired in 1972. I was obviously closely involved in the selection of his successor. I think we chose wisely and well in appointing David Miller who was headmaster for nineteen years, during which the school grew and prospered despite sometimes difficult circumstances. It was during David Miller's headship that the school became co-educational, at first with girls in the sixth form only but from 1985 throughout the entire senior school and also Brontë House. Apart from the change to co-education, The Grove also continued to change in the mix of boarders and day pupils. David Miller's headship began with a senior school containing 360 boys of whom 240 were boarders. The passing years saw a steady decline in boarding numbers. It is only comparatively recently that the decline has stopped and boarding numbers have stabilised at around 110 only a little over 10% of the total school population, which now exceeds 1,000 across an age range of three to eighteen.

Apart from being involved in every aspect of The Grove's development, I found myself increasingly involved with the Board of Management, ultimately serving for several years as its Vice-Chairman (the senior lay position) – which was, and is, the ultimate authority for the majority of the country's Methodist independent schools. There are presently fourteen such schools, nine of them on the same trust deed and consequently requiring the Board of Management's approval for any major capital expenditure or the sale and purchase of property. As a school Chairman, I have always been entitled to a place on this Board and during the period we are now considering I became increasingly active in its affairs.

For example, I felt that the Board badly needed an efficient committee structure and produced a paper outlining what I thought this should be. I strongly recommended the creation of a Financial Advisory Committee together with a General Purposes Committee. My suggestions were promptly accepted and I was asked to become the first Chairman of the Financial Advisory Committee – always known as simply the FAC.

I can truthfully claim to have changed the entire outlook as regards the financing of the development of Methodist independent schools. I argued strongly that all the schools' freehold sites were of immense value and that against that security, significant borrowings should be arranged centrally for the schools to draw down from time to time when they had a building project to tackle.

For many years the Methodist independent schools have followed this route and they continue to use the rule-of-thumb safeguard which I suggested at the outset, namely that a school's total borrowing should never exceed one third of its annual income, that is to say one term's fees. It all seems to have worked out and I like to think that there has been a lot more development at various Methodist schools than would have otherwise been the case.

When I first began to be seriously involved with all the Methodist schools, I was shocked to realise how little we knew about each other. The schools were in no sense an organised group and if anything, rather than mutual help and co-operation, there was some jealousy and rivalry on the rare occasions that paths crossed.

In the mid-eighties the then General Secretary to the Board of Management – let's hence forward just call it the BOM – was with me at yet another independent schools' gathering to discuss the threat to independent education which has hung over the independent sector for so many years. He introduced me to someone as, 'This is our Senior Chairman of Governors'. I asked him later if that was indeed the case and yes it was. At which I told him that if I was his senior Chairman it was time I pulled rank and organised something which I had long thought desirable. This was a three-day conference of the Chairmen of Governors of all fourteen schools. The first such took place at The Grove in 1987 and ever since these Chairmen's conferences have been an extremely valuable and important part of the overall governance of the fourteen Methodist Foundation independent schools. Today the schools exchange ideas for 'best practice' in all aspects of school affairs, they co-operate in all manner of ways and the Chairmen now look on each other as friends and colleagues.

With the gathering moving to a different school each year any long-serving Chairman sooner or later gains a background knowledge of several or even all of the schools in the group. The conferences are serious and valuable but also thoroughly enjoyable and it has been a pleasure for me to become reasonably familiar with schools as far apart as Truro in Cornwall, Rydale/Penrhos in North Wales, Ashville in Harrogate and the Leys in Cambridge.

Using whatever skill and knowledge one happens to have for the benefit of others is, I believe, very much the right thing to do. It is truly rewarding to accomplish something worthwhile and I found real pleasure in such circumstances as being heavily involved with the merger of Farringtons Girls School in Bromley and a similar smaller school, Stratford House. I remember with pride the Chairman of Governors of Shebbear College in North Devon saying to me with sincerity – 'without your help this school would have closed'.

Save for perhaps some concluding remarks in the final chapter, I shall say little more about my work at Woodhouse Grove and any reader of these words seriously interested in the development of that fine old school should, I suggest, look out for the publication in 2012 of The Grove's 200th anniversary book on which the author Nigel Watson is already working.

Incidentally, Nigel Watson now with some sixty or seventy histories of companies, colleges and schools to his credit, is a name which gives this old man a feeling of satisfaction. Nigel Watson, the son of my friend John Watson, a long-time tenant of the farm in Wensleydale which I owned for many years, came to me with a problem. Nigel – a history graduate and a very clever young man, had decided to pursue a career in accountancy. Part way through his time with a major London firm of accountants (Binder Hamlyn & Co., my son-in-law's old firm) he had, for the first time in his life, failed an exam. It appeared that clever though we was, Nigel was just not numerate. Figures and numbers came to him with difficulty. Not a happy situation for a prospective accountant! He came to me (his honorary uncle) in 1983 to be precise, I thought deeply and then came up with a good idea.

'Nigel', I told him, 'what you need to be is a corporate historian'.

'What's that?' was his reply. To be honest I had never heard of the phrase before, although it is now quite well known but I did know that many long-established businesses like to produce some kind of souvenir or commemorative book, booklet or whatever on their fiftieth, hundredth or again whatever, anniversary is due. The idea was simple. Nigel would begin checking up on the centenaries and other such notable dates of all kinds of schools, colleges and businesses and would offer his services as a historian but one with some knowledge of financial affairs, to write their anniversary publication.

His first such work was to write the fiftieth anniversary booklet for Brontë House, the junior department of Woodhouse Grove School and from then on he has never looked back and as I look across my study I see a long row of the books that he has produced for schools, colleges and businesses throughout the land. It is a very pleasing thing when one's advice bears substantial fruit.

I did have another educational involvement which gave me pleasure. During my days at Whittington I was asked to become a Governor of St Martin's College which was an Anglican teacher training college with close links to Lancaster University. I very much enjoyed my time as Governor there, particularly the several occasions when I was asked to talk to the students. My subject was business ethics and I enjoyed lecturing to the fairly scruffy and unruly mob I found waiting for me in the lecture hall on each occasion.

My technique was simple and perhaps unusual. After a few introductory words I told them that we were there and then going to form a company and I would point to whichever student looked likely to be the least interested, would ask him for his name and say – 'You've just been appointed Managing Director of our new company.' I would pick out a few others and give them labels which put them in charge of sales, marketing generally, production, staffing and all the other executive functions. I would then ask the whole group, 'What shall we manufacture in our new company?' Usually lacking a sensible reply, I sometimes picked up the water jug provided for me and said, 'All right, we are a glass manufacturer and we are producing these jugs.' I would then ask the newly appointed Production Director how many jugs he thought a work force of say 100 could produce per week if that were our only product line. The question at least produced some answers, many of which were silly but some were fairly sensible. Having established what we were going to sell and what our production capacity was the next question was, 'At what price could we sell the finished product?' I talked them through the elementary facts and figures of costing a manufactured item and established what our basic cost would be. Then came the key question – 'So how much should we sell them for?' I usually had their interest by this time but for the suggested price range all missed a key point. The fair-minded but left-inclined students all thought in terms of selling our product for just a little more than it cost us. That was my cue to tell them that the first thing we needed to know before setting our price, was for how much the competitors were selling theirs. The figure I offered them was way above their ideas on price and then I was ready to suggest that what we would do was pitch our selling price nicely below that of the opposition but at such a level that it showed us what seemed to their young minds a greedy profit margin.

Then of course it was time to explain. I recall the phrase I used – 'profit is not a four letter word' and before you knew it they were listening attentively to an explanation of basic capitalist thinking. An explanation of just how profit made the world go round, but with the very big 'but', that profit should be based on fair terms for staff and suppliers, a decent product which represented, if anything, rather better value than that offered by competitors and that profits could be sensibly re-invested to create more jobs and thus help the community.

It was all very interesting and I believe that quite a number of those students will have remembered such phrases as – 'some people say that business is just a rat race – that's perfectly true if you are a rat' – interesting days!

Anyone who has been heavily involved in the property world will have been involved in auction sales. I was no exception and have two or three auction memories which are worth recounting. On one occasion I went to an auction sale in Manchester, where we had an interest in two of the lots, one lot was the freehold for a shop in St Helen's, Lancashire which Greenwood's leased. The other and much more significant was the final lot in the sale – a block of several shops in Sunderland which included a large Greenwood's unit and also a branch of the Stylo Barrett shoe chain. Shortly before the auction Arnold Ziff, the then Chairman of Stylo, who I had come to know quite well rang me. He explained that his company also was interested in buying the block in order to secure the freehold of their unit and that being so why should we bid against each other but rather one of us should buy the block and then sell on the other's unit as a separate transaction later. We, therefore, agreed that I would do the bidding and if I secured the site, would sell Arnold the freehold of his shop for an agreed figure. I went to the auction in Manchester with son David and another colleague, only to find that Arnold and two or three of his colleagues were already there. Although I am sure he trusted me I think his natural instinct was that he must be involved.

The auction began and fairly early on I was able to buy the St Helen's lot. Then in due course we came to the Sunderland block and the bidding was fast and furious. I do not recall the exact figures but in today's money we would be talking somewhere approaching £1.5m.

With the very different values prevailing at that time Arnold and I had agreed that we would go up to about £260 or £270,000. Bids from all round the room soon pushed us up to that level and Arnold and I had a hasty conversation upping the amount that he was prepared to pay for his unit and thus permitting me to carry on bidding. I have never believed in the auction technique that some like to follow, bidding almost surreptitiously. My practice is always to bid positively with my hand in the air and usually calling out the amount of my bid. As we passed the £270,000 mark bids seemed to dry up and apparently I and someone towards the back of the room were the only bidders. '£285,000', called the auctioneer pointing in that direction and reluctantly I raised my hand for £290,000. Back came his response, '£295,000'.

I paused and thought. I well remember the auctioneer who had identified me from my earlier purchase, inviting me to 'fill it up' i.e. bid an even £300,000 and I remember him using the phrase – 'I'm sure you didn't come here just to buy St Helen's, Mr Greenwood?'

To his astonishment and the surprise of everyone in the room I stood up shouted, 'No way', slammed my briefcase shut and walked out down the centre aisle of the hall followed by my colleagues and Arnold and his team.

I had realised that for the last several minutes I had been bidding against myself and the bids that had kept driving me upwards had as they say been taken 'off the wall'. Theoretically the auctioneer was left with a bid of £295,000 but in – so I think – confirmation of my suspicion he hastily declared the property as withdrawn, left the rostrum and hurried down to the doorway of the hall where we were putting on our coats ready for departure. I recall him asking why we were leaving so quickly and my reply was simply – 'I don't like playing games'.

It was an example of how you must have your wits about you at an auction sale.

Then there was the time when my friend Ralph Sutcliffe and I decided we would buy The Royal Hotel, Kirkby Lonsdale as a joint investment.

Ralph and his wife Joyce came to stay with Enid and me at Whittington Hall the night before the auction sale and he and I agreed how much we were prepared to bid. Having settled on what seemed a likely figure I stressed to Ralph that he must leave the conduct of the sale entirely to me.

We went to The Royal Hotel the following morning and to our surprise and disappointment found that the place was packed. The auction had created a lot of interest. In the bar there was a sweepstake on what the likely purchase price would be and who might the purchasers be. I was not particularly pleased to see that I was the favourite named possible purchaser.

Ralph and I adjourned to the gents – the only place we could find for a quick private word and I said to him – 'I think we are going to have to pay a bit more than you and I agreed last night. How much further are you prepared to go?' We agreed on a higher figure and then went into the hotel's dining-room which was laid out for the auction. Ralph, Joyce and Enid sat somewhere near the front. I went to the back of the room and stood against the wall adjoining the doorway into the kitchens.

Jimmy Thompson the elderly, but very able auctioneer, whose firm had been selling farms, cattle and all kinds of property in Kirkby Lonsdale for many, many years was in charge. He gave his audience a fulsome description of The Royal Hotel and its history, naturally omitting the fact that it needed a lot of money spending on it, and then he invited bids.

He was hoping to see the property which was, after all, a fine old building with some twenty-four bedrooms, a ground floor restaurant and bar, together with generous garage and parking space realise quite a substantial sum. Again all the figures which now follow have to be up-dated for the ravages of inflation and can probably be multiplied by about five for a 2009 equivalent.

I was anxious for Jimmy Thompson to know I was there and bidding, so I called out – '£40,000'.

He peered at me over his half-moon glasses and observed – 'That's not much of a bid Mr Greenwood', to which I replied, 'It's not much of a pub Mr Thompson'.

He took the bid, then for a minute or two bids rattled in from various parts of the room. When the bidding reached £60,000 and he looked to me for an advance thereon, I waived my hand to signify that that was me out of the bidding. He focused his attention on the one or two other remaining bidders, assuming I suppose that I had only been there in the hope of buying the place very cheaply indeed. Suddenly with the bidding in the mid-sixties a new bidder spoke up. Leaning against the wall was a smartly dressed young man who topped someone's bid of £66,000 with an immediate and confident higher bid. A buzz went round the room – 'It'll be a brewery rep.' One or two more bids were forthcoming but on each occasion the young man immediately topped them in the confident manner of someone bidding with other people's money and plenty of that available.

£74,000 was his final and confident bid and all the other bidders withdrew, presumably thinking that if a major brewery had decided to buy the hotel (and that was not something that the locals wanted) then there was no point in bidding against them. Jimmy Thompson tried hard for further bids but none were forthcoming, so down came the hammer.

One of the waitresses who was standing in the kitchen doorway at the back of the room where I had positioned myself, shed a little tear. 'What's the matter love?' said I.

'Well you see', she replied, 'all of the staff here were hoping that you were going to buy the place.' I gave her a gentle nudge in the ribs and said – 'Don't worry love, I have!'

Jimmy Thompson asked the young man, 'Now, Sir on whose behalf were you bidding?' To which he replied, 'Mr Greenwood's'.

Jimmy Thompson paused for a moment and then as I walked towards the table, looked at me with his glasses perched on the end of his nose and said – what I took to be a handsome compliment coming from him – 'That were well done.'

The fact is that I had arranged for one of my colleagues from Shop & Store to come into the auction room, avoid me like the plague and then when he sensed the bidding was nearing its climax, he was to bid freely and boldly and go on doing so until I literally went across to him and told him to stop. That was not necessary, the ploy had worked very well indeed and my good friend Ralph Sutcliffe and I found ourselves owners and proprietors of The Royal Hotel for significantly less than we had been prepared to pay.

In due course we found a good tenant and let the premises to him on what was, in those days, a fairly unusual arrangement, namely a rental including a percentage of the turnover.

Now I can put it off no longer. I must tell you of the catastrophic decisions which I made early in 1982 regarding the division of the then so large and successful family business. It happened like this: I was anxious to press ahead with the expansion of Shop & Store and this would have needed more large-scale borrowing. My brother Denis was reluctant to see such adventures and whilst we never quarrelled bitterly, I do remember him telling me – 'Your trouble Brian is that you always want your own way.' I suppose I have to admit that he was right.

That led to the comment – 'The best thing we can do is split the bloody business.'

'All right,' I said, 'I'll come back to you in a day or so with a proposal', and away I went to try and decide how the whole business could be fairly divided between us. We both held exactly the same number of shares in the parent company Greenwood's and were therefore considering the situation from a position of equality and obviously if the entirety were to be divided in two, then the arrangements must be so contrived that the two halves were of equal value.

The plan was to ignore any goodwill elements and simply look at the net asset value of the companies involved.

At that time the total family business comprised 223 Greenwood's branches throughout the north, seventy-six Hodges shops throughout Wales and the south-west, and with Lowes store in Wigan there was therefore, a total of exactly 300 retail outlets. Also there was Hodges tailoring factory.

Worth more than all that put together was Shop & Store, whose property portfolio, at that time, was the equivalent in today's terms of some £82m. I recall that it came as a real surprise to Denis to learn precisely how much Shop & Store was worth.

Greenwood's properties in 1982 had a value in today's terms of around £38m and Hodges properties on the same basis totalled £17m. Therefore, the total value of the properties that we were seeking to split was in today's terms close to £140m. The value of stock in the retail businesses, fittings and fixtures etc. meant that we were trying to divide what today would be a £150m+ list of assets. This was subject to sundry bank borrowing and mortgage arrangements but nevertheless we were considering one of the largest private businesses in the north.

I came up with two schemes for the division. Scheme A which I personally very much preferred was that the parent company Greenwood's would remain just as it was i.e. jointly owned and controlled but with Denis's family having designated to them the Hodges business, also Lowes and whatever Shop & Store freehold properties might be necessary to secure a fair balance of values.

My family would have designated to it the remaining Shop & Store assets. Scheme A also provided that both families would have exactly equal benefits and rewards from the parent company but Denis and his family could obviously take whatever they wished from the assets designated to them i.e. Hodges and Lowes, and my family could do the same with the residue of the Shop & Store business, thus eliminating I contended any sources of friction as regards future remuneration and benefits. I also made the point that if Scheme A did not work out satisfactorily then at a later date a total division could follow.

Scheme B was for a total division at the outset. Sadly – in my view – everyone in Denis's family and in mine wanted Scheme B and thus a total division went ahead.

Stupidly and how I have regretted this crass mistake in recent years! – I felt that I needed to maintain an interest in retailing and elected to take the Hodges company on to my side of the division and then balance out the difference in values by transferring several million pounds worth of Shop & Store investment properties to Denis's side i.e. to Greenwood's. It was of course obvious from the outset that if the business were to be totally split, Denis would have to have the Greenwood's business.

The fatal – as it ultimately proved – weakness in the split that we finally agreed, lay for me in the fact that so many of Shop & Store's investment properties had to be transferred to Greenwood's, that the rental income from the remainder was no longer sufficient to produce an automatic and virtually trouble-free annual profit. Instead it became necessary for Shop & Store Developments Ltd. from that point on, to be fully committed to what its name implied i.e. shop developments. The remaining investment property income simply fell short of what was necessary to cover the interest on the quite large borrowings and the general running costs of the company.

Surprisingly enough Denis and I agreed all the details of this split with little or no disagreement or difficulty. I was naturally rather saddened when the time came for Denis to look at a list of all the Shop & Store freeholds, the development and acquisition of which had taken so much of my time in the recent years, and simply pick out those which he wanted, up to the necessary balancing value. One property that passed in that way was the Low Hall Restaurant freehold which particularly saddened me but having instigated the whole division procedure I could hardly quibble as to which properties Denis chose.

I am sure you can imagine what a meal the lawyers and accountants made out of all the work necessary to implement all the division arrangements, since of course, there were other smaller companies e.g. Lowes of Wigan to be included in the calculations and later all the complex documentation. Suffice it to say when the day came for signing all the necessary documents, a long and wide boardroom table at the offices of Clough & Co. (our accountants), was totally covered with piles of documents requiring a variety of signatures.

It was most certainly a wrench for my son, David and me to leave the business that bore our name and physically move our offices from Greenwood's headquarters at Guiseley to a property two miles away – Burley House – which we had recently purchased to be the headquarters of Shop & Store. In the event, the fine Georgian mansion gave its name to what I chose to call the Burley House Group of Companies which comprised initially: Shop & Store Developments Ltd. and its subsidiary for property dealing – Guiseley Properties Ltd. A further property company – Perseverance Properties Ltd. Greenwood Farms Ltd. which was the small company running the in-hand farming operation on the Whittington Estate.

Also in the Burley House Group was the shopfitting company – Brantongate Ltd. which had grown out of what was Shop & Store's small team of painters, Lowes of Wigan Ltd. and then of course Hodges Menswear Ltd., together with a newly formed company – Cambrian Clothes Ltd. which operated the Hodges tailoring factory.

At first the affairs of the Burley House Group prospered pretty well. We produced a Group magazine with the same old name – *Contact* that my father had first used for Greenwood's house magazine, as far back as the 1930s. In 'The Chairman's view' column for summer 1983 I see that I was able to say – 'I'm delighted to see Hodges has returned to significant profitability', and I noted that there would be eight new branches for Hodges in the second half of that year, bringing the total up to ninety.

The factory – Cambrian Clothes Ltd. for the first time in years was operating profitably. The property companies were all making good progress and even the Brantongate shopfitting business had attracted enough business from other multiple traders to replace the shopfitting jobs for Greenwood's branches, which had gone with the division. Denis – not unreasonably – decided that Greenwood's shopfitting orders would revert to Sharp & Law of Bradford, a company which had been doing shopfitting work for Greenwood's since well before the war.

However, as I now see so clearly, the Group was full of fundamental flaws and weaknesses. The first weakness was the point already made, that Shop & Store no longer automatically produced a profit but was dependent on the much more variable business of property development.

The Hodges' factory business, although briefly moving into profitability was effectively an attempt to 'flog a dying horse'. The bespoke tailoring trade was, despite our best efforts, in steady but inevitable decline. Before the division, the factory had the benefit of supplying Greenwood's branches in the north with both bespoke and ready-made garments. This began to reduce in volume.

At first special tailoring promotions and the increasing number of Hodges' branches kept the factory in the black. It was something of a race against time – could the Hodges' retail chain be expanded sufficiently rapidly to provide enough tailoring orders to keep the factory in work?

The answer was no. Fairly quickly the factory was once again producing significant losses and I had to go to Swansea and explain the situation to all the staff therein. We did manage to save some jobs by leasing the factory premises to a small scale manufacturer of ready-made clothing but his business did not survive poor trading conditions which came a little later.

The factory closure meant – as such circumstances nearly always do – quite a substantial loss for our Group and my only consolation was a comment from a senior figure in the Garment Workers' Trade Union. He told me that he had been involved in numerous similar factory closures in the British garment industry and I was the only Company Chairman he had ever met who had spoken to his members and colleagues face to face.

Another weakness in the Group lay in the fact that we had mistakenly decided not to have a group accountant in our executive team. I had certainly wanted to recruit such a person with particular emphasis on his role as an internal auditor but had been dissuaded by colleagues.

I learned that this was a mistake the very hard way when I was sitting in my elegant office at Burley House and the telephone rang with a call from the receptionist at Brantongate. By this time we had established this shopfitting business in excellent premises on the far side of Bradford and initial results had been such that we had extended the buildings so as to provide a really first-class single-storey factory building behind the handsome two-storey office block fronting the Wakefield Road. The call from the Brantongate receptionist, staggered me. She said, 'Mr Green-wood, there are two bailiffs in the hall'!

It appeared that we were weeks behind paying all manner of bills. I could hardly believe how this could come about when Brantongate's financial affairs were in the hands of a highly qualified and highly intelligent accountant who we had appointed first as Company Secretary and later promoted to be Finance Director.

In fact, what had happened was that the man had had some form of breakdown. He had lost control of the Company's financial affairs but had with great skill managed to produce entirely fictitious figures for each Board Meeting! Thus when I visited Brantongate for the monthly meetings I was shown sales figures which overstated the facts, cost figures which understated them and in effect a completely fictitious situation. It was hard to believe how this could have happened. It certainly would have been discovered much sooner if we had employed a group accountant with the responsibilities of an internal auditor.

Apparently our mentally disturbed Finance Director could not bear to put disappointing figures in front of the Board Meetings and had begun to falsify the figures, at first on a small scale and later massively. Of course the deception could not last since he was not able to pay the Company's suppliers on the due dates. When the time came to clear his desk, not only were there numerous unpaid bills of all kinds but one of his desk drawers was stuffed with cash!

Part of the man's duties was to collect the rents from the small row of cottages let to outside tenants which were part of the whole Brantongate site. Such was his weird, indeed quite extraordinary state of mind that he had simply not troubled to bank this cash but simply stuffed it week after week into a desk drawer. There was no question of him taking money from us. However, I thought later that I wish he had! It would have cost us a lot less if he had just pinched a hundred thousand rather than left us in chaos.

It was the summer of 1983 when he departed. I appointed a group accountant – David Parker who spent most of his first year with us sorting out the mess at Brantongate which – unfortunately – meant that he did not have the opportunity to check up carefully on the situation at other group companies.

I had another nasty blow when someone on whom I had come to rely, let me down badly. This was as regards the retail development which Shop

& Store had completed in Winter Park, Florida. As I have already mentioned we took some small apartment buildings and adjoining land and reconstructed them into what was a very attractive small unit scheme known as Brandywine Square. We used that name since one of the tenants already on the site was a restaurant trading as 'Brandywine' and the name was quite well known in the area.

Most of the work on the scheme had been done by Blair Rugh, the local realtor who I have already mentioned. We had come to know him quite well. He and his wife had stayed with us at Whittington and of course we met socially as well as for business when Enid and I were visiting Florida. During one visit, Blair invited us to his Southern Baptist church, which was quite an experience.

It was the only time I had been to a church which operated rather like a cinema showing a particularly popular film. For the morning services there were two full houses. When we turned up for the 11 a.m. service, we had to wait outside the vast church until the earlier congregation numbering, so it seemed about a couple of thousand people, poured out.

The second sitting was just as full and whilst I was certainly impressed by the enthusiasm of the hot gospel preaching and rousing hymn singing from both the massed choirs and the packed congregation, when the call came – 'Come forward to be saved' Enid and I were certainly not amongst those who rushed up the aisles to join this obviously powerful but for our taste very much too demonstrative church.

I recall standing across the street from our recently completed development with Enid and we agreed that it really did look fine. Small fountains were playing, the pantiled roofs and the bright colours gave the scheme an almost Mediterranean look. In fact it looked so good that Enid was quite surprised when I said, 'Right, now the next thing we'll do is sell this'. My hunch was that in its then shiny new state the scheme was just ripe for sale. Consequently I asked Blair Rugh to put it on the market as quickly as possible and we agreed the sort of figure that I would be looking for.

We returned to the UK leaving him to make all the arrangements for advertising the property, contacting likely purchasers etc. etc. A few weeks passed and I had heard nothing, so I rang him to check progress. I was concerned to get the property sold quickly since I felt that the market was turning down but more importantly the dollar exchange rate was moving against us.

I both wrote to Rugh and left messages for him on the several occasions I rang and all the receptionist at his offices told me was, 'I'm afraid Mr Rugh is out of town'. Finally I rang again to be told by a strange female voice that 'Mr Rugh doesn't work here any more'.

The so-and-so had simply decided to leave the district and move to heaven-knows where, leaving numerous incomplete files including the proposed sale of the Brandywine Square development simply lying there waiting for attention.

I have never heard from him since – which is perhaps as well since the aggressive side of my nature would certainly have shown. The simple fact was that the result of first his dilatoriness and secondly his disappearance was that when we finally got the property sold through another firm, the market had indeed turned down and we got a significantly lower dollar price than a quick sale immediately after my instructions might have produced. Furthermore, the exchange rate most certainly did move badly against us and the end result was that the delay must have cost us something like £1m.

The above incidents were bad enough but I suppose the very worst business shock I have ever experienced came in the summer of 1984. I was reading my post at the breakfast table in my flat at Burley House. I opened one handwritten letter which I suppose I should have preserved permanently since it was one of the most shattering pieces of paper I have ever held in my hand.

It was a note, handwritten and unsigned which said – and this is just about word for word since I remember it so clearly – 'Dear Mr Greenwood, You are a man for whom I have some respect and I therefore want to tell you what is going on in your property business. Your Managing Director, Mr Tyldsley, and his assistant Graham Forster are running their own property business from inside yours. Helping them is your Chief Architect, Mr Mudd and Mr Tyldsley's secretary. If you want to see an example of what they are doing I suggest you go to Stamford and have a look at the High Street.' This was an horrific piece of information which I had to follow up as quickly as possible.

L.B. Tyldsley had joined us over twenty years before. He had previously been no more than a draughtsman but he proved to be an able property manager for Greenwood's and I was happy to make him first a director and later managing director of Shop & Store and its associated property companies. He was – deservedly – the best rewarded executive in the Group and at the time I received that anonymous letter I had three further benefits in mind for him.

His company car at that time was a Daimler Double Six and the company provided a further small car as a perk for his wife. I had decided that his next company car could be a Rolls Royce or a Bentley. I was also working on a scheme to give him – not for the first time – 'a piece of the action' that is to say an equity stake in one or more of the property companies. Thirdly knowing that he had just completed twenty-one years service with the company, I had bought for him – and had suitably engraved – the most expensive watch I have ever handled. The inscription on the back – 'In appreciation of 21 years of loyal service' was to be proved singularly inappropriate.

The anonymous letter obviously had a ring of truth about it. I remembered my late father saying only a few months after the bright young Tyldsley had first joined us – 'This fellow will be very good if he doesn't twist us!'

There was only one way to find out if the letter really was true. I cancelled my plans for the day and taking Enid with me drove at once the 100 miles to Stamford. I left her in the car and went straight into the High Street. I didn't have far to look. A building was under reconstruction to provide a handsome retail unit but unusually there were no signs on the hoarding to say who were the developers or the architects or anything else. I went on to the site and spoke to the site foreman, suggesting to him that I might be interested in taking the shop that they were just finishing. I asked him if he knew who the developers were or who were the agents dealing with the property. He had no idea but he helpfully suggested, 'I know who the architect is, it's a man from Bradford called Mudd'.

That of course was all I needed to know, Brian Mudd was the senior of the three or four architects who we employed at Burley House, designing jobs such as that one in Stamford. The anonymous letter was obviously a quite accurate tip-off.

What to do next? My son and son-in-law agreed with me that we must let the next monthly meeting of Shop & Store's Board – fortunately only a few days away – take place. If both Tyldsley and Forster were going to go, it was essential we learned as much as possible of all the current deals and possible deals, many details of which they were carrying in their heads.

That Board Meeting was a grim day. I think Tyldsley and Forster had begun to realise that at the very least we were suspicious about them and the atmosphere was not cordial. What they did not know was that waiting outside my office which served as our Board Room, were two solicitors from Macfarlanes of London who had advised us on the procedures to be followed.

A typical Shop & Store Board Meeting agenda consisted mainly of a long list of locations where we either had work in progress or negotiations underway. Son David, son-in-law Stewart and I were scribbling notes as Tyldsley and Forster reported on the situation at each of the listed locations. Also in the meeting was the then number three in our property team, Roger Kilty and of course the Company Secretary, Geoffrey Busfield taking the minutes. Slowly we worked our way to the bottom of the agenda and the time came when I could say to Kilty and Busfield, 'Will you leave us now please'.

Also present was David Parker who had recently joined us as Group Accountant. He was tied down to dealing with the problems at Brantongate and had not yet begun any internal auditing of Shop & Store's affairs which would probably have uncovered the Tyldsley/Forster situation. It was probably his appointment which had decided the two villains to resign shortly, which, as I later learned had been their plan. I asked him also to leave us. Tyldsley was seated at one end of the board table, I was at the other. I remember very clearly what I said – I looked at him and said, 'Barry the one thing I want you to tell me is why?!'

At first he tried to bluff – 'What do you mean, I don't know what you are talking about'. I reached in my pocket, pulled out the very handsome and very expensive inscribed gold watch and threw it down the table. I said, 'That's just an indication of how much I trusted you and thought of you'. I then called in the two London lawyers and in their presence formally dismissed both Tyldsley and Forster for gross misconduct and the dismissal to be of immediate effect. I told them both to go and clear their desks immediately and to be out of the building in a matter of minutes. We took Forster's car keys from him, since he of course also had a company car. There was an ugly scene in Tyldsley's office since he wanted to remove numerous papers which were clearly not his personal effects but rather, items referring to the business that he had been running from inside mine – Fairfax Securities Ltd. Fortunately both David and Stewart are big men and the situation did not come to blows. Tyldsley simply took his personal effects from his office and was then driven home by the company chauffeur and a colleague who returned with both the Daimler and his wife's car.

All that was exciting but also terribly sad. I dealt with our Chief Architect and Tyldsley's secretary by simply asking them – 'Don't you think it would be a good idea if you offered me your resignation with immediate effect?' to which they both answered, 'Yes' and they too were out of the office within minutes. So we had eliminated the conspiracy but now it was necessary to try and pick up the pieces.

We quickly learned that the legal work for the numerous property transactions which were improperly being carried out on our premises with our facilities etc. etc. was being handled by a well known firm of Bradford solicitors, Last Suddards. This amazed me since the senior partner in that firm was someone I knew reasonably well and I could not see how he and his colleagues in that practice could have failed to know that Tyldsley and Forster were both executives of Shop & Store Developments Ltd. We were advised that we had grounds for action against Last Suddards and were ready to proceed with an action for damages – and the damage we had sustained was very significant – but fortunately the matter did not reach the courts. I will simply say that without any admission of liability on their part which of course we noted, that practice offered us a very substantial six figure sum which we were pleased to accept and abandoned the proposed litigation.

We then had to try and pick up the various deals which Tyldsley and Forster had in progress for their own company. They were to say the least, reluctant to give us full details of these but over a stressful period of months the end result was that several hundred thousand pounds of profit from such transactions ended up where it should properly have been in the first place – in Shop & Store's coffers rather than in their pockets.

The enforced departures described above obviously meant some changes to the management of our property business. I had to assume the temporary role of Managing Director, in addition to the Chairmanship. Roger Kilty previously number three on the property team became number one and was appointed a director of Shop & Store and over the next two or three years various property professionals were recruited from outside to fill such roles as Development Manager (North), Development Manager (South) and Estates Manager. Of these, the most valuable was

Michael Jenkins who certainly had more property developer's flair than his other colleagues.

For several years after the departure of Tyldsley and Forster, Shop & Store did quite well. A particularly good deal was the property we chose to call Nidderdale House in Harrogate. There we had purchased the cinema adjoining Marks & Spencer's original Harrogate store and at first had high hopes that we could re-build the cinema as an extension to M & S. However, they decided to move elsewhere and instead we built a block of shops – I think I can say a quite handsome block of shops, since the facade was all in dressed stone. The principal tenant was McDonalds who took a large corner unit and the position is still one of the best in Harrogate.

In order to generate a decent profit in 1985 we needed to sell the completed development. Acting for the prospective purchaser was my old friend Kenneth Hanson, senior partner of Dacre, Son and Hartley. He and I agreed a sale at £3.5 million (around £8m today) after only a quarter of an hour's discussion and he knew and I knew that when we shook hands on the deal that was a binding transaction. Sadly in subsequent years deals settled with a handshake have totally disappeared from the commercial property world and in my view business is much the poorer for that.

Hodges was also doing quite well. They opened their hundredth branch in Abingdon in October 1984 and thus twice in my life I had achieved the multiple retailer's ambition of a hundred-strong chain. The previous time had been way back in the early 1950s when Greenwood's opened their hundredth branch in Huddersfield.

We began an experiment at Hodges in 1986. Many of their units had surplus floor space so we decided to introduce ladies departments at a number of branches. We called the operation 'His and Hers at Hodges' and after a couple of years had incorporated Hers units into thirty-three branches. The experiment was neither a roaring success but nor was it a flop. Probably we would have done better with ladieswear if those at the top of the business – particularly me! – had known more about the ladies' trade. My experience was limited to the modest operation at Lowes store in Wigan and that experience came to an end in 1984 when we finally decided to close the store down, demolish the old buildings and build a new development on the site.

In fact that had been our intention when we first bought Lowes' business but as I have already mentioned we decided to have a go at the departmental store business. We never made a lot of money as department store operators but to be honest my family and I thoroughly enjoyed the experience. The only thing that finally decided us to close Lowes down was the fact that the property really needed a great deal of money spending on it if it were to compete successfully with the other main store in Wigan – Debenhams.

Thus the old store which had been a landmark in Wigan for so many years came down and we replaced it with what we intended to be a row of shops but which ended up as a large Barclays Bank.

Recording some of these business issues prompts the thought that I was never motivated simply by money-making. I genuinely enjoyed both running chains of shops and also the cut and thrust of the commercial property world. However, I always felt – and still do – that if you are able to make a lot of money you should most certainly give some away. Before the family division, both my brother Denis and I had set up charitable trusts to which we gave substantial blocks of preference shares. The dividends from those shares were, in my case, distributed annually to a long list of good causes and worthy charities, mostly medical, educational and sporting. For many years my family would get together and decide which of the charities we would help and with what size of cheque. We usually distributed the equivalent in today's money of about £100,000 a year and thus over the life of the charitable settlement the equivalent of about £1.5m which could have gone into my family's pockets went to places where it would do much more good.

Having to close down this charitable settlement when the preference shares were rendered worthless following the business disasters which I shall shortly be describing to you, was just one of the many bitter pills that those disasters forced me to swallow.

CHAPTER 20

Ups and Downs

THE 1980S AND THE EARLY 1990s were certainly a very interesting period. There were some very good times and then towards the end some very bad ones.

Let's look first at affairs in South Wales and the south-west. Just before we had been obliged to close Cambrian Clothes Ltd. i.e. the old Hodges factory operation, we had acquired a new headquarters for the Hodges chain, a few hundred yards away from the original factory and head office but still part of the Fforestfach Trading Estate just outside Swansea. Hodges moved into those new premises in 1982 but in only five years had outgrown them and we did a deal with the Welsh Development Agency to exchange the inadequate premises at Kingsway, Fforestfach for a splendid new headquarters at Bruce Road on the other side of the same trading estate.

The Bruce Road headquarters with some 75,000 square feet of storage space and ample office, auxiliary accommodation and generous car parking was a facility big enough to serve perhaps as many as 300 shops. My son David and I had ambitions that the time would come when we would need all that capacity. In the meantime, at least before the impending recession hit the company, Hodges was running quite smoothly. Philip Clayton had retired and been succeeded as Managing Director by Jack Cruse, previously the Company Secretary. The Swansea-based local board was a good one with two long serving Hodges' ex-managers – Rodney Stone and Richard West serving as Merchandise Director and Sales Director respectively and with a newly appointed Finance Director, Jonathan Griffiths completing the team. David and I and for a while occasionally son-in-law Stewart, also attended the regular monthly meetings in Swansea and of course David and I both spent a lot of time travelling around the branches and also following up property possibilities throughout the south-west.

We used to run advertisements in the trade press – *Menswear* magazine in particular, on the lines of – 'Would you like to sell your business?' These produced numerous replies and such additional branches as Kenilworth,

Andover, Swindon and the Abingdon hundredth unit already mentioned. It is probably fair to say that over the years I bought for Greenwood's and Hodges individual menswear businesses or small chains with shops over most of England. Probably therefore I have bought more menswear businesses in this country than anyone else ever.

I enjoyed those transactions and I think the vendors particularly appreciated the fact that they were dealing directly with the person who would ultimately sign the cheque. Being in that position also gave me the negotiating advantage of being able to make an instant decision. I like to think I got most of them right and I believe all the vendors with whom I did deals over so many years went away from the situation with the feeling that it had been a fair deal.

In 1987, the year when I turned sixty, we decided as a family that there should be another division, namely a split of ownership and responsibilities for the now quite prosperous Burley House Group between my son and his family on one side and daughter Patricia and Stewart on the other. Personally, I was never wholly convinced of the merits of this idea and would have preferred to see the business continuing as a single entity. However, everyone else in the family wanted this sub-division so with some reluctance I agreed to it. The outcome was that Stewart gave up his professional life in London and became Managing Director of Shop & Store and its associated property businesses. Hodges' ownership passed into the hands of David and his wife Judith. I continued to act as Chairman of the different companies (handing over the Shop & Store Chairmanship to Stewart a little later) and was designated Group Chairman.

Probably the high point in my family's business affairs came the following year in 1988. The various property companies had just produced an annual profit of which today's equivalent would be something over £2m and Hodges' best ever year was only a little less which is to say a total profitability of around £4m, to which could be added the progressive appreciation in value of two substantial property portfolios. First, Shop & Store's investment properties and then on the other side the steadily increasing value of Hodges freehold shops since around seventy of the hundred + chain were the company's own property.

During this prosperous period Stewart found an opportunity for us to make a modest but useful investment in Holland and Holland, the world-famous gun makers. For a few years we owned 10% thereof and did very nicely thank you when the company was finally taken over by a French conglomerate.

Despite the then very successful trading at Hodges my son David had – quite rightly as time ultimately proved – anxieties as to the long-term future of, what we might call, middle class menswear retailing. Therefore when an unusual opportunity for a major diversification presented itself, he and I were both enthusiastic for it. It happened like this.

We knew a family called Shergold, having met the elder members thereof on a cruise. They ran a chain of hardware shops, mostly in the Midlands. They had merged their business with a similar family-owned hardware chain, named J.W. Carpenter Ltd. and the result was a total branch list of some fifty hardware stores operating from a warehouse and head office at Thame in Oxfordshire. Michael Shergold who was working as Managing Director of the combined enterprise came – out of the blue – to see me one day, although he and I had hardly met. It was his father and mother who were our casual shipboard acquaintances.

Michael Shergold explained that he was unhappy with the set-up in the business that he was running and suggested that we might seek to acquire an interest in it. This possibility obviously coincided with David's thoughts about diversification and it also was relevant to the fact that Hodges' fine new Swansea headquarters was operating at significantly below its capacity. Clearly if we were to acquire a fifty-strong chain in a different form of retailing, it would be possible for the warehouse operation to be conducted much more cheaply from Swansea, even if the administration of the business remained in Oxfordshire.

After some careful thought and visits to Carpenter's headquarters and looking at most of their branches, we became convinced that there was a deal to be done. Not only could we supply the Carpenter shops more efficiently but there was quite a number of Hodges' branches which would almost certainly have traded more profitably as hardware stores than as menswear branches.

J.W. Carpenter Ltd. i.e. the previously merged Shergold and Carpenter chains was not a p.l.c. it was technically a private company but had an unusually large number of shareholders counted in hundreds, some of whom were distant relatives of the Carpenter family, others being former members of staff or with different, usually fairly remote connections with the business.

To acquire Carpenters it was obviously necessary to secure the support of more than half of those disparate shareholders. The Shergold family held some shares which they were ready to sell but we obviously needed the agreement and support of many more individuals. Naturally we tried at first to persuade the main members of the Carpenter family to agree to the sale of control of their business and hoped for an amicable and uncontested acquisition of a controlling interest. We were disappointed!

With the exception of Michael Shergold, the existing directors and the Carpenter family chose to oppose our proposals bitterly and we therefore decided to proceed with what was in effect a semi-public takeover battle. We wrote to every one of the shareholders explaining our proposals and even went so far as to produce a video showing the Hodges' operation – its headquarters, its warehousing and many of its branches etc.

Much correspondence with shareholders was generated. David's office became something of a 'war room' for the operation. The acceptances began to roll in and soon the number of shareholders who would accept our bid had passed 40% at which stage we were more than somewhat excited. A few days later a letter of acceptance from a clergyman in the south-west took us just past the magic 50% level and it looked as if the battle was won.

It had become a battle – and not a very pleasant one – since the Carpenter directors seemed to regard us as villainous characters who were probably only interested in asset stripping. We never had the opportunity for meaningful meetings with them, when they might have learned that our intention was to increase the size of that business dramatically with consequential benefits for most of its staff and executives. They were of course furious with Michael Shergold and when they noted that many of the telephone calls logged to his company phone were to us in Yorkshire they apparently suspected that he had been divulging privileged and secret information. He had not done so for the simple reason that it was not necessary. We had learned all we needed to know about the business by looking at figures that were on the public record and our own appraisal of the various shops. Nevertheless the Carpenter directors apparently managed to persuade some judge that he should grant that extraordinary thing – an Anton Pilar order.

I had never heard of such a thing until one day – again out of the blue – a bevy of solicitors descended on Burley House with the right to examine anything they wished therein.

An Anton Pilar is a fearsome legal instrument of obvious rarity and probably only the lawyers amongst readers of this book will ever have heard of it. I had never heard of it in more than forty years of very active business life. I believe it is normally only used in extremely serious cases of potential fraud and the like, and I have to say with all due deference to the law and the judge concerned whoever he or she might have been, that this was a classic case where the law was an ass.

The bevy of lawyers found absolutely nothing of any value to their clients in the takeover battle and duly departed after an hour or two when they had caused my colleagues and I intense annoyance. It is not funny to have to open every drawer in your desk etc. for the inspection of some smart alec solicitor who you have never seen before.

The bitterness into which what should have been a series of sensible and civilised discussions had descended did have one effect. The clergyman who had tipped the balance in our favour rescinded his commitment to us and we found ourselves when the dust finally settled with 49.99% of the shares committed to us. It was as close as that.

On that basis our offer was withdrawn and as far as we were concerned that was the end of it. There was a sad aftermath to the story in that Carpenters went bust a year or two later and the shareholders who could have done well from our offer ended up with little or nothing. David and I to this day are satisfied that if we had taken over the firm we could have made a success of the business. We would have brought to it economical warehousing, an immediate addition of several new branches (changing over Hodges' units) and the financial backing to expand the chain elsewhere.

The Carpenter saga was one of the 'downs' of the 1980s but there was also a very significant 'up' in that decade, when as a family we became proprietors of a substantial Scottish estate. I had come to know one part of the Highlands pretty well having regularly taken salmon fishing for a week or two each year on such rivers as the Carron, the Cassley and the Oykel. I had also on occasion rented Glencalvie Lodge and its substantial acreage for deerstalking. On the back of that local knowledge when we heard that it was possible to buy an interest in the River Oykel, we jumped at it and purchased a 20% share in that splendid river. This was actually quite a good commercial deal as well as providing us with the opportunity of regularly fishing on what some people – and certainly me – regard as amongst the best salmon fishing in Scotland.

Salmon fishing is usually valued on the basis of so many thousand pounds per fish caught against the river's five- or perhaps ten-year average catch. Thus for example, if the river were averaging say 500 fish per year and the then going rate for fish was £3,000 then the approximate value of that river or stretch of fishing would be £1.5m.

We were lucky in that we bought our 20% share of the lower Oykel at a time when the five-year average had not been particularly good but during the period of our ownership, catches greatly increased and at the same time so did the generally accepted price per fish caught. Those two circumstances put together meant that after a year or two we were able to sell half of our interest i.e. a 10% stake in the lower Oykel for the same price that we had paid for our 20% stake.

The arrangement on the lower Oykel was fairly unusual but it worked extremely well. The river was not split into say five equal sections. Our original 20% stake simply meant that we had the benefits of one fifth of the whole. The income from all the lettings of the fishing went into a central pool, from which all the outgoings were deducted and then the balance split amongst the proprietors but in proportion to their percentage holdings. The biggest outgoings were the costs of employing a fisheries manager or head ghillie and three other ghillies. The river was divided into four beats with a ghillie being in charge of a beat for one week and then moving on to the adjoining beat. A similar arrangement applied to the anglers. Two or at the most three could fish each beat and if, for example, they began on beat two on the Monday of their week, on Tuesday they would go to beat three and on Wednesday to beat four, Thursday to beat one and Friday back to beat two, ending their week on the Saturday on beat three.

This arrangement meant that anyone taking two weeks on the lower Oykel would fish each beat three times in that visit with each succeeding day being different from the previous one. Obviously much more interesting than fishing the same beat day after day for a fortnight.

Most of the pools on the lower Oykel are easy to reach with hardly any lengthy walks and there is a great variety of fishing between the pools which begin at the base of the Oykel Falls and then continue through a rocky gorge under the famous Oykel Bridge and then through a delightful variety of pools until the bottom of beat four where the river runs out into the Kyle of Sutherland. During the time of our interest in the river the average catch moved up to around the 1,000 fish in a year mark with a decent run of spring fish and lots of summer fish when fishing became a shirt sleeves operation and fairly alcoholic picnic lunches by the riverside a real joy.

The Oykel Bridge Hotel was the base for most anglers and very comfortable it was.

However, after a year or two of enjoying this rather different part of Shop & Store's property portfolio we had the opportunity to purchase the Invercassley Estate which adjoined the river. The Estate totalled some 17,000 acres of which about 2,000 were farmland and forestry and the remainder good ground for deerstalking or – as the Scottish expression has it – a deer forest. Incidentally many a 'deer forest' has no trees or only very few on it. That was the case with most of the area of the Invercassley Estate. However, the sheep farming operation on the lower ground was quite significant.

We had decided that Shop & Store Developments Ltd. should be the business which purchased and operated these Scottish properties and thus Shop & Store found itself with a sheep farm carrying 1,000 ewes and producing nearly 2,000 lambs each year. Readers with farming knowledge will wonder how a lambing ratio of nearly two lambs per ewe could be attained in the Scottish Highlands. The reason was that the previous owners of the Estate had built some enormous sheds which could comfortably accommodate 1,000 ewes at lambing time and still leave room for son-in-law Stewart to use some of the vacant floor space for an indoor tennis court! Thus lambing was all indoors away from the vagaries of the Highlands' weather.

A very nice five-bedroomed house – Invercassley House – came with the property and at first it was a holiday home for Stewart and Tricia and my two granddaughters Sophie and Emily. However, another piece of property – the Inveroykel Hotel came on the market and Stewart decided that we should buy this and renovate it as a company property from which the Estate could be managed as and when he and Tricia were able to get there. That was not as difficult as it might sound, since there were regular flights from London to Inverness which then only needed a car journey of a little less than an hour to get to the Estate.

I bought Invercassley House out of the company and made it my holiday home and enjoyed it hugely. Stalking deer on your own estate and catching salmon on a river of which you own part were for me just about as good as it gets.

Various of my friends would come and stay with us and enjoy the Highlands life. Some of them were good, indeed expert, fishermen, others were not.

I remember particularly my old school friend Tom Whitfield as a fisherman. I had tried to teach him the rudiments of fishing on the River Lune at Whittington and there he had conclusively proved that he might not have been a good angler but he was certainly a lucky one. Late in the season on the Lune it is permissible and sometimes necessary to spin for salmon as opposed to trying to catch them on a fly. Tom Whitfield came with me on one occasion to the banks of the Lune and watched me spinning for a minute or two before saying, 'Can I have a go?'

I taught him the basics of casting with a spinning rod on a quiet stretch fifty yards upstream then took him back to a more likely spot and told him to cast away as instructed. I turned away from him to go further downstream and have a few chucks with my fly rod but before I had taken three paces a small voice behind me said – 'I think I've got one.' I turned round and there was Tom with a bent rod. I assumed he had just caught the bottom or a piece of debris and took the rod from him to attempt to clear it. At which point the line moved and he had indeed hooked a salmon with his very first cast and in due course we had it on the bank. When I think of all the hours I have spent casting fruitlessly and all the blank days which have been recorded in my fishing diary I could have cried. There was this absolute beginner who immediately took the view that salmon fishing was really quite easy.

He was not quite so lucky on the Oykel. He was fishing away with an experienced ghillie to assist him and this time he was casting with the usual two-handed salmon fly rod. He got into a fish in a deep pool near the bottom of beat four on the Oykel. The fish which was obviously a good one was zipping around the pool pretty vigorously and then all of a sudden the line stopped moving. 'I think your line's caught round a rock or something Sir,' said the ghillie. 'If you'll let me hold the rod perhaps you'll go round across the bridge and see what's holding it.' Tom gave the rod to the ghillie, crossed over the bridge 100 yards or so away, walked up the opposite bank and peered into the deep pool.

'It's caught round an old tree,' he shouted.

'Do you think you could free it?' the ghillie shouted back. Tom hesitated for a moment and then shouted, 'I think so'.

To the ghillie's amazement and to provide him with a story which he never tired of telling thereafter, Tom Whitfield stripped off down to his long johns and thermal vest (it was a fairly cold spring day) and then dived straight into the pool.

You must understand that gentlemen salmon fishers who are plying their skills on extremely expensive stretches of fishing do not normally jump into rivers in their underwear.

In the event Tom managed to free the line but in his struggles with it the fish came off and escaped, at which point Tom was caught by the current and carried some 200 yards downstream before he could get out of the river and return to the slightly shocked ghillie. To his great credit he retrieved his outer clothes, dispensed with the long johns and vest and then carried on fishing, thus displaying very much the kind of enthusiasm needed for country sports.

With hindsight I can now see clearly that although we got a lot of pleasure out of the Invercassley Estate and the lower Oykel River, we put far too much company money into the operation. We spent a small fortune renovating Inveroykel Hotel and also providing good roads throughout the blocks of fir trees which comprised the forestry element of the estate. Money also went into the farming operation which later included a handsome-looking herd of Highland cattle which became the object of many tourists' cameras on coach trips running up through Bonar Bridge and then across the Highlands to Ullapool, which route took them over Oykel Bridge and past our farmland.

Turning back to more normal business, from my part-time role as something of a Scottish laird, finds me in a period full of interest but now with more 'downs' than 'ups'. By 1989 Brantongate, our shopfitting company, had been re-organised and in particular its management strengthened. We had appointed an experienced managing director with a wide knowledge of the shopfitting industry and he had brought with him two senior colleagues. Then to my great disappointment he and his two main assistants told me that they all wished to leave simultaneously for what they saw as better opportunities elsewhere in the country. David and I decided that we were not going to go through all the pain and anxiety of re-organising the business once more, so decided to sell the company.

We agreed a sale of Brantongate as a going concern to another and larger shopfitting business but just when we thought our troubles with the company were over, our prospective purchasers changed their mind and backed out. Business conditions at this time were generally poor and looking likely to get worse. It quickly became apparent that we had no alternative other than to liquidate the company and thus its brief but chequered career came to an abrupt end.

At the same time things were not too good at Hodges. The year 1990 was a poor trading one and the company's problems were not helped by the fact that Managing Director Jack Cruse had been obliged to retire due to ill health. We recruited a very able replacement in John Flatley from outside the company, but it must be said he took hold of the company at a bad time.

We were now into the era of very high interest rates and lower than anticipated spending by the public. Furthermore the long journeys from Yorkshire into the West Country and South Wales were becoming less and less attractive.

The impact of high interest rates on Shop & Store was particularly savage. Shop & Store had – like most property development companies – large borrowings and the abnormally high burden of interest on these borrowings was beginning to crush the company.

Generally our situation was very different from our happy position only a couple of years previously.

Despite our mounting problems, David and I agreed early in 1991 to become involved in a very high-tech medical company. It happened like this – our family doctor David Fieldhouse had a friend – Brian Clarke – who was an inventor. He had made himself an authority and expert on the use of liquid nitrogen and had formed a business named Cryogenic Technology Ltd. This small business operating from modest premises in Belper, Derbyshire had as its main product a hand-held device capable of delivering with great accuracy and precision small shots of liquid nitrogen which could painlessly remove warts, moles and the like from the skin of both people and animals. The sale of these gadgets and the supply of the liquid nitrogen for them was the little company's main business. However, Brian Clarke's inventive mind had produced a design for the use of liquid nitrogen in the treatment of liver cancer.

I knew nothing about such matters when David Fieldhouse came one weekend for lunch at Whittington Hall. He explained to me that tumours in the liver were sometimes inoperable and no one had as yet come up with a satisfactory treatment. Apparently Brian Clarke's invention of a liquid nitrogen dispensing machine which would deliver through a special probe a precise shot of liquid nitrogen directly into the liver tumour which would then be destroyed, could be a major medical breakthrough. The inventor's problem was that he simply did not have the resources to develop his invention and the question put to my son David and I was – 'Would we help?' Initially the funds required were no more than £30,000 and of course we readily agreed to help with that but it soon became obvious that more and more money would be needed. We, therefore, ended up with control of the company and with David and I, together with our Group Accountant David Parker, joining Brian Clarke, his wife and Dr Fieldhouse as Directors of Cryogenic Technology Ltd. which lengthy title we always abbreviated to – Cryotech.

In fact, we could ill afford the ever-increasing cash demands that Cryotech needed but there were two motivations for continuing what became an ever-increasing involvement. First, was the obvious point, that if indeed the invention were successful, it could save many, many lives and secondly like all high-tech medical equipment, if it could be sold in bulk it could be massively profitable.

The plan was to continue to expand the sale of the hand-held devices whilst completing the development of the hepatic machine, for which a worldwide market seemed entirely possible. David acted as Chairman of the company, I was just a Non-Executive Director.

I see from an old scrap book that the *Mail on Sunday* issue for 20 December 1992 ran a half-page feature on Cryotech in its money section. The article described how Brian Clarke had started the company and how we had come in to help. It also confirmed that the hepatic machine had earned a SMART (Small Manufacturing Reward for Research and Technology) in 1990 and went on to mention that through a USA distributor, the machines were being tested in that country and already sixty serious liver cancer patients had survived thanks to the treatment.

We had acquired a piece of land adjoining Cryotech's original small premises and had built new headquarters for them. However, the problem was that throughout all the development period the company was losing a lot of money. Our hope was that the breakthrough would come and perhaps in due course there would be hardly a hospital in the world which did not have one or more of Cryotech's hepatic machines.

For anyone who produces a new drug or a new medical procedure, there is one hurdle which must be cleared. That is the approval of the Federal Drugs Administration of the United States. If you have FDA approval for your drug or device it can be safely assumed that the medical authorities in other countries throughout the world will approve your project. There is, however, one horrible snag with seeking FDA approval and that is – quite simply – the time that it takes. Your new drug or device takes its place in a massive queue of applications from all over the world which have to be fully examined and tested before they are either approved or rejected.

Cryotech's hepatic machines or 'consoles' as we called them took their place in the queue and then month after month went by as we slowly moved up the queue. We had to wait for more than a year before we had FDA approval.

All the time that we were waiting for that vital decision we were meeting the costs of an enlarged workforce, paying for further research and development and struggling to keep the business afloat by trying to increase the sale of the original product – the hand-held dispensers.

Finally, we had the approval and quite quickly we saw a handful of the consoles in use as far apart as France, Germany and Australia as well as the UK and of course the USA. Then the blow fell. An American company commenced litigation against us on the grounds that the fine probes which were actually inserted into tumours, breached a patent right of theirs. Whilst right was on our side in this – Brian Clarke was sure that the specific design of the probes had come from his inventive mind and nowhere else – might was not.

American litigation is something to be avoided at all costs, since all too often issues are decided largely by the amount of money that the contestants can throw at each other. We simply could not afford the massive legal costs of fighting a long and complicated patent or copyright issue through the American courts. We could not sell a product with the litigation pending and we could not afford to defend ourselves against what we felt was a false accusation. There was nothing to be done other than liquidate the company and take a heavy loss – probably around £4 million in today's money. The rump of the company and its intellectual property was sold to the UK subsidiary of a Swedish medical business and Brian Clarke went to work for them. For our part we had lost a great deal of money and almost as important – had wasted a great deal of time during a desperately difficult business period, when our other affairs needed our full attention. Cryotech was altogether a bitter and costly disappointment.

As a footnote to this sad story I note that today cryogenic technology i.e. the use of liquid nitrogen for various medical procedures remains in use. Apparently the system we had produced for the treatment of liver cancer and later prostate cancers has been largely superseded by what I believe is known as laparoscopy surgery. The hand-held devices for external use are still very widely used. Perhaps, therefore, it can be said that our adventure into the world of high-tech medicare was not a complete dead loss but in financial terms and its impact on our general affairs at a very difficult trading time, it most certainly was.

The Cryotech saga was bad enough but it pales into insignificance alongside the outcome of our merging the Hodges business with the rump of that fine old menswear chain Dunn & Co. In the summer of 1991 the century-old Dunn & Co. menswear chain was in trouble. For most of the company's life they had primarily been retailers of headwear and were often described as Dunns the Hatters. In more recent times they had increasingly extended their ready-to-wear clothing sections and had deservedly earned the reputation of being a sound business selling good quality clothing and headwear to a middle class market. They had branches in almost every major town and city. With their timber and leaded glass shop fronts they appeared to be a settled and permanent part of the British retail scene.

Dunn & Co. was an unusual business inasmuch as its founder George Arthur Dunn on his death left all the shares in the business for the benefit of its staff and thus for many years the company was controlled by trustees acting on behalf of Dunn's Pension Fund. The company was also unusual in that it did not take the protection afforded by what is known as limited liability (that being of course what the letters 'Ltd.' mean after a company's name and which has the effect of limiting the liability of the shareholders to the amount of the company's capital). All limited companies have to file their reports and accounts regularly. Those very rare and unusual businesses of which G.A. Dunn & Co. was perhaps the best known, do not. Thus, little or nothing was ever known in or out of the menswear trade about the state of Dunn's finances.

In fact for years, like many other people in the menswear trade I had been curious about Dunns and had longed to know just how well they were trading but whereas an enquiry in respect of any normal company can produce for you, at modest cost, a set of that company's filed accounts, in the case of Dunns this was not available. Thus all that was generally known about them was that it was a fine old established business which

72. At my desk in Burley House in the mid 80s

73. Far from work, in Eastern Province South Africa with the Kudu bull which almost had me!

74. *Our Ruby Wedding at Whittington. L to R: G.B.G., Enid, son-in-law Stewart Urry, 'Tricia, daughter-in-law Judith and David*

75. *Invercassley Estate beyond the junction of the Rivers Cassley (on right) and Oykel (on left). Invercassley House is the white house surrounded by trees*

76. Invercassley House south side

77. Invercassley House from the road

78. Norman Tebbit and G.B.G. during a November 1992 pheasant shoot at Whittington

79. A 'Whittington Week' group on Croasdale grouse moor. L to R my springer 'Sam', David, Tom Burst, Bill McClanahan, Ralph Sutcliffe, Gene Godbold and G.B.G. October 1994

80. W.G.S. Board of Governors 2006. L to R standing Paul Robertshaw, Rev. Peter Whitaker, Dr Neil Tunnicliffe, Keith Davy, Rev. Paul Glass, Tony Kassapian, Alan Wintersgill, John Robinson, Graham Russell, Ian Small, Judge Stephen Gullick, John Weaving. L to R seated Tish Burton, Elaine Cleland, Roger Davy, G.B.G., Dr Georgina Haslam, Judge Helen Wood

81. Enid and G.B.G.'s Golden Wedding at Ripley Castle, near Harrogate 31 August 1999

82. Enid and G.B.G. at Beck House on their Diamond Wedding anniversary 31 August 2009

83. Beck House from across the Thornton Beck valley

84. Beck House south side, from the golf course

owned the freeholds of most of its chain of shops stretching from the south coast as far north as Inverness.

All of us in the trade knew that in the past few years there had been some changes in trading policy at Dunns with something of a departure from its well-established image as a retailer of traditional better quality menswear. We began to suspect that perhaps the company was not trading as well as it had in earlier years but nevertheless it was certainly a surprise to me to learn that the company was in fact available for sale.

I telephoned its chairman to express my sympathy at the circumstances and told him that at that time we simply did not have the resources to acquire the whole company with its long list of valuable freehold properties which clearly were worth tens of millions. I simply expressed the hope that there might be perhaps some of their branches in the south-west which could be offered to us if no other solution to the trustees' problem arose.

The Dunns' chairman noted my interest and then nothing happened for a month or two until I learned that Ayrhouse Ltd. a company formed by two of our suppliers, had in fact, reached an 'in principle' agreement to acquire the whole of Dunns, albeit on the understanding that some of the less successful branches would have to close. It seemed to me that one of Dunns problems must have been the very high cost of a London head office and warehouse and of course Hodges headquarters in Swansea was large enough to serve many more shops than our then branch list of 106. Furthermore, I felt that our management team and the systems we operated would be perfect for restoring Dunns to success and profitability. I therefore approached the directors of Ayrhouse and suggested it would be to our mutual advantage if they were to acquire Dunns, that it and Hodges should be merged and the whole enterprise operated from Swansea. The Ayrhouse team were very enthusiastic for this project and we quickly reached an in principle agreement with them. We would retain the freeholds of our Hodges branches but would sell to Ayrhouse our entire retail business for – in today's money – £12 million.

The Dunns chain was shrinking in numbers with a branch closure somewhere almost every few days, since to satisfy their bankers they were being obliged to sell many of their shops.

We moved quickly and reached an agreement. We arranged what was to be the final formal meeting in Manchester and arranged for our Hodges management team, that is to say the Swansea-based directors thereof, to meet with us and the Ayrhouse directors in Manchester.

Ayrhouse planned to purchase most of the Dunn & Co. freeholds. Consequently that part of their deal was significantly larger than the simultaneous acquisition of the Hodges retail business. In fact – at today's prices their agreement was for over £30 million to Dunns as well as £12m to us, thus their funding requirement was c. £45m.

With their assurance that they had all the necessary funding in place, David and I set off to drive to Manchester for what was intended to be the final meeting and an opportunity to introduce our Swansea colleagues to the men who would be their new bosses. Thereafter, David and I would have been out of retail menswear and instead simply administering a substantial property portfolio.

I shall never forget driving across the M62 on the top of the moors on the way from Yorkshire to Lancashire when the car phone rang. David was driving and I took the call to hear the senior of the Ayrhouse team explain that at the last minute one of their proposed funding partners had pulled out and they were not in a position to finalise the deal. Thus what had seemed a fascinating prospect which would have meant more than 200 shops operating from Swansea and a lot of money coming to my family – came to nothing. To say the least this was a very dark moment and another 'so near and yet so far'.

However, in the course of the Ayrhouse discussions and negotiations we had learned enough about the Dunns business to feel that we could sensibly make our own quite independent offer for part of the business. By this time more Dunns branches had been closed down and sold to different trades and numerous others were scheduled to go down the same route. We were finally invited to submit an offer for some seventy of the remaining shops. A number of these were impossible for us on grounds of geography and there were others which we felt could not be economically viable if a full modern market rental had to be paid. Thus after a period of quick but very intense discussion, consideration and negotiation we finalised on a list of forty of the Dunns branches and took them over together with the right to trade under the name Dunn & Co. or George Arthur Dunn.

The end result, therefore, was that at one stroke, Hodges had acquired forty more branches bringing its total up to 146. More than 100 experienced and able people, area managers, branch managers and assistants joined us and were made very welcome and our menswear turnover (in today's terms) jumped up to something over £40 million per annum. The acquisition was completed in August 1991 and we began at once to use the Dunn name on all new branches and also to convert existing Hodges units to the name Dunns. We had taken the view that whilst Hodges' name was extremely well-known in South Wales and one or two parts of the south-west, Dunns name was nationally known.

In a little over a year the number of units trading as Dunn & Co. had been increased to seventy-two and there were many of the other eighty units which were still under Hodges name being prepared for changeover.

It was a priority for us to get Dunn & Co. back into London. Some of the Dunns branches we had acquired were in the outer London area but representation once more in central London was, we thought, a must. We were able to secure handsome premises at 90 Regent Street. We naturally had to pay a substantial rent and in fact Regent Street was the first time I ever had a branch where the rental was well into six figures. In fact the shop did very well and allowed me to achieve another ambition.

Ever since my early days in the trade I had wanted to have a shop somewhere which took over a million pounds a year. Regent Street very quickly did that. With that flagship branch open we frequently used as an advertising slogan – 'Dunn & Co. Regent Street, London and over 150 branches nationwide'.

Trading conditions in the early 1990s were as bad as anything I could remember and not until the 2008 credit crunch and the recession which followed, were trading conditions anything like as difficult as say 1991 and 1992. The harsh economic circumstances had come at a very bad time for us. We had this wonderful opportunity to merge the Hodges and Dunns businesses with the object of restoring Dunns to its old position as a major national business but to accomplish this an awful lot of money needed to be spent on re-fitting so many shops. We were trading at a loss just at a time when we particularly needed a lot of cash.

By the middle of 1993 we were satisfied that we had the right formula for successful trading at Dunn & Co. The new or converted branches were all fully carpeted, the decorations and fittings included numerous old-style prints, the odd bookcase, Chesterfield settees or armchairs with coffee tables, as well as the usual menswear fixtures and fittings. We were trying to achieve something of the feeling of a gentlemen's club. The formula was definitely successful, as the results from newly opened branches, such as Guildford, Brighton and Richmond proved. However, one thing was certain – the formula would not be appropriate for some of the older and smaller Hodges units in the Welsh valleys and we began a programme of disposing of such branches.

We were clearly very close to re-establishing Dunns on a national scale. We had, however, two major problems, the first and most important was the simple fact that recent poor trading had meant that we lacked the funds to maintain or better still, accelerate the Dunns development programme. A further problem lay in the fact that David and I were trying to develop a quite complex business with its headquarters some 250 miles distant from us. I suppose it must also be said that I was approaching my sixty-fifth birthday and the best of my hard-working days were obviously behind me.

David and I therefore decided that the logical thing to do was to sell Dunn & Co. to someone who would have the resources, both in money and time to continue the company's re-development.

We produced a handsome sales brochure which fully explained the history of the business and provided all relevant facts and figures. I see from the Executive Summary and also the five year business plan outlined therein, such items as –

- Dunn & Co. is one of the premier menswear brands in the UK.
- Currently the Company operates from 152 shops
- The business is presently poised for significant expansion to a projected 239 without a corresponding increase in overhead costs due to the low cost base of the head office and warehouse.
- The Company is one of the best placed of all retailers, to take advantage of the increase in average age of the UK male population.
- It is the intention of the vendor to retain all their freehold interests in the premises from which Dunn & Co. operate.
- The Company is for sale as the Chairman of the parent group is due to retire from full time business responsibilities and the Vice Chairman wishes to concentrate on other activities.

The five year business plan was for the opening of between fifteen and twenty new shops each year, which would have meant a potential turnover of just under £60m (approx. £90m in current figures) by 1998. If that rate of expansion had been achieved, pre-tax profits of over £3m (about £4.5m in today's values) would have been the result.

It was our bad luck that we were offering the Dunn & Co. business for sale at a very poor time. Late 1993 and early 1994 was the period in question and this was the time when the British economy was just beginning to recover from a deep and serious recession. Nevertheless, we felt that the product we had to sell must be right for someone. Our plan was to retain all the freehold properties – seventy of the 152 shops then open and trading and simply sell Dunn & Co. merged with Hodges as an ongoing retail business. I should mention that apart from the retail sale of menswear, there were other aspects to our trading, including a fairly substantial catalogue business which I had begun way back before the 1982 Greenwood business division. Hodges had continued with this and when we acquired the rump of Dunns, one of the first things we did was to add the catalogue element to the Dunns units. More recently we had established a department for contract clothing, where we used the prestige attached to the Dunn name to seek bulk orders for corporate uniforms and we had a small team of salesmen travelling the country for that purpose. Ladieswear was still being sold at those shops which shortly before the Dunns acquisition we had converted into 'His & Hers' units and another aspect of the business which was progressing well was hire wear.

Everyone of course thinks first of Moss Brothers when it comes to hiring dress clothes for weddings or other formal functions. Nevertheless, we had established hire wear firmly as a rapidly growing part of Dunns business.

With its 152 branch strong chain, its excellent head office and warehouse facilities and perhaps most important of all a very able and mostly long-serving staff, it seemed the business was in excellent shape to achieve the planned expansion which was carefully outlined in the sales brochure.

However, at that point in time there were few UK businesses ready to take a major step into multiple menswear retailing. We came quite close to agreeing a sale with one of our leading suppliers but their motivation was more to protect their own business rather than any wish to be active retailers. We finally met two men who were very keen indeed to acquire the Dunns business. Anthony Phillips and Jim Bellingham were experienced and knowledgeable in retailing and the plan that emerged was for a 'management buy-in'. The financial resources of the two were limited but they obtained the backing of CINVEN (Coal Industry Nominees

Venture Capital Arm) which perhaps was more easily described as the Coal Board's Pension Fund. Cinven put up only part of the funds needed and the way the deal was finally structured was the best we could do at the time but it was certainly not – as later events proved – a complete answer to our problems.

To reduce the size of the purchase price we retained a minority interest in the Dunn & Co. business and in addition we accepted loan stock in the company as part of the price. Which meant – to put it crudely – that we were paying ourselves with our own money. Furthermore, Cinven and Phillips and Bellingham did not take all of the branches. They 'cherry-picked' the branch list and selected the best 109 units, leaving us – that really meant my son David – to find tenants as quickly as possible for some forty-three shops – not an easy task.

Apart from the some £3m of loan stock mentioned above we retained some 25% of the equity of the business with Cinven holding just over 50% and the new management team of Phillips and Bellingham the balance. David continued as a director of Dunn & Co. to keep an eye on our continuing substantial interest in the company but in a non-executive capacity.

Obviously the on-going success of Dunn & Co. was vital to us, not only as regards the financial arrangements outlined above but even more importantly in the fact that we still owned the freeholds of seventy of the Dunns branches and the rental from those shops was essential to us.

The only actual cash that we then received from the management buy-in was a modest amount of circa £3m.

Early results following the deal which was finally completed on 16 June 1994, were not bad but were behind the figures that the new team had forecast and they found themselves under pressure from their bankers, the Bank of Scotland. So much so that it was necessary for Cinven to put in some more cash and as a condition of this they required that their share of the equity should be increased and ours decreased. Nevertheless we remained hopeful that the business which was certainly fundamentally sound would steadily improve and in due course thrive. With hindsight it is probably true to say that Phillips and Bellingham rushed the expansion programme too quickly and they would have been better advised to try and grow the business more slowly and steadily.

There was nothing we could do to influence the operation of the business. We simply watched anxiously from the sidelines and David was desperately busy striving to clear our own borrowings from HSBC. Despite the tough trading conditions we succeeded in letting all the empty units and then selling them, although it was not until as late as 2003 when our debt to HSBC was finally cleared – and cleared in full.

I suppose the mid-1990s were by far the worst years in my business life. Blow after blow and change after change were so severe. Dunn & Co. with our large continuing involvement therein was trading less well than we had expected. David's property portfolio which included the Whittington Estate was heavily indebted, the loss we sustained on the liquidation of Cryotech had come at a time when we could ill afford it and as if those problems were not enough Shop & Store now directed by my son-in-law Stewart Urry was running into ever-increasing problems.

The fundamental mistake which I had made back in 1982 when dividing the 'Greenwood Empire' with my brother, now hit us. This was the point previously made that in that division a large part of Shop & Store's established rent roll had been transferred to my brother's family thus leaving Shop & Store dependent on ongoing development profits for its survival. Throughout the early and mid-1990s retail property development had become increasingly difficult. Stewart's team simply could not find enough profitable development opportunities to meet the ongoing costs of the company, particularly its heavy interest burden. The problem had not suddenly arisen. Until the recession of the late 1980s and 1990s, development activity had been fine. Shop & Store was finding and developing sites for such tenants as Boots – The Edinburgh Woollen Mill – Clinton Cards – Waterstones – Superdrug etc. However, as the recession bit deeper retailers expansion plans were either cancelled or deferred and the result was less and less development activity.

Shop & Store's problems were aggravated by the fact that the need for funds to cover the development activity had resulted in Stewart deciding to replace the old long-term and low interest rate mortgage deals which I had arranged during the 1960s for significantly larger borrowings at a much higher interest cost. These and the company's bank borrowings were now proving crippling. Shop & Store was locked into a descending spiral. To satisfy its lenders, property had to be sold into a weak market with, as consequence, only low prices being achieved. Every sensible economy was needed and by late 1995 it was clear that our group headquarters at Burley House would have to be sold. This meant that a smaller Shop & Store management team moved into modest accommodation in Ilkley where I was simply an occasional visitor and David had to take his anxiety-ridden property companies to rented offices in Otley.

The sale of Burley House obviously meant that my Yorkshire home – The Mews flat there – was no longer available for me.

Even more depressing was the fact that the Whittington Estate, owned by one of David's companies was going to have to be sold. I needed somewhere to live and at last there was a modest silver lining to all the clouds. Enid and I found a property then known as Black House Farm near the village of Bishop Thornton, about eight miles from Harrogate, which had been converted into an extremely comfortable home some twenty odd years previously. We bought it and promptly renamed it Beck House which seemed appropriate since the small river known as Thornton Beck ran through the south side of the twelve or so acres which surrounded the property. Not only that but to me the name Black House had a rather sinister ring.

Selling a country estate on which you have lavished a quarter of a century's care, experience and planning is not a very happy thing to do and if you are unlucky as I was, it is even worse.

We put the sale of the Whittington Estate into the hands of leading estate agents – Savills, who duly produced a handsome brochure and advertised the property in *Country Life*, *The Field* etc. etc. These arrangements produced a number of enquiries, despite the fact that we were seeking to sell a major property into a poor market. I was anticipating selling at that time for about £5m which for a magnificent country house with just under 1,500 acres of land seemed reasonable enough. Most of the land was occupied by three let farms but in addition there were extensive woods which David and I had over the years improved or planted so as to provide an excellent pheasant shoot. Also included with the estate was almost a mile of salmon and sea trout fishing on the River Lune, together with trout fishing in the park lake and the old quarry. Altogether Whittington really was a splendid sporting estate.

Unfortunately, it seems that when you have such an interesting property on the market you are likely to attract some peculiar people. We had several enquiries which were really a complete waste of time. I recall two in particular. There was the man who called himself 'Sir Robert Balshaw' who turned up in a large chauffeur-driven limousine having rung for an appointment to view the property. Something about him did not ring true and whilst I wasted half a day showing him all round the estate and the Hall itself, fortunately my very efficient housekeeper Mrs Wilson had invited in his chauffeur. Whilst she plied him with coffee and biscuits, she also gently pumped him for information and quickly learned that the limousine was his – not the property of the potential purchaser and that he (the chauffeur) was a hire car operator. His client, so my housekeeper learned, made something of a hobby of visiting major houses that were on the market and pretending to be a potential purchaser.

Another of the time-wasters was even worse, a phone-call arranged for a man and his wife to come and inspect the property and in due course the couple turned up. When I saw the clapped-out Ford which they had parked outside Whittington's handsome facade, I decided that they were either lottery winners or just time-wasters. They assured me following my polite questions that they certainly had the resources to consider a purchase of such a property and I had begun to think that perhaps they were indeed someone who had won a jackpot. However, a little detective work as regards their address soon proved that they were indeed a complete waste of time and simply somebody else who found entertainment in pretending to be purchasers.

We had serious interest from Warners, who were considering buying the estate with a view to extending the Hall towards the rear so as to form one of their hotel/retirement complexes. This was not a use I would have wished for the Hall and the estate but it did seem that they would be willing to pay a pretty good price. In the event, after some quite close negotiations, they withdrew, possibly on planning grounds.

Then we had another very serious enquiry. A lady who at first I thought was American came to look around the property. She explained that her origins were in Lancashire but she had lived in California with her artist husband until his fairly recent death. She had now decided to purchase a country house somewhere in the north of England and apparently Whittington seemed perfect to her. She made a further inspection a little later and no doubt took professional advice. She was a charming person with whom it was a pleasure to deal. We ended with one of those scenes which, like quite a number in my varied life, is graven on my memory. We were in the billiard room at Whittington, she seated in a comfortable wing-chair, with me perched on the club fender which enhanced the Victorian fireplace.

I told her — and I most certainly meant it — that I would very much like to see her as the new owner of the Whittington Estate but I obviously needed to sell it for the best possible price. She asked me what would be a figure that I would accept and I told her — £5 million pounds. She thought for only a moment or two and then agreed and we shook hands. She gave me details of the California-based lawyer who would act for her, and I told her who would be acting for us.

My only anxiety was the fear that this might be yet another time-wasting situation and that this lady might not have the financial resources to complete such a purchase. I rang her Californian lawyer and he quickly put my mind at rest. He explained that his client was the widow of the famous modern artist Sam Francis who had died in 1994 and his widow — my prospective purchaser — was to inherit a considerable fortune. Much of the fortune consisted — or so I gathered — of a stock of Sam Francis' paintings which had never yet been put on the open market. His works at that time were selling for several hundred thousand dollars each and apparently Mrs Francis' inheritance would include dozens, possibly even hundreds thereof.

I was, of course, delighted to be reassured but then — as seemed to be so often at this unhappy period of my life — things went wrong. A little later her lawyer explained to me that Sam Francis had been married before and his former wife was contesting the will. He was absolutely confident that in due course the courts would find in favour of his client, my purchaser but the trouble was — how long might that take? Anxious weeks dragged by and sadly it became obvious that there was no hope of the litigation being concluded in the near future.

We were under constant pressure from our bankers and simply could not afford to wait and therefore once again the estate was on the market. It was all another case of so near and yet so far.

In due course a genuine buyer with immediate access to the necessary funds appeared in the shape of Lord Reay. He drove — characteristically I understand — a hard bargain and finally I was forced to accept a figure of £4m and thus another million pounds had slipped through my fingers.

Before completion of the sale of the estate in May 1996 we had to deal with the many items of furniture, pictures etc. for which we would have no room in our new house. We arranged for the bulk of these to be sold by auction at Tennants of Leyburn, North Yorkshire on 18 April 1996, having first organised a viewing day for all these items at the Hall itself a few days previously. I suppose it could have been a painful experience seeing familiar paintings and pieces of furniture go under the hammer but this was not the case. Both Enid and I were, by that time, quite reconciled to the impending move and we were simply interested to see what kind of prices various items brought. In fact they all sold quite well save for one significant disappointment.

For years the sitting-room at Whittington had been adorned with the original, very large painting, reproductions of which will have appeared at some time in virtually every home in Britain. The painting was 'The Christmas Tree' by Albert Chevalier-Taylor. Sadly the rights to reproduce this painting on Christmas cards and the like had been sold many years before we purchased the painting. Nevertheless it was interesting to see just how many Christmas cards appeared each year bearing that familiar illustration of a Victorian family group around a candlelit Christmas tree. The painting was so appropriate for Christmas time that for one Christmas Marks & Spencer used it on all their Christmas wrapping paper and paper bags. Quite often we would receive two or three Christmas cards each year which were reproductions of our painting from people who did not know that.

Unfortunately, it was far too big for our new home and it had to be sold. I was hoping it might achieve a six-figure price but in fact it failed to do that and was ultimately sold in America.

In 1995 shortly before Whittington went on the market I sold my farm and cottage in Wensleydale. My tenant and friend John Watson had reached retiring age and I had no wish to deal with a new tenant. As regards our cottage at the farm which had certainly given us a lot of pleasure over the years there seemed to be no point in keeping this, not least since we planned to live on the north side of Harrogate and would therefore be permanently on the edge of the Yorkshire Dales. My friend the well-known Wensleydale vet Jack Watkinson bought the cottage and has over the years extended it into an excellent country dwelling.

I used the proceeds of the farm and cottage sales to purchase Invercassley House out of Shop & Store's Scottish estate and I also purchased our present home Beck House, Bishop Thornton, Harrogate.

We moved into Beck House in November 1995, a few months before Whittington was finally sold and soon agreed that we had made a very good move. The house has sufficient accommodation to provide a study, a library, a billiard room and an office as well as the usual rooms.

I gave much thought as to what to do with the adjoining field. Any kind of development was of course out of the question since Beck House is in an area of outstanding natural beauty and there is an automatic presumption against any kind of planning permission in AONBs. At first I simply let a local farmer have the land for grazing and I sometimes practised golf shots there. In the summer of 1997 the farmer no longer had any use for the land so I telephoned a golf course designer and asked him – 'What is the smallest golf course you have ever designed?' When I told him of the very modest acreage available, his first reaction was to laugh but then he told me he had a major commission in the north and when next he was up here, he would look at my site.

To cut a long story short, he designed a course which had three greens but no fewer than ten tees. I later added a fourth green. Some of the ten tees are outside the field itself and they necessitate playing over belts of trees. Thus the Beck House private golf course is significantly more than a par three with several holes being well over 200 yards and either up hill, over obstacles or dog-legs. In fact the course has eight par four holes and ten par threes. The greens are all against the boundary fence beyond which is out of bounds and thus there is a premium on accuracy. Altogether a small golf course of this kind is a real asset to a country property and it will provide much enjoyment. We have a pavilion which serves as the nineteenth, a golf buggy which helps those in my age group up and down the slopes and even an annual competition, which is keenly contested amongst my friends. I shall certainly miss it when the time comes to move into some smaller place for the last years of our lives! – and I commend the idea to anybody who has a bit of surplus land.

I should mention that I took up golf late in life under rather odd circumstances. I hit a few golf balls as a teenager but at that stage decided I much preferred tennis. For a brief period in my early forties I attempted to play once a week with a solicitor friend and duly joined Otley Golf Club for that purpose. Within a few weeks either he was ringing me to cancel because he had an urgent completion or I was ringing him to apologise because I had to visit a shop somewhere or other. Thus, our attempts to play regularly fizzled out and I never held a golf club again until the early 1990s when we were fishing on the Oykel. It was what we used to describe as 'Costa Oykel' weather. Bright blue skies, warm sunshine and the river reduced to a very low ebb, all of which made salmon fishing pretty well a waste of time.

One of the ladies in the fishing party suggested that we all go and play golf at the small club at Bonar Bridge. She had learned that clubs could be hired from the general store at Bonar Bridge and thus I found myself asking for two pints of milk, a loaf of bread and two sets of golf clubs. All were immediately produced but 'sets' would be flattering the assortment of golf clubs in the two bags given to me. Nevertheless, I thoroughly enjoyed hacking and slashing my way around the beautiful little Bonar Bridge course and in due time joined Ripon Golf Club, had one or two lessons and began to play regularly. My only regret now that I have my own little course as well as playing on numerous others is that I did not take up the game seriously when I was younger.

CHAPTER 21

Mostly Downs

BEFORE CONTINUING A CATALOGUE of business disasters, there are a few aspects of my varied life which are, I think, of interest but I have not previously covered them in this story.

Let's think first of politics. I have said a bit about that subject in one or two places but I see that I have failed to mention that on two occasions I was offered direct entry into the political world. Way, way back when I was a youthful, successful and fairly well-known north-country business-man some people came to ask me quite seriously if I would be willing to stand for Parliament as the Member for the Shipley (that's a small town on the edge of Bradford) constituency. I had to think hard about this possibility, since at that time, the Conservative party was doing well and I certainly had confidence in my ability to speak to the good people of Shipley in such a way as to secure their support. In other words I was pretty sure I could get elected. The big question was – did I want to?

I did not know to whom I should go for advice and then I remembered that the MP for the Pudsey constituency which was where I lived in those days, was – and he would have taken this description as the compliment which I mean it to be – 'a wise old bird'. Joe Hiley was that MP and I knew him well enough, having worked for his election more than once. 'Should I go for this Shipley seat Joe?' was my question. His advice was plain and simple – 'Don't do it'.

He pointed out to me I was at the beginning of what could be a happy and successful business career and that that would just not mix with Parliamentary duties 200 miles away. He also told me, 'You will probably do more good running a decent business and looking after your staff than you ever would as a back-bencher. Unless you are prepared to give your whole life to the job, don't do it'.

I took his advice and it was many years later before I had a second opportunity to be seriously involved politically.

Mark Lennox-Boyd who was both my MP and a personal friend when we lived at Whittington tried very hard to persuade me to take on the chairmanship of his Constituency Association. I have no doubt that if I had done so and given that constituency the amount of work and effort which I have put into Woodhouse Grove and the other Methodist Foundation independent schools which have had so much of my time in the last many years, that I would have made a success of constituency chairmanship and probably enjoyed doing so. However, I decided against it and in favour of an ever greater involvement in independent education.

My educational involvement became ever deeper as the years rolled by. Most of my efforts were devoted to Woodhouse Grove but as I have already mentioned whilst at Whittington I enjoyed several years of significant involvement as a Governor of St Martin's College, Lancaster. Then, of course, I became very heavily committed to the whole group of Methodist independent schools.

Some of the highlights at The Grove included the appointment of three first-class headmasters. First, came David Miller who took over from F.C. Pritchard in 1972 and then led the school through a period of continuing growth and improvement for nineteen years. David Miller's successor was David Welsh who – by Woodhouse Grove standards – had a comparatively brief tenure. Unlike most of The Grove's headmasters he did not remain at the school until retirement but after seven successful years moved to another headship in 1996.

The Grove's ever improving stature in the educational world was certainly evidenced when we arranged the usual advertising for a new headmaster. I think there were some sixty applications from first-class men at fine schools throughout the land. A long-list was, in due course, whittled down to a short-list and at the final interview stage, all of us involved were sure that in the youngest of the applicants we had found the right man and we were delighted to appoint David Humphreys, then only in his mid-thirties.

With hindsight I think just about the best combination possible for the conduct of a major school in this age of ever increasing complexity is a youthful, enthusiastic and innovative headmaster and a much older, widely experienced Chairman. Despite – or perhaps because of – the fact that David Humphreys had not been born when I began as a Governor at The Grove he and I have been able to work together extraordinarily well. The recent years have seen a succession of changes and improvements as well as an increase in pupil numbers to over 1,000. Academic, sporting, musical, theatrical, indeed just about all standards have gone from strength to strength. The reputation of the school, which has its 200th birthday in

2012, has never been higher and, despite all the dramatic changes, the school's overall character and ethos have nevertheless been maintained.

Some of the changes of recent years would certainly have surprised the governing body which I first joined fifty years ago. In those days not so much as a bottle of sherry was to be found on the premises. Today the gallery which serves the school theatre includes a modern cocktail bar. (Not, I should stress, for pupils' use!). Today the school premises are busy for fifty-one weeks of the year, since an enormous variety of outside clubs, associations, businesses, other schools etc. etc. share our facilities. The school's assets are always fully employed, sometimes in quite original ways, such as the fact that for some years the Bradford Bulls Rugby League Club used our fine sports hall and other facilities as their Academy.

As regards my efforts for the other Methodist independent schools. I gave up the Chairmanship of the Finance Committee when I was in my mid-seventies and in my eightieth year retired from the Board of Management of all the schools but will continue as a Trustee for them for – I hope! – quite a number of years yet.

Now back to business and the final 'downs' which wiped out 95% of the family fortune. In 1996 the outlook still seemed fair, if not good. I was anxious about Dunns trading performance but could do no more than watch from the sidelines since the management buy-in team were in charge. Similarly Shop & Store's cash problems were causing increasing worry. Before the year was over the Invercasssley Estate, Shop & Store's major Scottish property had to be sold. The best price that son-in-law Stewart could obtain came from – of all people – Mohammed Al Fayed, proprietor of Harrods. He was not a person with whom I would have wished to do business but since he already owned an adjoining Scottish estate he was an obvious purchaser for the Invercassley Estate.

Once the estate had been sold there was not much point in my retaining Invercassley House and with some sadness I sold it the following year to a much more welcome purchaser, Simon Marks, a younger member of the Marks & Spencer family.

I should mention that there were two abortive attempts to correct the mistake of the 1982 division. In 1991 Denis's son-in-law, Stephen Rawson was serving as Managing Director of Greenwood's and he was quite enthusiastic about the possibility of re-uniting Hodges' retail business with the Greenwood chain which would have meant massive savings since Hodges' entire warehouse and head office operation would have been rendered superfluous. Denis and other members of his family were not keen on this idea and it came to nothing.

Four and a half years later when Hodges' retail business was in the hands of the management buy-in team of Phillips and Bellingham a suggestion for re-uniting in the opposite direction was seriously considered. Early that year Dunns (as Hodges had now become) was doing reasonably well and its two new principals were ambitious enough in their wish to achieve full national coverage that they made the suggestion that most of Greenwood's branches should be merged into Dunns with the remaining small units to be closed. Such a deal would have suited David and me very well since it would have secured our remaining investment in the Dunns business and it was certainly a fact that the two chains of men's shops would have fitted together admirably – as they should have been if we had not been so foolish in 1982! In the event the scheme sadly came to nothing as Denis and most of his family preferred to continue as they were.

Phillips and Bellingham therefore simply continued to run Dunns trying to expand it with new branches. However, whilst trading conditions were not desperately bad they were regularly falling below their planned and promised figures and their bankers were increasingly impatient.

The really ghastly blow came at Christmas time in 1996. On 19 December, their bankers – Bank of Scotland – who had been brought in with the management buy-in 'pulled the plug', that is to say they terminated the overdraft facility with immediate effect.

To me this was a classic case of greedy, unthinking bankers taking a callous, selfish and short-term view. With the Christmas figures and the January sale receipts, by mid-January the overdraft was in fact cleared and what the company really needed was some patient support which would have meant some fairly modest additional borrowing almost certainly only on a temporary basis. Instead some loathsome swine – and that is how I shall always think of the individual or individuals concerned – chose to destroy a century-old business and throw dozens of long-serving and hard-working people out of work.

The administrators appointed by the bank had of course only one duty and objective. That was to make sure the bank got all its money back as quickly as possible and then get rid of what was left of the business, also as quickly as possible. They found a purchaser for many of the branches in Ciro Citterio, a Birmingham-based menswear retailer who also bought the head office and warehouse in Swansea.

The effects on my family were of course disastrous. The equity that we had left in the company became worthless overnight and the value of our loan stock therein became zero. If that were not bad enough it meant that David's property business had lost the tenant of many of its properties.

To make a ghastly situation even worse we had been obliged to guarantee some of the leases to other landlords of Dunns units in order to secure their consent to the arrangement at the time the management buy-in took place. In several cases Ciro Citterio had not wanted the branch concerned and consequently we were liable for the rentals until such time as we could find new tenants.

All these problems inevitably meant that our own bankers pressed us continuously for the repayment of all borrowings. I was turned seventy when the full impact of these business disasters hit us and it fell to David to do almost all of the work necessary in finding new tenants for the vacant shops and selling properties frequently for poor prices, at a time when the market was still weak.

We were in a pretty deep hole on David's side of the business and by this time the dearth of the necessary property deals for Shop & Store was also an ever-increasing problem. It was to my son's very great credit that he coped with what was fast becoming a desperate situation. If he had not succeeded in finding tenants and buyers for all the former Hodges and Dunns units that we were landed with, then I suppose it would have been a complete melt-down. However, he gradually succeeded in getting the bankers more or less off our backs by a series of skilful and hard earned successful negotiations.

By 1998 there wasn't much left of what had been a multi-million pound business. David put most of his resources into – for us – a completely new type of property venture. He began buying small terraced houses in East Lancashire, which at that time could be bought for trivial prices and soon had a portfolio of some seventy terrace properties, mostly in Colne, Nelson and Burnley. Every one had to be refurbished and before they were let they all had gas fired central heating, safe wiring, modern kitchen units and new floor coverings, as well as being fully re-decorated. In their refurbished form they were quite pleasant little houses and soon they were all fully let.

With some input from me, David also worked on some minor housing developments which turned a modest profit. Thus at the end of the 1990s we had survived, but only just. David's side of the family business was dramatically reduced in scale but it was afloat. On the other side of the family, Stewart and Patricia's business, Shop & Store, was sinking under the burden of its borrowings.

Perhaps this is a good point to take a break from business problems and record some interesting charitable work with which I still have an involvement. As far back as 1988 whilst making one of my frequent visits to Woodhouse Grove, I had a look at the school's dyslexia or special needs department, then under the very able direction of Mrs Celia Stone. I knew virtually nothing about dyslexia other than the fact that The Grove had this special department which was fast earning a very good reputation for helping children with this particular learning difficulty. I was not alone in my ignorance of the subject, since back then and very certainly much earlier, dyslexic children were frequently simply categorised as stupid. As we have all come to learn in recent years that is very far from the truth. Many dyslexics have above average IQ and many of them achieve great things. Sir Richard Branson is, perhaps a particularly good example. I believe it is now accepted that as many as 12.5% – that is one in eight – of the entire population is dyslexic to some degree.

On that day in 1988 a hefty boy, I think a member of the first XV had just been fitted with a pair of Irlen glasses. Those are the glasses with brightly coloured lenses which you sometimes see children wearing and which take their name from the American child psychologist Helen Irlen, who had made the discovery that different coloured lenses could greatly help people who suffered from Scotopic Sensitivity Syndrome. The story goes that she kept her records of children with whom she was working in different coloured plastic files and one day one of her students pointed out that he could read much more clearly through the coloured plastic than he had ever read before. Apparently as many as 50% of children with serious reading difficulties can be helped with Irlen lenses. The hefty rugby player who I saw in our dyslexic unit was such a case. The dramatic transformation in his reading ability when he first put on his Irlen lenses was such that the poor lad burst into tears.

I was moved when I saw this and listened closely when Celia Stone told me that she and her two helpers, Myra Nicholson and Elizabeth Franks had evolved various teaching procedures which greatly helped the dyslexic children they were teaching. I suggested that Mrs Stone should write a handbook or books and I see from her letter to me of 20 June 1988, in which she said, 'I have been thinking very seriously about your suggestion that I should write a handbook for teachers and parents of children with specific learning difficulties', and that she was going to take up my suggestion. She and her two colleagues went on to do just that and I became their business advisor and my charitable foundation the principal source of funds for what ultimately emerged as the *Beat Dyslexia* set of books and audio tapes which have been used widely throughout this country, America and elsewhere.

By 1995 the three ladies were an organised partnership and their work was achieving deserved success. They had agreed a royalty deal with publishers from which they continue to receive their just rewards. I found helping and advising them on all the business aspects of the operation a welcome relief from the ever increasing business pressures from which I suffered during the mid-1990s. It was good to receive a letter from Mrs Stone in July 1999 enclosing the last book in the *Beat Dyslexia Activity Pack* series. She ended her letter with the kind phrase – 'Another certainty is that it wouldn't have happened without your prompting and great generosity'. That was a very welcome fillip when I was suffering so much from business anxieties.

I was pleased when – some years later – Celia Stone contacted me once more and told me that she and her colleagues had now completed the preliminary work on a system for teaching children who suffer from dyscalculia which, in layman's terms, is a condition affecting about 6% of all children i.e. one or two in every classroom who have particular difficulty in dealing with numbers.

We arranged for Mrs Stone to come and see me at Beck House in, I think it was, May 2005 bringing with her the first wooden mock-up of an 'Addacus'. I was greatly impressed by the ingenuity of the device and all its accompanying components. So much so that I immediately promised to give the project all the help I could. There was a lot to be done. The first thing was to decide on the name for the project, we plumped for Addacus just as soon as we found that no one else was using it as a trade name. As you will probably have noted the name for what I can now describe as 'our' project was very similar to the word abacus, which is of course a counting frame.

For this project Celia Stone was partnered initially only by her colleague from Beat Dyslexia days Myra Nicholson but her Newcastle-based daughter Nicola Barnsley and Nicola's children as guinea pigs helped greatly. Celia's husband Bryan at that time a departmental head at Woodhouse Grove gave her much time and support and after his retirement from the teaching profession in the following year, he was ready to accept the responsibilities of Company Secretary.

I had quickly decided that the Addacus project was more than just something which would help many thousands, perhaps ultimately millions of children who have problems with numbers. As well as having that very worthy objective, the project clearly had a very significant commercial potential. For that reason I proposed that the best way forward was to form a company to organise the manufacture and later the marketing of the product and thus Addacus Limited came into existence with Celia Stone as Managing Director, Bryan Stone as Company Secretary, Myra Nicholson and Nicola Barnsley as Directors and myself as Chairman.

I was anxious from the outset to ensure that no one could steal the very good idea which the Addacus project represented. Consequently our first major expenditure was in having solicitors Walker Morris of Leeds ensure that our intellectual property rights were protected, not only in this country but throughout Europe, America and elsewhere.

We then had to find premises from which to operate and were able to lease a very suitable unit on a small industrial estate in Guisley, near Leeds, which was laid out very well for our purposes. Apart from two or three small offices, there was a large room big enough to host sales or teaching, seminars and in addition there was ample storage space for the storage of Addacus packs.

Addacus packs required only four suppliers. The Addacus itself and a number of other components which were made of plastic. The books of course had to be printed as did the carefully designed box and a few minor items. A third item was what we termed 'strings' which came from a manufacturer of shoe laces etc. and finally we had to find a supplier for the compact disc which was included.

It took us a while to find the best plastic supplier and Mrs Stone and I considered several before giving our order to a plastics manufacturer in Hexham, Northumberland. In fact it took us a year to establish the company, move into its Guisley premises, solve all the production difficulties and finally to have Addacus packs with Book one available for sale and it was not therefore until the end of 2006 that we began to sell the product.

Just about everyone who saw it was impressed but our problem was that we simply could not afford what was obviously so desirable – a major advertising campaign. We had spent all the monies which the shareholders had put into the business, mostly on the substantial legal costs but also in purchasing the very expensive tools needed for the manufacture of the plastic components and simply could not afford significant advertising. Consequently the product has sold only slowly but happily, steadily with sales resulting either from word of mouth recommendations or mainly from demonstrations of the product given by Mrs Stone to numerous schools, education authorities and at educational exhibitions.

Towards the end of 2007 when I had passed my eightieth birthday it was becoming clear to me that the time for my active involvement with the company was coming to an end. None of us was taking any remuneration or benefits from the company and it seemed probable that it would be some years before the hoped-for steadily increasing sales would permit any rewards or even expenses to the directors who were also of course the only shareholders. After some debate and some misunderstandings we finally agreed amicably an order of priority for the distribution of any surpluses that the company would – hopefully – in due course achieve. With that issue resolved I was content to resign from the board in January 2008 but I maintain my interest as a shareholder and of course keep in touch with the struggling little business's progress.

The whole project has gone much more slowly than we first hoped but it remains the case that everyone who has bought the product seems very pleased with it and everyone who sees it for the first time is impressed by it. Therefore, I look forward to the day when sales begin to take off and Addacus is a term known to every teacher in the land and thereafter to teachers in other lands! If you are interested in learning more about this quite admirable teaching aid you need do no more than visit the Addacus website at www.addacus.co.uk.

In the late 1990s I began to think about the possibility of a very special kind of school. These thoughts crystallised into the concept of the International Methodist College. I was able to persuade my colleagues on the Board of Management for Methodist Schools that establishing somewhere in the UK a brand new institution which would have a similar character to the Methodist independent schools but which would serve pupils from overseas would be a very worthwhile objective. A working party which I chaired was established and we soon defined more clearly our objective.

The plan was for a college with some 300 students initially but with a capacity to accommodate 500. This was to be built in the Midlands (in view of lower costs of all kinds than in the London area) and within easy reach of an international airport. The age range would be from sixteen to nineteen year olds and the curriculum to be based on a two year international baccalaureate.

By the middle of 2001 we had made a great deal of progress. I had been able to persuade a leading architectural practice – the Sheppard Robson Partnership of London to produce a design for the proposed college on an assumed green field site. These architects, like other professionals with whom I spoke were sufficiently impressed by the whole idea, that they agreed to do all their preliminary work on the basis that no fees would be charged until actual construction of the college was ready to begin. Sheppard Robson, who had in the past thirty years designed no less than ten universities and 100 schools in various countries were clearly an ideal choice and they quite quickly produced outline plans showing how the college could be laid out. Their scheme included every facility from a group of three-storey halls for students, through to lecture halls, admin. offices, chapel etc. etc.

With their scheme before them, my working party at least knew what a perfect international college could look like. We then began a search for a suitable site realising that the end product might not be an entirely purpose-built college but perhaps some existing institution adapted to satisfy the accommodation provision which the Sheppard Robson scheme indicated.

The next and obviously most important consideration was how was this fine new operation to be paid for? From the outset my plan had been that it would require an international fund-raising appeal. Just as it was hoped that the college, as and when it appeared, would attract students from all over the world, then the intention was to attract funding from all over the world. It seemed to me that there must be many wealthy individuals' businesses and institutions throughout the world who would look with favour on the project. Obviously we were going to be talking about a lot of money. Perhaps a figure in the order of £40 million would be needed for buildings and equipment but in addition to that I was sure that we would need significant bursary or scholarship funds. Thus, our appeal would have to be for something well over £60 million.

Then we ran into difficulties. The Methodist Board of Management had funded the expenses for all our preliminary efforts and discussions but it very quickly became clear that we would need several hundred thousand pounds more to finance the international fund-raising operation. Such a sum was not available from any Methodist source and sadly the days had long gone when I could have looked to either my business or my charitable foundation to provide such an amount.

The project stalled on this stumbling block and it remains stalled. It also remains the case that the concept is an entirely desirable scheme. Everyone with whom we discussed it – politicians, church leaders and even the Prince of Wales' Private Secretary (we had hopes that Prince Charles might ultimately be a patron of the international appeal) all were impressed by our ideas. We desperately needed a funder of the fund-raising and at that time found no solution to the problem. We, therefore, left the project 'on ice'. I am now too old to provide the necessary impetus to re-start the project and of course the state of the world economy means that presently the time is not right.

However, the concept of boys and girls aged sixteen to nineteen from many different countries and backgrounds, some fee paying, others supported by bursaries and scholarships being educated to the very high standards seen in Methodist independent schools and with the whole operation within the Christian and caring ethos which is natural to those schools, must surely remain a very desirable objective.

Who knows, perhaps some reader will be inspired to try and move this forward and if so he or she will find that much of the initial spadework has already been done and the results of much thought and deliberation by my working party colleagues are there in the Board of Management's files.

The last time I mentioned Shop & Store Developments Ltd. was with the sad observation that the company was sinking under the burden of its borrowings. In the year 2000 it finally sank. I suffered the bitter pain of receiving a P45 termination of income form from the company which I had built and later in that year the company went into receivership. All that my family managed to salvage from the wreck were some properties in Florida which remain in the hands of my son-in-law Stewart and daughter Patricia. For me it just meant pain and grief which continues to this day. It is quite hard to walk past buildings which one used to own and realise that never again will you have the opportunity of owning properties of that quality.

During all the problems of the 1990s I did manage to establish a small property company owned by Enid and me which managed to do two or three profitable deals. All of these were only a fraction of the size of the sort of transactions I had become used to during the forty years spent in building up the Greenwood's and Hodges' portfolio and of course building Shop & Store. Nevertheless, one of the deals I managed just before the turn of the century had a surprising outcome. I bought from the wreckage of the business, the property known as 'The Shambles' in Settle. This was the charming little block of shops with a row of cottages built on top of them which have always been a main feature of the market square in this attractive little dales town. In fact, this was the property which, when I had bought it into the business many years previously had caused my father some concern when he learned that it was not a freehold. It was however a 2,000 year leasehold at a peppercorn rental. When I bought it out of the business, I had, of course, to pay the price put on it by a professional valuer. It went into my newly formed tiny business principally because it generated a good rental income. However, after giving it some intensive attention which included re-negotiating the shop leases and the cottage tenancies, as well as smartening it up with fresh paint work and a few minor repairs, I then put it up for sale by auction with a result which I had never seen before and doubt I shall ever see again.

So many people wished to buy this unusual but very attractive property that it sold for well over £800,000 which was exactly 100 times the price I had paid for it back in the 1960s and thus Settle became the only property I have ever dealt with which showed a 100-fold appreciation over the years.

CHAPTER 22

Lessons Learned

A FINAL 'DOWN' OCCURRED early in 2009. The original family business, Greenwoods Menswear Ltd. had been under the control of my brother Denis's family since the 1982 division. Greenwood's had continued to have a very good name for value in men's clothing and outfitting but over the years they found business increasingly difficult as the pressure from Marks & Spencer and other variety stores intensified. Increasingly supermarkets and other discount stores were moving into the lower end of the clothing trade and that competition also continued to press on Greenwood's. It was, of course, not my business and to some extent I had anticipated that they would find it increasingly difficult. Denis's influence on the firm's affairs obviously diminished with the passing of time. He is two years older than I and as the years passed he had turned over control of the business, first to his son-in-law Stephen Rawson and later to a second son-in-law John Hanson, whose family textile company Parkland had obviously given him much experience in running comparatively large businesses.

As business conditions tightened, so the Greenwood's branch list began to shrink until the time came when its Guisley head office and warehouse complex was sold for a housing development and its headquarters moved to a part of the old Parkland buildings at Greengates near Bradford. By 2008 the branch list had fallen below 100 and apparently an effort was made to merge the much diminished business with an overseas – Chinese – supplier's business which was seeking UK representation. Clearly the merger possibility must have failed since early in 2009 came the news that the Chinese company had bought Greenwood's from the bank-appointed administrator, although John Hanson would continue as its Chief Executive.

This was a sad moment for me and I suppose even more so for my brother. I cannot pretend it came as a complete surprise since I had watched a steady decline in Greenwood's affairs for a number of years. However, I had always said that their property portfolio was so strong – I knew that since my name was on most of the deeds as having purchased the property originally – that I felt the company would certainly survive longer than I would.

With hindsight the story of all the Greenwood family businesses seems to bear out quite dramatically the truth of the old adage – 'united we stand, divided we fall'. If we had not divided the business back in 1982 we would certainly have been able to merge Hodges' business with Greenwood's and operate from a single northern headquarters. Then we would have been able to acquire Dunn's name and a number of their branches and thereafter probably operate some 300/400 shops throughout the country, possibly with the larger ones trading-up and operating under the Dunn's name and the smaller ones trading at a lower price level under the Greenwood name. Backing up that powerful retail business would have been an undivided Shop & Store Developments Ltd. which would have not needed to go into the risky high-borrowing business of large scale development activity.

So many things would have been different, I would have been wealthy enough to ensure that the Addacus project was fully funded and able to benefit from an extensive advertising campaign. I would have been able to support Cryotech long enough to extricate ourselves from it profitably and even such ideas as the Ring Tennis project could have been advanced. Finally, I suppose I would have been able to provide myself, the necessary funding of the fund-raising for the International Methodist College scheme.

However, one of the lessons learned from all the pain and grief is that there is not much point in fretting over what might have been. Instead it is far better to look back with pleasure or amusement on the good and happy parts of what has proved to be a long and extremely interesting life.

I certainly enjoyed my life at Whittington and in Scotland which I referred to earlier as living in ducal splendour but in fact I'm not sorry that the latter part of my life must be lived on a more modest scale. Two cars rather than seven, is not really so painful. Some part-time help rather than a dozen personal staff is in fact much more enjoyable.

However, those are modest consolations. I am certainly not going to pretend that losing a fortune has been fun but one of the lessons you do learn from a series of problems and disasters is to value the truly important things in life.

The blessing of reasonably good health for yourself and for those for whom you care the most, is certainly much more important than the number of noughts on your bank balance. Long and deep friendships give more satisfaction than successful deals. The memory of the good things you have done and the people you have helped eases the pain of disappointments.

To bring the story to a close I should mention that I did, just as the business disasters began to enfold me, find myself about in the middle of the *Sunday Times* Rich List. The joke was that by the time I was included in that not very accurate piece of information, most of the wealth I was supposed to have had already disappeared and in any event if the figure had been produced a year or so earlier it would have been an underestimate. The moral of that is – don't always believe what you read in the papers!

I was pleased to see David extricate himself profitably from his venture into the housing end of the property world. He then spent some time acquiring twelve freehold public houses and operating them as a small chain. Some were tenanted and some were managed but all bought their beer from David's beer wholesaling operation which was all right at the time.

I'm glad to say he wisely moved out of that venture and back into commercial property where he will, I sincerely hope, prosper and succeed for the rest of his days. Enid and I hope to move from Beck House in the near future but the national indeed international financial chaos of 2008/9 has meant that Beck House will certainly not fetch the kind of price we had hoped for. Nevertheless, we hope to move into a smaller and easier to manage home in the not too distant future.

I shall have retired from active involvement as a Governor at Woodhouse Grove by the time you read these words. However, I anticipate taking an interest in the school's affairs for the rest of my life. I believe that the school will have granted me some honorary lifetime position and I shall enjoy that ongoing connection.

I plan to write 'thrillers' to keep 'the little grey cells' active. One such, *Death on the Hill* already exists and I have begun work on *A Level Murder* and *Take-over*. The first is about murders on a Scottish sporting estate, the second is set in a co-educational day-boarding school and the third will be around the subject of an opposed corporate bid. All of which are subjects where I shall be drawing on personal experiences as you have read. With those mental activities and one or two other possibilities added to my intention to play tennis and golf just as long as I can swing a racquet or club and to enjoy a little shooting and fishing I shall have – God willing – a few interesting years yet to come.

I suppose I shall never forget all those years as a shopkeeper and also a property developer. Oddly enough I find it much easier to remember details now long past, rather than the details of the final unhappy period. For example, whenever I am driving any distance and see a motorway sign for a particular town or city I immediately recall the branch which either Greenwood's, Hodges or Dunns had in that particular place. Often as part of that recollection I clearly remember the manager of that shop, its layout and sometimes details of how we came to acquire it. I suppose it is quite normal to have a clearer recollection of interesting and pleasant situations, rather than testing problems.

And so to end with a few words of advice which come as a result of the lessons I have learned. Lesson number one must surely be to look after the only body you have got, avoid the obviously unhealthy things, such as smoking, keep your drinking within sensible limits and for a stressed man I recommend wholeheartedly whisky and red wine. Get plenty of exercise, both mental and physical. I think it is perfectly true that if you don't use it you will lose it and that goes for both mind and muscle. Remember always that the most important person in the world is the one with whom you share your life. Stay as close as you can to the rest of your family and your friends. Try always to have some positive objectives in mind.

I do believe that as the years begin to catch up with you the motto to follow is – 'The more you do, the more you can do!'

I have tried to live up to a phrase which I noted, when as a young man I read the Bible carefully from start to finish – Ecclesiastes chapter 9 verse 10 which reads: 'Whatsoever thy hand findeth to do, do it with thy might!'

Index